# SUFFOLK INVASION

Soldiers leaving Landguard Fort.                                                    *Soldier Magazine*

# SUFFOLK INVASION

The Dutch attack on Landguard Fort, 1667

by

## FRANK HUSSEY

TERENCE DALTON LIMITED

LAVENHAM  .  SUFFOLK

1983

Published by
TERENCE DALTON LIMITED

Reprint arranged by
LANDGUARD FORT TRUST
2005

ISBN 0 86138 027 4 limp covers

*It is now some years since my father Frank died. His ashes were scattered on the foreshore at Landguard, an area he loved and knew well.*

*This book is a testament to Frank's deep interest in the sea and Landguard Fort's history. Extensive work was carried out on Landguard by English Heritage in 1997 and the Fort is now managed by the Landguard Fort Trust and its volunteers, under an agreement with English Heritage.*

Graham Hussey 2005

*Text photoset in 11 / 12pt Baskerville*

*Printed in Great Britain at
The Lavenham Press Limited, Lavenham, Suffolk*

# Contents

## Landguard Fort

Along the sands, and by the sound
  Of ocean, moaning night and day,
It stands: — its lonely burial ground
  Scatter'd with low stones, mossed and grey,
Whose brief inscriptions waste away
  Beneath the ocean-breeze's spell;
And there, beneath the moon's pale ray,
  Still walks the nightly sentinel.

*Letters and Poems,* Bernard Barton

Landguard Fort, from
Raw's *Ladies Pocket
Book Companion.*
  *Mrs Gladys Wilton*

# Author's Introduction and Acknowledgements

I AM deeply conscious that Major J. H. Leslie's *History of Landguard Fort* of 1898 has a sure place as a minor classic of local history. My aim, therefore, is amplification so far as the Dutch landing of 1667 is concerned and to give rightful meaning to Willem van de Velde the Elder's fine grisaille of 1669. Much more in the way of contemporary accounts is now available, so the full tale of both sides in these stirring events can at last be told.

For a full appreciation I found it essential to study the whole course of the Second Dutch War, so I also give some account of the run up to and the aftermath of the Landguard attack. I have rounded off with a few oddments from later years both for the amusement of the reader and as some guide to future writers who wish to tackle a fuller history of the fort.

It was Michael Robinson, the well-known Van de Velde specialist of international repute and former Head of the Picture Department at the National Maritime Museum, who initiated a very considerable renewal of research by noticing bottles on the bowsprit jacks of five of the ships in the Van de Velde grisaille. It struck him suddenly that, whereas the picture had long been considered to represent the Dutch attack on the Medway, such bottles were in fact the device on Flushing jacks of the Zeeland squadron, which did not join De Ruyter's fleet until after the capture of the uncompleted fort at Sheerness. The original attribution then became untenable; even more so when Mr Robinson referred to an old Dutch biography of Admiral de Ruyter by Gerard Brandt. There he discovered that while a small squadron under Lieutenant-Admiral Willem Joseph baron van Ghent and Cornelis de Witt was forcing an entrance to the Medway, De Ruyter's famous flagship *De Zeven Provincien*, which is clearly shown in the left-hand distance of the Van de Velde picture of ships attacking a fort, was lying quietly at anchor by the Middle Ground some miles away up the Essex coast.

Further inspection and research clearly showed him that the picture concerned the attack on Landguard Fort, a view which was soon shared by experts in Holland. The grisaille has long been part of the Van de Velde collection in the National Maritime Museum, but nothing is known of its history prior to its appearance in Christie's saleroom in 1927 except that it came to the vendor as part of the estate of the Rochfort family.

I have a personal interest in this battlefield as both my father and my grandfather were once stationed at Landguard Fort. If after roaming the lonely Dry Common my father and his elder brother wanted a dip in the sea a hundred years ago they had only to strip off their clothes and have one in the buff. At that time my grandfather and others of the garrison were involved in the farcical "civil war" between Colonel George Tomline and the military authorities. The former, *bête noire* of Edward FitzGerald, was the far-sighted founder of the Felixstowe railway and dock and also the owner of the land surrounding the fort. Then, most happily, my grandfather was employed as surveyor by the same Tomline estates when he left the Army in 1879.

Accommodation for the family was provided at Pier House, Felixstowe, until they moved to Levington in 1883. There was family talk for many years afterwards of the enterprising cat which used to bring in fish from Walton Creek, known in the seventeenth century as Ireton's Ditch. Other favourite stories concerned the besieging of Pier House one evening by a crowd of furious dock-diggers whose wages had failed to arrive on the usual train and of my father being inadvertently left "sitting on the dining-room mantelpiece" in the eighteen-seventies, after a hurried evacuation during a tidal flood. It was my imperturbable grandmother who replied thus to an anxious "Where's Harry?" query when the soldier rescuers had rowed half way back to Landguard Fort.

Pier House, Felixstowe, amid the almost subsided flood of 1953. The sea has always been the greatest and most relentless invader of the Suffolk Coast.     *East Anglian Daily Times*

Nearly sixty years ago, and twenty-three homes later, when my father had retired to Felixstowe after a lifetime of Army postings, a walk past the old grey house, round Landguard Point and back along the beach was a favourite constitutional. In April, 1925, I followed the Felixstowe fire-engine pell-mell across the common and was one of a handful who saw the old wooden lighthouse burning down.

Fifty years ago Godfrey Clarke and I sailed down coast in a very old yacht through channels mentioned in this book. The boom of the Shoeburyness guns after we left Havengore on a sultry afternoon, and the sight of projectiles in the air, jerked Godfrey into unexpectedly grim talk of a First World War experience. Within the Medway, during our sail up to Gillingham, we saw HMS *Renown* and HMS *Valiant* at anchor in the lower estuary. Either of these great ships could have taken on De Ruyter's fleet with just one gun. Now, as I recall the sunny personality of Godfrey, a keen member of the original Felixstowe Ferry Yacht & Dinghy Club, I realise that forty years have elapsed since he was laid to rest in Old Felixstowe churchyard overlooking the Deben. It is indeed appropriate to mention Godfrey in this book, for "Sparks", as we nicknamed him, contracted his final illness while working on electrical installations for the guns of Landguard Fort. Maybe these were the Darell's Battery six-pounders of phenomenal firing rate which made a fleeting appearance in *The Sea Shall Not Have Them*, a film about the air-sea rescue service.

It has been an unexpected and enormous pleasure to have been engaged in this and other research with a host of kindly people in what would otherwise have been just humdrum and handicapped old age. I could not even have attempted this narrative without the most generous provision of many archival transcripts, lengthy translations and much advice and encouragement from Michael Robinson, who originally brought the grisaille to my notice. Vice Admiral A. van der Moer, of the Royal Netherlands Navy, who himself has been researching and writing about the Landguard action, sent me translations of his article *Een nabrander van de tocht naar Chatham* in the periodical *Marineblad*, and also of archival extracts made by the late Dr Van der Kooij of the Bureau of Maritime History at The Hague. He has also helped me greatly in correspondence.

I gratefully acknowledge, too, the expert aid and kindly advice of my historian kinsman William Hussey, who looked up original papers in the Bodleian, but I hasten to add that any errors or misconceptions that do remain must be put down to my own amateur approach and headstrong enthusiasm. As with my previous books, Hugh Moffat, of Clopton, has furnished me with many a delightful snippet from the *Ipswich Journal* and, despite the pressures of the times, the staffs of the Ipswich branch of the Suffolk Record Office, the Ipswich Central Reference Library and Westbourne Branch Library have throughout provided most friendly and exemplary service. It was Charles Trollope of the Harwich Society and the Fortress Study Group who very recently unearthed most valuable plans of the 1626 fort and its little-known immediate successor. I am indeed grateful for this timely discovery and for the generous provision of information by him and also by David Wood, who is chairman of the Felixstowe Museum and History Society. The latter has most kindly contributed drawings of the later forts.

The collection of helpful illustrations was in fact a major task which itself produced useful by-products outside the scope of this book. In particular, thanks are due to the Trustees and Staff of the National Maritime Museum for the privilege of reproducing not only the three-hundred-year-old picture which provides the main theme for this book but also some of the other superb Van de Velde drawings in their great collection. Other repositories and collections, both great and small, have kindly provided illustrations and these include the British Library, the Victoria and Albert Museum, the Ashmolean Museum, the Public Record Office, the Henry Huntington Art Gallery, of San Marino, California, U.S.A., the Parker Gallery, the Suffolk Record Office, the Ipswich Museums, the Colchester and Essex Museum, N. R. Ormell and Felixstowe Town Council. For photographs I am particularly indebted to the Imperial War Museum, the Royal Artillery Institution, *Soldier* Magazine, Beken of Cowes, Mrs Winifred Cooper of the Harwich Society, Mr G. F. Cordy and the *East Anglian Daily Times.* My wife Doris has helped me in many ways and my son Graham, his wife Honor, my grandsons Jake and Dan and my nephew John Hussey have all contributed, thus making, with my father's and my grandfather's reminiscences, a five-generation participation.

In Bob Malster I have been blessed with an editor who not only has a wide knowledge of the Norfolk, Suffolk and Essex sea-borders but also, as proved by his own books, a deep feeling for all the craft and seafarers of yesteryear. Because space now presses others to whom I am equally grateful for answers to queries and for help at various times are only too briefly mentioned below: — Dr R. E. J. Weber, of the Commission on Maritime History of the Royal Netherlands Academy of Arts and Sciences; Commander F. C. van Oosten, R.Nl.N., Director of the Historical Department Naval Staff; Lieutenant-Commander Ph. M. Bosscher, R.Nl.N.; Mr Tim Shaughnessy, of Old Fort Erie; the staff of Portsmouth Reference Library; Lieutenant-Commander C. O. Abbot; Captain R. E. Sanders, former Superintendant of Pilots at Harwich; Major Sidney Harvey, one-time CO of No. 9 Super Heavy Battery, RA; Colonel K. W. Maurice Jones; Brigadier W. G. Shackland, one-time CO of 98th HAA Regiment, RA; Colonel J. H. Boag; Major J. D. Braisly, RA, Editor of *Gunner*; Mr M. G. Little, of the Royal Marines Museum; Miss M. J. Perry, Curator of the Hydrographic Department; Mr David Sherlock, of the Department of the Environment; Mr Peter Northeast, of the Suffolk Local

Landguard Point lighthouse, built in 1861 and destroyed by fire in 1925. *Masons Photo Service*

History Council; Mrs Gladys Wilton; Miss Gwen Dyke; Miss E. D. Guinness; Messrs Hervey Benham, S. Brown, T. E. Cook, Paul Fincham, G. R. Garnham, A. H. (Chubb) Horlock, John Leather, E. H. Lewcock, George Mack, Henry Maxwell, Norman Scarfe, Francis W. Simpson, Francis Steward and Leonard T. Weaver.

Finally, I hope that, for the contemplative East Coast cruising yachtsman, this will become a cabin book to while away a few hours in some still deserted anchorage, if he can find one, or else that it will provide him with a new back-in-time theme for winter's fireside cruising. For the historians and for students of naval and military operations, and perhaps for a politician or two, I am sure there is much still left on these old and formerly neglected bones for future picking over.

Ipswich, March, 1983                                              F.V.H.

**Overleaf:** Landguard Fort from the air, with the 1875 buildings on a roughly circular plan inside the older bastioned walls.

*East Anglian Daily Times*

# CHAPTER ONE

# Invasion Fever

THOSE with adult memories of Felixstowe in the early days of the last war will know that particular sense of dread, mixed with a morbid excitement, which the threat of invasion brings. Visions of the spoliation of well-loved countryside, even of precious hearth and home, with all the attendant risks to life and limb, were uppermost in mind, and with them came realisation that an orderly peacetime existence was very much a thing of the past. There was, moreover, a feeling of abandonment when Ipswich, twelve miles inland, was no longer considered to be a safe reception area and the London evacuees and quite a few local residents departed westwards.

All was finally rammed home on a beautiful sunny day by the sight of men, stripped to the waist, smashing through the immaculate promenade to provide foundations for concrete anti-tank blocks throughout its length. Wire-rope-linked obstacles were rapidly placed on the beach itself, together with contact mines and much barbed wire. On the road to Felixstowe Ferry a notice warned of a minefield in the adjoining turf. Angular concrete pill-boxes, with a variety of ingenious disguises, dotted the countryside which was already denuded of signposts. A particularly large concrete defence post on the Woodbridge by-pass sported a name board—HOTEL ENDISNERE. Bellringers stood by to sound the tocsin. A great gun of No. 9 Super Heavy Battery appeared with its own shed on a spur of the railway by the Ipswich road and with it came rumours of an armoured train full of belligerent Poles who one night almost fought a battle with the skirmishing Local Defence Volunteers, soon to become the Home Guard.

Felixstowe, it was clear, was in the front line of a Defence Area and all vehicles entering the town were eventually obliged to display an official pass. Much more can and should be added by those with first-hand memories of forty years ago and indeed by the very few who can now recall the invasion scare of the 1914-18 War. Then the pill-boxes were round and there were barbed-wire-fronted trenches along Felixstowe beach. History should record that the board of the local electricity company gravely debated the purchase of a rifle during the first world-wide conflict.

So much for the sea-borne threat, but in both wars the invasion of air space was very early begun. The dreaded triple-dipping of the electric light, followed by complete darkness, a hurried descent to the coal cellar and the

1

sinister drone of an airship remained vivid in the memories of many people for the rest of their days. The thrill of the questing searchlight with high-level gunnery and night-fighter activity against the relatively few intruders of the first war seems never to have been eclipsed by experiences of the much more dangerous air-raids of the later struggle. The eerie quality of those early "Zepps" was perhaps matched only by the next generation's fears of large-scale parachute landings.

From the outbreak of hostilities in 1939 the Observer Corps maintained a ceaseless vigil from the top of P Martello Tower in Felixstowe, working in close co-operation with the newly invented "RDF". Tall lattice masts at Bawdsey in Suffolk and at Great Bromley in Essex were once the outward visible signs of this early radar, while P Tower itself still exists as a coastguard station and a reminder of the Napoleonic invasion threat. Bombs soon fell here and there, and Heinkel floatplanes laid magnetic mines in the harbour approaches.[1] A special lookout was kept near Felixstowe Dock to plot the fall of the latter, but it did not prevent the sad loss of a destroyer, HMS *Gipsy,* near Landguard Fort.

It seemed that the stronghold on the point would at long last be in action as local men were employed on urgent work to increase its effectiveness. New gun emplacements and observation posts were constructed, one being named after Darell, the hero of this tale. There was supporting armament on Beacon Cliff, across the estuary at Harwich, at the now-vanished Brackenbury Fort and on Bawdsey Beach. A 1939-45 range chart in one of the buildings at Landguard forecast the destruction of any naval threat at the very limit of normal eyesight, and this certainly could not have been said for the same target

area when De Ruyter roamed our seas. Thoughts of broken windows during peacetime target practice from Landguard and Brackenbury now gave place to the possibility that the fort guns would next be used in earnest. No longer could it be said, as learned counsel for Colonel Tomline averred in 1876, that Landguard Fort was there "not for the defence of the realm so much as for the defence of Felixstowe against Harwich . . . or of Suffolk against Essex".[2] The cherished right to fly the Union Flag every day, a privilege granted to very few saluting bases, had indeed taken on a new significance.

*     *     *

The present Landguard Fort, however, is not the main subject of this tale. Closed down since 1957, it is at least the fifth stronghold to be built on the same spit of land and much mental adjustment of today's scene must be made before a full appreciation of the events of 1667 can be realised. Useful aids are Francis Place's seventeenth century drawing entitled *Langer Fort by Harwich*, John Kirby's estate survey of the lordships of Sir John Barker in 1740/41,[3] Henry Davy's nineteenth-century etchings and some of Charles Emeny's old photographs in Charles Corker's *In and around Victorian Felixstowe*. In the mind's eye all the various stages of the development of the modern town of Felixstowe, as distinct from the original, slightly inland village of Old Felixstowe, must now be stripped off like successive skins of an onion. Where houses, shops, seafront developments and port installations now abound just heathland and fields, small woodlands, a few homesteads, scrub-covered cliffs and a great stretch of benthills, common and marshland on the Felixstowe

**Opposite:** A 12-in. railway gun of No. 9 Super Heavy Battery, R.A., alongside the Ipswich-Felixstowe road at Trimley Heath. The roof of its purpose-built shed has been rolled back.

*Imperial War Museum*

**Right:** An armoured train with eager Polish crew and armament reminiscent of the sponson guns of First World War tanks.

*Imperial War Museum*

low ground become the setting for this scene. Remove P, Q and R martello towers, a boathouse and a few dwellings from Henry Davy's sketch at the time of King William IV's death in 1837, put back the old trees and the resultant picture will show the invasion beach and cliffs much as they existed one hundred and seventy years before.

Looking seaward from the High Road, at the Orwell Moathouse corner, all the shops of mainstreet Hamilton Road must now give way to dusty Mellor's Lane, then running only to the cliff edge. Somewhat to the left, appearing above the trees, great gouts of black smoke blow away in a gentle wind from nearly north. They emerge from a tar barrel on a gaunt structure in Beacon Field, and there is a flurry among a knot of men at its base. The time is around eleven o'clock in the forenoon of Tuesday, the Second of July, 1667, of the old-style Julian Calendar still in vogue in England. This, however, was the Twelfth of July of the new Gregorian Calendar then in use in Holland. The all-important flood tide will be coming up Felixstowe beach until four in the afternoon. Away to the right of the smoking beacon the cliff face suddenly turns away inland while the beach and low ground beyond it stretch away in a great curve towards Landguard Point. There a large Union Flag flaps uneasily near the King's Bastion of the fort.

This tale, however, cannot yet be enjoyed to the full without some

**Opposite:** A view of Felixstowe in 1837 from P Tower to Cottage Point (now Cobbold's Point), from an etching by Henry Davy, of Ipswich.
*Author's collection*

**Right:** A bank-holiday invasion of Felixstowe in the days before the First World War. In the distance on the extreme right is the much-eroded Felixstowe Cliff and the area of the Dutch landing in 1667.
*Collection of the late Harry Wilton*

knowledge of its background events and of the nature of the threatened coast and the waters within four or five miles of the shore. In days when most men know the essentials of space travel to the Moon, and some will have read in their history books of the Mutiny at the Nore, how many in ten thousand ashore can tell also of the Middle Ground, the Gunfleet, the Sledway and Hollesley Bay? Yet these names, applied to the anchorages which the Dutch treated as their very own, were common knowledge in 1667 of all who dwelt in Felixstowe and Harwich. Notwithstanding the very roundabout and tedious journey by road, they were only too well aware that, by sea, the entrance to the ravaged Medway was a mere forty miles away. The Whiting, Bawdsey Sand and the Shipwash were then very familiar hazards for ships near Orfordness and, after 1794, they certainly conjured up local memories of the Lowestoft pilots who were said to have been clapped into irons for putting Sir John Orde's HMS *Victorious* upon the Bawdsey Sand.[4] As for talk of "clapping", while yachtsmen will have no trouble with such nautical terms as are necessary for this tale, how many would now say of a vessel which suddenly altered course to tack, "and then she clap upon a wind"?

The casual watcher on the shore sees the coastal flats uncovering their expanse of shingle, sand and mud twice daily and, far out from the elevation of the Naze, he may discern part of the Gunfleet Sand at low tide. From sea

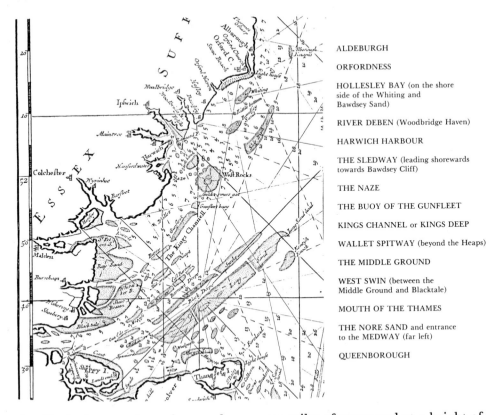

ALDEBURGH

ORFORDNESS

HOLLESLEY BAY (on the shore
side of the Whiting and
Bawdsey Sand)

RIVER DEBEN (Woodbridge Haven)

HARWICH HARBOUR

THE SLEDWAY (leading shorewards
towards Bawdsey Cliff)

THE NAZE

THE BUOY OF THE GUNFLEET

KINGS CHANNEL or KINGS DEEP

WALLET SPITWAY (beyond the Heaps)

THE MIDDLE GROUND

WEST SWIN (between the
Middle Ground and Blacktale)

MOUTH OF THE THAMES

THE NORE SAND and entrance
to the MEDWAY (far left)

QUEENBOROUGH

level he looks over about three and a quarter miles of water and at a height of
fifty feet his horizon is some nine and a half miles away. He may perhaps think
that here and there the surface is more ruffled than elsewhere, and wonder
why isolated groups of whitecaps appear but, except for the ships upon it, he
does not give the North Sea a great deal of thought. The seagoer, on the other
hand, knows that the whole area landwards of a line drawn from the North
Foreland to Orfordness is a maze of shoals converging towards the mouth of
London River, with channels known as "deeps" between. The only parts of the
great Thames Estuary shoal system not so contained are the seaward end of the
appropriately named Long Sand, the very tip of the Sunk Sand, the whole of
the Shipwash and the far-flung Kentish Knock.

On the seaward side of the first line of offshore banks is the Kings Channel
or Kings Deep, which craft coming coastwise from "the back of the Shipwash"
used on their way to the Thames. At roughly half-way point its name
nowadays changes to West Swin, because East Swin has long been an
alternative title for the Kings Deep. The Dutch, however, used the latter name
for the whole course to the Thames and they boasted that they had learned to

navigate it "with as little danger as sailing in and out of the Texel".[5] To this end they took soundings, made charts and prepared written instructions for their officers. Many references to the Kings Deep follow later, and near its juncture with the West Swin the shoal called the Middle Ground is found. Alongside this bank is the very lonely, and, for some historians, rather elusive anchorage often used by De Ruyter's fleet during the Second Dutch War.

Landward of The Heaps, formerly a separate north-easterly projection of the Middle Ground shoal,[6] is the narrow and shallow gut called the Spitway, which leads between the Gunfleet and the Buxey sands. This gives access to an inshore course for light-draught vessels, through the Wallet and the later-named Medusa Channel to Harwich. Such traffic, described as coming "over the Spitts", played an important part in beating the Dutch blockade. Looking towards the Thames, from the Middle Ground onwards, the channel skirts the great Maplin Sands which are here shown in two parts, the Blacktayle and the Shooe. Five miles across the estuary is the Nore Sand and the entrance to the Medway, which the Dutch called Rochester or Chatham River.

Next, looking north-eastwards up-coast from Felixstowe, a wide channel called the Shipway, here unnamed, passes on the landward side of the Shipwash shoal on a course for Orfordness. Further inshore, on the other side of the Bawdsey Sand and the Whiting, lies the famous anchorage of Hollesley Bay. Beyond Orfordness and its early lighthouse the coast leads five miles along the shingle bank to Aldeburgh, a place from which many reports add their quota to this tale. Now, off the chart and twelve miles further up-coast, past Thorpeness and the few remains of bygone Dunwich, the coast traveller comes to Walberswick and Southwold. There the rather exposed anchorage of

The original nature of Landguard Common, now covered by port installations, is shown in this oil painting of 1854 by John Duvall. Here the Suffolk Artillery Brigade Militia are engaged in a sham fight. *By kind permission of the Trustees of the Suffolk and Norfolk Yeomanry (Parker Gallery photograph)*

Sole Bay was much used by the English navy during the Second Dutch War. Lowestoft, ten miles still further northwards, was not the port it is today because the cut-through from Lake Lothing to make its harbour did not take place until 1831. Yarmouth, in nearby Norfolk, had its Dutch invasion scares and was garrisoned to repel the enemy. It found itself, however, on the fringe of greater activity down-coast and it provided a most useful haven for colliers blockaded on their way to London.

Another chart, dedicated by Captain Greenvil Collins to Samuel Pepys, gives a closer scrutiny of the Felixstowe and Harwich inshore waters. The royal yacht *Merlin* was used for this survey some sixteen years after the Dutch attack of 1667. During this Second Dutch War whole fleets lay at anchor in partially sheltered waters near the tip of the Gunfleet sand, little more than five miles out from the Naze. The Gunfleet then dried out to a greater extent than it does today and the enemy could be clearly seen from the higher ground ashore. For an understanding of some of the action it should be remembered that the deep-draught course from the Gunfleet anchorage to Harwich is most roundabout. It runs in anti-clockwise fashion behind the West Rocks and Cork Sands towards the Sledway, an ancient channel leading landwise from the open sea.[7] Then the course runs through Felsto Road[8] towards Landguard Point, keeping well out to avoid the inshore flats, and finally it passes through the narrow channel between the Ridge and Andrews shoals. This tortuous approach was the cause of many a false alarm at Harwich.

Thus, for the enterprising Dutch, the Shipway and the Kings Deep, alias the Swin, provided an ideal beat for over fifty miles all the way from Orfordness to the Thames. With anchorages so conveniently situated in the vicinity of Orfordness, in the Sledway, at the buoy of the Gunfleet, the Middle Ground and the Nore they could menace the entire coast. It was in the Sledway and Gunfleet anchorages that the people of Harwich most dreaded to see them, and for day after anxious day they trod the well-worn path to Beacon Hill to find out whether the enemy were still "quiet neighbours". If, however, the Dutchmen were seen to be under way then, furiously, the coast watchers would cogitate their motion.

# CHAPTER TWO

# The Early Bulwarks

L ANGESTUNA of the Domesday Survey of 1086 developed into a variety of names of which Langer and Landguard are the most recent. One can only guess, however, at the form of the locality when the confluence of the Orwell and Stour estuaries, as tradition has it, flowed under the cliffs of Walton and Felixstowe until it finally reached the sea "about Hoasley Bay". If Langer then existed at all it was probably as an island of sorts amid saltings of a greater projecting Essex coast. On the other hand the bulk of the low ground leading to Landguard Point may well result from a build-up of coastal drift, combined with considerable soil deposit from the ebb of the estuaries. The former is certainly the reason for the attenuated seaward bank of the River Ore which now enters the sea at Shingle Street, about a mile below its seventeenth-century termination.

It seems that Camden provided the earliest description and that only the future excavations of archaeologists and geologists can add to his picture:-

> ". . . the shore is very well defended by a vast ridge called *Langerston,* which for about two miles, lies all along out of the sea, not without great danger and terror to mariners. 'Tis, however, of use to fishermen for drying of their fish, and does in a manner fence the spacious harbour of Orwell."

The first part of the estuary running up from the Harwich Harbour entrance towards Ipswich was for centuries known as Orwell Haven. Here, despite the mile or so width of salt water between Landguard Point and Beacon Cliff, the passage for ships is surprisingly narrow. The channel, moreover, runs extremely close to the Suffolk side and vessels cannot turn into the River Stour to approach the modern Parkeston Quay until they have cleared an extensive mudflat, known as The Guard, which stretches out from the Essex shore. In times long past the way into Harwich Harbour was further complicated by dangerous shoals which lay between the old Main and South Channels, and these were especially hazardous because fishing weirs were built upon them. Known as the Altar, the Glutton, the Bone and the Gristle, they were both a curse and a boon to local pilots who earned their living by knowing "the very secret way of our port of Orwell".

For centuries an arm of Walton Creek stretched from the Orwell estuary as far as the site of Felixstowe's present Ordnance Hotel, and this made Langer spit into virtually an island. The high tides formerly filled and often overflowed this creek and various other minor fleets which were said to be relics of the time when the rivers ran out to the north-east. Thus the low-lying part of Felixstowe provided an inviting beachhead for a hostile landing which, with only a few guns of even short range artillery, would be likely to command the harbour entrance and beat off any counterthreat from Harwich. Meanwhile, unless there was a very speedy mobilisation and transportation of county militia, the thinly populated country between the Orwell and the Deben, with Walton the only place approaching a township, would be wide open for an eventual march upon Ipswich.

This is a problem which has always exercised the minds of those entrusted with the defence of Suffolk, and perhaps the first of these was the Roman Count of the Saxon Shore. Walton Castle, from the nature of its remains and the artifacts found in the vicinity, is known originally to have been a Roman fort. Its last vestiges rest a short distance out to sea from the beach at Reedpond, the area often spoken of as "The Dip" on the coast road to Felixstowe Ferry.

In his estate survey of 1740/41 John Kirby shows some of the fallen ruins of Walton Castle very close to the shore; it is also said that the western wall of this stronghold once stood well back from the edge of the cliff. Therefore it seems likely that it was the former coastal projection on which this castle was built, rather than the vicinity of the present-day Cobbold's Point, which originally formed the eastern extremity of Felixstowe Bay. This impression is strengthened by the naming of the area between Orwell and the old Deben port of Goseford as *The Corner of England* in a map drawn between 1173 and 1200. Here was a site well chosen to oversee the former entrances of both rivers

Walton Castle, from a drawing of the remains made in 1623 and attributed to J. Sheppard. These "stoneworks", as they were called locally, have long since fallen into the sea near the dip in the cliff road to Felixstowe Ferry.     *Suffolk Record Office, Ipswich (qS9)*

and it was here that Hugh Bigod, whose descendants had so much to do with the beginnings of the port of Harwich, maintained a baronial castle. Seized by Henry II after the troubles of 1157, it continued as a royal stronghold until 1175. It was then purposely demolished not only to avenge the wrongs which Bigod and others "had frequently inflicted on the Lord King" but also because the new castle of latest design at Orford had probably superseded it. In addition it was no doubt threatened by coastal erosion. Its static garrison was unable to prevent the landing of the rebel Earl of Leicester and a force of Flemings at Walton on 29th September, 1173, but Orford Castle, when attacked, repelled them. They were finally defeated at Fornham St Genevieve, near Bury St Edmunds, on 17th October. There was another landing of "318 experienced knights" in the Orwell on 15th May of the following year and these Flemings, sent by Philip of Flanders, linked up with Hugh Bigod's forces for the eventual taking and plundering of Norwich. Ralph de Diceto, Dean of St Paul's and onetime incumbent of Finchingfield, recorded these stirring events of his own lifetime.

In Harwich Harbour itself, Bloody Point, now politely known to other than than grounded yachtsmen as Shotley Spit, is reckoned to be named after a battle between ships of King Alfred's navy and those of marauding Norsemen in 885. Ipswich was plundered by sea-raiders in 991 and 993. King Canute landed in the Orwell in 1016 and King Sweyn followed him in 1069. In 1326 the dread Queen Isabella came from Dordrecht to Orwell Haven with her paramour Mortimer and a force of mercenaries, this in spite of an attempt by Edward II to mobilise East Coast ships against her. Again, in September 1338, it was necessary to assemble a large fleet to repel a threatened invasion. Then followed an attempt by French galleys in 1339 to fire the town of Harwich. This however was avenged in the next year when Edward III sailed from the harbour to join with the rest of his fleet from Goseford and demolish the French navy in the Battle of Sluys. For some time there were fears for the King's safety and the household accounts of the Black Prince, who stayed for a while at Shotley, show payments to men who were to watch out for his royal father's return.

Such warlike use of Harwich Harbour brought increasing risk of reprisals and a need to strengthen the local defences. To this end the "Bailifs and good men of Harwich" had already announced in 1338 their intention to enclose their town with a wall, but their first grant of murage was revoked because Ipswich claimed sole control of the haven. Nevertheless, Harwich got its wall in the end but, although looking most impressive to those approaching from the open sea, it did not run along the western perimeter. It apparently availed nothing during a French raid of 1450 when, because of the negligence of the watchmen, "the town was spoiled and destroyed by our enemies and our neighbours to the number of nine were slaughtered". A thumbnail sketch by a

Richard Lee's proposed fortifications for Landguard Point (left) and Beacon Hill (right). The former design is almost identical with that used for Southsea Castle, which was built in 1544-45.

*By permission of The British Library*
*(Cott.MS. I, i, 56)*

Mr Lee, who is mentioned again later, shows Harwich as a walled town before the power of the gun had become fully manifest.

Meanwhile Ipswich, being the older town, always regarded Orwell Haven as the natural point of arrival and departure for its coastwise and foreign trade and there was perpetual wrangling with Harwich in consequence. This went on vigorously during the thirteenth and fourteenth centuries with the claim always made that the Ipswich jurisdiction extended down the whole river to the very tip of the Polleshead, the original name for Landguard Point, or rather for a drying-out portion of the Andrews Shoal beyond it. The rivalry continued and as late as 1513 Henry VIII granted Admiralty rights to Ipswich over all land "at any time overflown with water as far as that place." Such rights were already being asserted by the "Bayliffs, Portmen and Officers" of Ipswich, for in 1433 it had been ordered that "The bounds of the liberty of the Towne by water shall be sailed, and that every craft of the Towne shall find botes".[9] The Ipswich jurisdiction at Shotley and Landguard was never questioned but their attempted landings on the sometimes tide-covered north-eastern corner of Harwich produced local opposition. Also in demonstration of these privileges the Ipswich Admiralty Courts were occasionally held on Landguard Point.

The great interest of Henry VIII in coastal defence is evidenced by his gun-mounting castles at Deal, Walmer and elsewhere and by his visit to "Harwict" in June, 1543, when "all his army by sea" was to assemble and receive his commands. Four years earlier he had sent down three "sad and expert" men to advise on the defences. They had a powerful presence, for

"even women and children were seen using the pick and shovel at the bulwarks". The ancient septaria walls were now outmoded and well-sited batteries were becoming the vogue. These were usually protected by substantial ramparts of earth, turfed to keep them in shape and having the additional advantage of making them less noticeable to the enemy. Two such bulwarks were set up at Harwich, one on the Beacon Cliff and the other in or near the town. One of the towers of the wall was made into a blockhouse.

There is among Sir Robert Cotton's manuscripts in the British Library a "plott" concerning proposed fortifications at Beacon Cliff and Landguard Point. Although this plan is endorsed "Ano 25 Hen 8us", which is 1534, it is now thought that it was actually drawn up ten years later, thus fitting in better with the King's visit and work at Harwich in 1543 to designs by Lee. The latter later became Sir Richard Lee, Surveyor of Fortifications, whose work at Berwick is better known. His two projected strongholds for Harwich Harbour both had central keeps, complex batteries, bastions, curtain walls and indications of a drawbridge and moat. The proposed castle at Landguard is in fact almost identical with the original design for Southsea Castle.

Since the earliest known bastioned work in Europe is said to be that built by the Italian engineer Michele San Michele at Verona in 1523, Mr Lee seems to have been well in touch with the latest practice. He provided for no fewer than forty-seven gun embrasures at Landguard, and his project for Harwich was even more elaborate because he planned a large semi-circular battery on the very face of Beacon Cliff. Neither fortification appears to have been built in brick and stone, however, perhaps because of the crumbling nature of both

13

sites. According to a chart of the time of Henry VIII the first defence work on Landguard Point was of somewhat rounded shape, probably just a turfed sconce.[10]

Whatever its form, it is certain that the first fortification near Landguard Point was not built until after 1539. On 27th March of that year the Earls of Oxford and Essex signed a now fire-charred report which reads as follows:

"There is between that h[aven and] Colnes being on Suffolk syde a point called Lan[ger Point] where ther maye arryve and londe 20 thousand [men] and resorte to theyre shyppes agayne, without dawnger [for] neyther they of the Suffolke syde where they maye a[rrive] nor yet they of Harwyche shoulde do theym dis[turbance]. For the ad voyding whereof, if it myght lyke the [King's] highenes that a substanciall Blokehowse myght b[e buylt] and made at the same poynt, and fortefyed with Ordyn[ance], it wolde keepe all that stream on both sydis from [any] dawnger."[11]

Blockhouses were eventually erected both in Essex and at Landguard, and State Papers of 1547 record that a captain, a lieutenant, a porter and six gunners were stationed at "the house at Langer Point" and the same sized garrison at "the house at Langer Rood". The situation of the latter is a matter for considerable debate. If not near Landguard Point itself it is difficult to

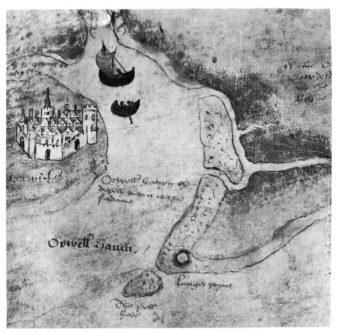

Portion of pictorial chart (temp. Henry VIII) showing Harwich as a walled town and an indication of an artillery sconce near Landguard Point.
*By permission of The British Library*
*(Cott.MS. Aug I, i, 58)*

accept Major Leslie's alternative suggestion that it stood in the vicinity of the "Garrison Rood" or "Garrison Spring", the source of the water supply to the later fortification. At that distance, right across the marshes of Langer Wet Common, sixteenth-century artillery would have been inadequate to repel shipborne invaders, whether by sea or in the estuary. A low-lying site near the water, like that occupied by the other blockhouses at East Mersea and Bradwell, seems indicated. Perhaps, as Mr Charles Trollope has recently suggested, the second blockhouse, if not somewhere else on the Langerston bank, defended the landing place near Walton Ferry. It is said that a search for a secure foundation for Walton Battery, known locally as the "Doolie Fort", produced a suggestion from a fisherman that they should build it on top of a former fortification which he called "Old Harry".

In 1553, at the very end of the reign of Edward VI, the seven bulwarks at Langer, Harwich and Mersea received orders to return the "Ordinaunce and Municon" to the Tower of London, but almost immediately the need to refortify arose following the accession of Queen Mary and "the Commotion made by John Dudley, Duke of Northumberland against her". The townsmen of Harwich then greatly strengthened the defences at the south-eastern corner of their walls, surrounding the Tower of the Angle with a spacious and elevated bastion. Not only did this have a field of fire over the estuary and along the southern and eastern faces of the town but it also equalled in height a hillock which, from a distance of only five hundred feet, menaced the entire southern wall and the main gate. This large defensive work, known as the Queen's Bastion or Battery, also shortly as "The Mount", was armed with "great guns"[12] from Landguard Fort on the express orders of the Queen given in Framlingham.

Despite Queen Mary's loss of Calais to the French in 1558 and the continual friction between Spain and England later, the first twenty-six years of Elizabeth's reign saw no serious threat posed to the English coastline. True, there was a minor scare in 1571, when Ridolfi's Catholic plot envisaged the landing of troops from the Low Countries at Harwich and Landguard, but apart from an inspection of the area the authorities did nothing. In June, 1578, Lord Darcy was requested to examine the defective fort "besides Harwich" and in the next year yet another survey was ordered. The main anxiety in 1582, however, was that shingle was being washed from the north and east through a sea breach at Landguard and that Harwich Harbour was in consequence deteriorating. Whether a repair was made is not said, but the Ipswich bailiffs and the local landowners denied responsibility.

Then, in 1584, the breach with Spain quickly revived interest in shore defences but, by that time, many earthworks, being particularly susceptible to weather damage, were in a parlous state and were in other respects inadequate. At Harwich an estimate of 1587 contemplated the construction of

An eighteenth-century drawing of the Burial Ground near Landguard Fort, attributed to Francis Grose. This shows the eroded remains of a former turfed sconce. Silas Taylor, writing in 1676, mentioned an ancient fort on this site. *Suffolk Record Office, Ipswich (HD480/2)*

no less than 682 yards of turf-faced earthwork, with an additional 250 yards for the faces and flanks of four small bulwarks. There was to be a ditch of 10 feet depth and 33 feet width in circuit with this earthwork and it was to have a rampart 10 feet high and 20 feet broad, topped with a parapet 4 feet high and 5 feet thick. All this was in addition to repairs to the existing earthworks and to three old towers. Three gates were to be replaced, complete with "bridles, drawbridges and ironwork", one being the principal gate of the town. There was provision also for "piles, poles, planks, fagots and ironwork for a palizade of great length to defend the ranges". Finally the estimate, which totalled £1328, included the construction of "a scluse to receive and keep back the water" and for "a bulwark of stone to skowre the haven".

In December, 1587, a survey of the coast of Suffolk again stressed the vulnerability of Langer Poynt and called for the construction of "a sconce with walles of Torfe where there must be planted 6 peeces of Ordynance". This was backed up by another report from the Deputy Lieutenants in the following month, and there soon came references in the State Papers to military pay at "Langgarsid Bulwork" and "Langgerodd Bulwork" with the same establishment as that of some forty years before. In 1588 the Ipswich Chamberlain's accounts show that an earthwork was in progress at Landguard and that a Mr Gregory received ten shillings for "the drawinge of a plateform" for it. On 26th October there was another payment of 8s. 6d. concerning "wyne, suger, cakes and beere bestowed upon Sir Philip Parker and his men". This was the Sir Philip Parker who lived at Erwarton across the estuary near Shotley and was

Sheriff for Suffolk in 1580. The work at Landguard seems to have been completed by 19th December, under which date the following quaint entry appears:

> "Item, to Mistress Lymefilde for a supper, a breakfast and hors meat bestowed on Sir Philipp Parker and his men, £1 11s.
>
> "Item, for the hier of 7 horse to Langer, when the knightes and the rest of the gentlemen rid thether, for to carye their meskettes and there to shoote at their apoyntments."

It is likely that the sconce recommended in 1587 is the "ancienter fort" referred to in Silas Taylor's manuscript history of Harwich in 1676. He said that it existed "where now is the common Burial for the Soldiers and where yet can be seen two Faces and Flankers of a Bastion;the remains doubtless of the ancient one; the rest of it being eaten away by the Sea". In this connection a portion of the seashore near Landguard Point in a fortifications plan of 1716, recently discovered by Mr Charles Trollope, and a later drawing of the burial ground are of particular interest. Whether these show the last surviving corner of a turf-bastioned fort or, more likely, just the vestiges of an hexagonal sconce and ditch is a subject for lively discussion.

However, the Armada threat had already subsided, for it was on the evening of 8th August, 1588, that thirty-five ships had come to anchor in Harwich Harbour with news of the Spaniards' defeat. At a solemn thanksgiving service celebrated in London's old St Paul's "eleven of the Spanish ensigns were hung to the great joy of the beholders as 'psalmes of Praise' for England's deliverance from sore peril". Harwich had certainly been well equipped to face a Spanish landing, for 46 guns had been placed on the new earthworks, 17,000 soldiers had been stationed in nearby Essex and at one time the famous *Ark Royal* was at hand for the defence of the harbour. Sir Harbottle Grimeston, who was in her, expressed the opinion that "she wolde have doun more good service than all the land forces". In Suffolk only two thousand of the militia had been assigned to defend the county's ports and landing places. Ryce's *Breviary of Suffolk* tells of the rest, 2,500 in number, who were sent to Tilbury.

Lord Howard of Effingham, commander of the victorious English navy, was in no doubt as to the importance of Harwich Harbour. After a visit to the port he wrote to Lord Burghley saying "the haven hath not its fellow in all respects not in this realm and especially as long as we have such enemies so near in the low countries". He was no doubt thinking of the Spanish army which was still operating against the rebellious Dutch, it having been the intention of the Armada to transfer these troops to England. The war with Spain was in fact continued until Elizabeth's death in 1603, but after 1596, when Lord Howard and the Earl of Essex destroyed Philip's new armada at

Cadiz, there was not much action. The *Corslet* and the *James* of Ipswich were attached to Lord Howard's squadron in this latter operation, in which a contingent of the Suffolk Militia also took part.

Even before the Spanish threat, and for nigh on two centuries afterwards, the Suffolk and Essex coasts were plagued by the Dunkirkers who were privateers, pirates almost, operating from the French port. Six or seven of these raiders, blockading the coast north of Harwich in 1596, were said to have plundered between twenty and thirty coasters and fishing boats and taken their masters captive. Again in 1600 the Harwich bailiffs were urgently warned that twelve ships had sailed from Dunkirk with a thousand musketeers aboard and it was thought that they might make "some attempt upon the coasts of Essex about Harwich". By and large, however, the Dunkirkers did not threaten serious invasion of English soil and the coastal defences everywhere were once more neglected.

All this time, slowly but surely, plant and bird life was making a pleasant invasion of the whole Landguard area. Golden plover, snipe and wildfowl became established for the future delight of many a sporting subaltern. Nature built up its own sea defences in the shape of grass-bound benthills and produced a wonderful variety of wild flowers in summer. According to Leslie the "sea thistle", found at Landguard, was eventually adopted as the badge emblem on the sabretache and pouch of the old Suffolk Artillery Militia. Sea Thistle was once an alternative name for the Sea Holly or *eryngium maritimum* which John Kirby singled out for special mention in his large-scale survey of the district in 1740/41. Like other plants found on the Felixstowe common, it had useful medicinal properties, in this case with a notorious side effect. The candied roots of this apothecary's delight were to be eaten in the morning "to prevent the Plague and Contagion in the Air", but they were also said to "provoke venery". A box of this aphrodisian sweetmeat became the traditional welcoming present for incoming foreign princesses, no doubt with the very laudable object of prolonging the royal line.

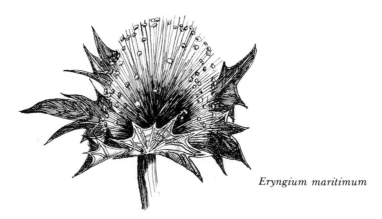

*Eryngium maritimum*

# CHAPTER THREE

# The Fort of 1626

ALTHOUGH the England of James I was officially at peace with the rest of the world, this was in stark contrast to the King's relations with Parliament and certain citizens, who did not hesitate to criticise him in forthright manner. In exasperation, therefore, he commanded his loving subjects "every one of them, from the highest to the lowest, to take heed how they intermeddle by Penne or Speech with causes of State, and secrets of Empire, either at home or abroad, but containe themselves within that modest and reverent regard of matters above their reach and calling". Any person heard so offending was to be reported forthwith and was to receive harsh punishment "for example to others".

This proclamation of 1620[13], combined with almost continual activity on the part of the Dunkirkers, led Peter Johnson, master of the *Cat* of Hamburg, into dire trouble. In 1623 his vessel was riding "near his Majesty's Fort of Lantguard" when, as his petition to the Privy Council reveals,

> "he unhappily espied a Hollander shipp taken by a Dunkirker in sight of the said Fort, whereat being very much aggrieved and having formerly suffered by the same Dunkirker in that very place and manner, and being in great passion and extraordinary drunk, he uttered these words against his royal Majesty: 'then your King is naught', for which remark he hath ever since suffered imprisonment in the gaole at Harwich."[14]

It is not known whether clemency was ever extended to this poor fellow, but it is clear that there was then a fort of some sort at Landguard.

All the same, according to a report of 1624, the defences of Harwich were again in ruins despite the outbreak in that year of hostilities with Spain. In the next year the new king, Charles I, became faced with an additional threat from France and the reinstatement of harbour bulwarks then became a matter of the greatest urgency. Some preparations had in fact already been made, since it had been decided in 1621 that all the coasts should be put into a state of defence. In 1623 a commission consisting of four knights, "an ingenieur or two and other expert men" reported on the state of all forts and castles. In due course they received instructions to demolish all those of little use and where necessary to "renewe and fortifye *alla moderna*". Thus regard was to be paid to the new style of artillery fortifications evolved first by the Italians and then

19

A seventeenth-century drawing of Landguard Fort and the low ground at Felixstowe by Francis Place, who lived from 1647 to 1728.

greatly developed by the Dutch during their Eighty Years War (1566-1648) with Spain.

Wisely an entirely new construction was agreed upon for Landguard and instructions were given in 1624 to go ahead. A Simon von Cranvelt was probably involved in the design of the new works because a man of this name was induced by our ambassador in Holland to come over to England "for the making of fortifications within this kingdom". He soon died, however, and his representatives were paid £100 in 1626.[15] Thus, thanks to Spinola's threat of invasion, Landguard, unlike Sheerness, was able to face the Dutch with worthy opposition forty-one years ahead. Had the construction of the new fort in Suffolk been left until the outbreak of the Second Dutch War, as happened with the defence works at the Medway entrance, the work would not have been completed.

The situation in 1625 was so tense that even before the new fort was built a thousand men of the Suffolk trained bands were ordered to be ready to proceed at an hour's notice for duty at the Landguard bulwarks. Replacement of brass ordnance for the iron guns of the existing battery was sought because it was feared that the Dunkirkers might take advantage of the French hostilities to make a raid. Over at Harwich, where all ordnance was dismounted, platforms decayed and forts abandoned, people feared not only the sack of the town but also the destruction of "the fifty or sixty sail of Newcastle" laid up in the harbour. Between Orfordness and Thorpeness there were only "eight honeycombed iron pieces". The authorities at Aldeburgh were requesting a cannon because their shore was so deep and "by reason of the marshes at both ends of the Town there may be landed by boats and ships 10,000 men in an hour's space". Dunwich and Southwold each had only two old and useless guns.

Construction at Landguard Point proceeded rather slowly and certain people were reported to the Privy Council in 1626 for refusing to carry timber. It was also necessary to seek a warrant to take fresh turf. In October of the same year the Earl of Warwick, who had so far been controlling the construction, handed over that duty to the Earl of Sussex, who happened to be

Lord Lieutenant of Essex. There had previously been some arrangement whereby both lords acted in the lieutenancy but the latter had long been agitating for a change, maintaining that "an Army can hardly be well governed by two Generals". With the full co-operation of the Earl of Suffolk it had already been decided that, although the building, provision of armament and peacetime garrison would be administered as part of Essex defences, troops and companies of Suffolk horse and foot militia should always be in readiness to defend Landguard Fort. They were "to give repulse to any enemy upon sodern alarum or attempte". This accounts for future references in official papers to "Landguard Fort in Essex" and, perhaps, in this situation lay the seed of considerable dissatisfaction regarding the generalship at the time of the Dutch attack in 1667.

On relinquishing his responsibility, and not wishing to be blamed for any future delays in the completion of the fort, the Earl of Warwick requested a survey of the considerable amount of work already carried out. A report made on 11th October, 1626, confirmed that, although four months' further work was necessary for completion, "ther hath beene great care and judgment used not onlie in the well husbanding and spending of the Kinge's money, but also in the substantiall and exquisite workemanshippe of the said Fortes". The plural covers other defences also under construction at Harwich, where a massive "half-moon" bulwark was erected on the King's Quay with platforms for fifteen brass and iron guns. A new parapet was built "upon the oulde mounte called the Dunn Bulwark", together with three platforms for twelve guns, and three more guns were mounted south of the town. Also provided were palisades, guard and store houses and a stock of ammunition, tools and various utensils "fit for land service".

The work in progress at Landguard was described in such detail, with dimensions of the bastions, curtains, ramparts and even the foot-banks, that very little is left to the imagination.[16] The steady build-up of the carefully graded embankments, surrounding and connecting the mounds and wooden platforms of the batteries already set up in each corner, can easily be visualised, as also the placing of fresh turf cladding on each completed section and the pegged-out markers for work yet to be done. Particulars of the buildings to be erected in the sixty-yard or so square of the interior are all given, but for a brief description of the whole it is best to turn to Samuel Dale's *History and Antiquities of Harwich and Dovercourt* which was published in 1730 and included the text of a manuscript history written by Silas Taylor in 1676:

> "The *Landguard-Fort* mention'd by our Author, was a handsome square *Fortification* consisting of four Bastions, viz at each Corner one mounted with divers Guns, those towards the Sea being the largest; the Entrance into it was over a Draw-Bridge, thro' a Gate over which was their

Magazine; fronting the Gate was a handsome Brick Building in which the *Governor*, when he was there resided: Adjoining the South End of which was a neat *Chapel*, in which the *Chaplain* read *Prayers* twice a Week, and preach'd a Sermon on the *Sunday*. On each Side of the *Parade* was a double Row of Brick *Barracks*, each containing eight, those on the right hand, being for the Habitations of the *Deputy-Governor, Master-Gunner*, and the *Quarter-Gunners*; and those on the left for a *Sutling-House* [17], and the rest of the Lodgings for the Garrison; between these last and the Gate was the *Guard-Room*, for those upon Duty. Fresh Water is brought in Pipes under *Ground* from *Walton* aforesaid, about three Miles. About sixty men used to be here in Garrison."

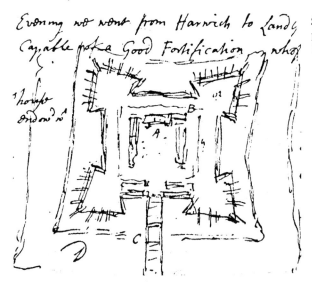

Sketch plan of the 1626 fort on page 6 of James Thornhill's diary, 1711.

*Victoria and Albert Museum*
*(L.1380. 1961)*

The rod mentioned in the progress report of 1626 is the Rhineland rod of approximately twelve feet, and this points to a Dutch design. For a perspective view of the whole fort reliance has so far been placed on John Kip's representation in his *Prospect of Harwich* of 1712-14, but this is now shown to be faulty in more than one respect. A rough sketch-plan in John Thornhill's diary of 1711 gives indications of a perimeter wall, with a covered way between the foot of the ramparts and the ditch, and this is fully borne out by a scale drawing discovered recently by Mr Charles Trollope during a visit to the Public Records Office. Ninety years of weathering and various improvements and rebuilding of ramparts, etc., account for differences of a few feet in the measurements as compared with those quoted at the time of the original building.

As for armament, the first corner batteries mounted thirty guns in all,

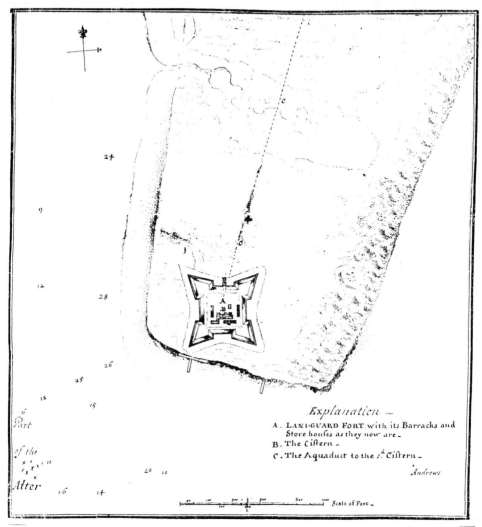

**LANDGUARD FORT, built 1626.** The bastions are: top left, WARWICK'S; top right, QUEEN'S; bottom right, HOLLAND'S; and bottom left, KING'S. Unlike the present day, the tip of Landguard Point was then very blunt and the fort itself was so near the sea that, despite the provision of a strong breakwater, the King's Bastion was constantly threatened by erosion. Also faintly shown on the plan are two sea breaches into the north and west sides of the moat. The creek system, crossed by the pipeline to the fort, is almost certainly the result of the serious breakthrough of 1582. The narrow ship channel running close to the Landguard Beach is indicated by soundings and beyond it lies the Altar Shoal with the remnants of fish weirs upon it. The cruciform building to the north of the fort is the brewhouse and around the burial ground, amid the sand dunes, can be seen the last vestiges of the former artillery sconce.

Adapted from a Crown copyright record of 1716 [Ref. PC.1.3/45] *in the Public Record Office by permission of the Controller of H.M. Stationery Office.*

twenty-four demi-culverins of iron and four demi-culverins and two sakers of brass. Nine of these guns were placed in each battery "towardes the channell" and six in each of the other two. A later list of 1626 raised the total to "43 peeces of Ordinance" made up of fourteen culverins and fifteen demi-culverins of iron and a mixture of brass guns consisting of two demi-cannons, two demi-culverins, six sakers, two portpieces and two fowlers. The four last-mentioned guns were presumably intended to produce rapid fire against a close-quarters attack, since each was provided with four chambers. A further nineteen "peeces of Ordinance of fine mettle" were then added in 1627, and these included a huge brass basilisk weighing four tons which would have fired a 60lb shot through its 8¾ inch bore. There were six brass culverins among them which came from the French prize *St Esprit*, renamed *The Holy Ghost* by the British navy. The remainder consisted of eight sakers and four saker-drakes, the latter being three-pounders. Altogether it was an impressive list with a grand total of sixty-two guns, backed up by stocks of "Shott of all sorts 2950" and "Corne Powder 3 lastes 72 barrells".[18]

An establishment of seventy-seven was sanctioned in June, 1627, with ranks and daily rates of pay as follows, but the warrant of 1628, which appointed Henry Rich, Earl of Holland as the first Governor, speaks of 126 men "there to be conteyned":

"The Captaine at 10s. The Leiftenant at 4s. The Ensigne at 2s. The two Sargants at 2s. for them both. The Clarke at 1s. The Drummer at 1s. The Chyrurgion at 1s. The Ammunition Master at 1s. The Prov. Marshall at 1s. The Armourer at 6d. The Master Gunner at 1s. 6d. The Gunner's Mate at 1s. Six Ordinary Gunners at 8d. 57 Soldiers at 8d. The Chaplayne at £40 per annum."

Whatever its total, the garrison did not get away to a happy start, for Major Leslie writes at some length about a mutiny of sorts in 1628. Captain Robert Gosnold of "Landguarde Neweforte" compelled the six "Chiefest auters" to draw lots for "one of them to dye". Then the winner, who happened to be "the veriest villayn of them all", was handed over to the Walton constable for transmission from constable to constable to Melton gaol but the constable at the next parish, Trimley St Mary, most contemptuously sent back the warrant to Captain Gosnold and himself discharged the prisoner. So, for the latter at any rate, the tale may have ended happily.

Apart from a requisition having been submitted in 1629 for gun-wheels, axle-trees, "flaggs of the King's coulers", pikes, handspikes and the like, little of note seems to have happened at the fort until 1634 when it was visited by "a Captaine, a Lieutenant, and an Ancient, all three of the Military Company of Norwich", apparently on a private excursion. They said they found the fort "for her warlike munition, strong ffortifications, watchful garrison, and prudential preservation, is most gallantly ordered and pruided for, at His Majestie's great charge, and care". Over at Harwich, however, they found utter ruin — "10 Peeces of Ordinance upon the wall and ffort, and as many more in another place by the key side and lying all along grouling and groaning, as if they were bed-rid and not able to hold up their heads, ever since the other over-thwaart neiboring ffort . . . began to flourish". The deterioration of wooden gun-carriages, particularly the axle-trees, can be very rapid if they are constantly exposed in all weathers.

Maybe because of hospitality received, the visitors of 1634 took far too rosy a view of the fort. In June of the very next year the Commission for His

Henry Rich, Earl of Holland and first Governor of Landguard Fort.
*From J. H. Leslie's History of Landguard Fort*

Majesty's Treasury received a "Remonstrance regarding Landguard Point" from the Earl of Holland. Describing "the great defects of the sayd fort", he remarked that forty guns lay unmounted for want of carriages, that both moat and counterscarp were unfinished and that the bulwarks and curtains were all decayed. Furthermore, he complained that the soldiers of the garrison were "reduced to extreame poverty, weakness and almost nakedness", all because the annual allowance for the upkeep of the fort was £5,600 in arrears. His plea had no immediate effect, although he pointed out that "these wants have been much increased by length of Tyme, and the longer they doe goe unsupplyed the greater the charge will be to His Majesty".

25

Then in May, 1636, the Surveyor General of Ordnance, Forts, etc., lent a hand. He submitted an estimate of £2,018 for "needfull reparacions to be done at His Majestie's Garrison at Landguard". The largest item was £1,362 for the building of a brick wall completely round the fort, "the earthen walles being much decayed and fawlne downe in divers places (in soe much) that they may ride into the Forte, horse and man". The wall was to be "12 foote in height and two foote in the grounde, six bricks in thicknes at the base and three bricks thick at the topp". The same estimate was put forward again in 1637, but it is unlikely that the work was done even then because at the end of that year no less than seven years' wages were still "in arreare unto the Captain of the Fort". Apart from thirty-five field carriages then wanted for the guns, there was a need also for double the number of soldiers because there were not enough to maintain a continuous watch at night on the four bastions and the gateway. Some enemy enterprise was apparently intended against Landguard because "the sea two leagues out of the harbour's mouth hath of late been sounded two days and a night together by a sloupe either of Dunkerke or Calais". "God knowes what money it might cost His Majesty to recover [the fort] if the enemy should once take it", wrote the Earl of Holland, but it is more than likely that this plea, like the rest, fell upon deaf ears. The only record concerning the fort in 1638 has as its subject the replacement of the four brass sakers and the two port pieces and two fowlers by iron guns. In the following year three "able Gunners" were transferred for service in the field against the Scots, but whether they went willingly is most doubtful. Puritan Suffolk refused even to provide coats for some local men raised to fight the Covenanters.

A rare print showing Landguard Fort and Harwich from the Rolling Ground. The church and fort are greatly exaggerated, and the silo-like structure is a mystery as both Willem van de Velde the Elder and Francis Place show a smaller tower with a pitched roof.

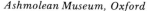

*Ashmolean Museum, Oxford*

Landguard Fort was not involved in the fighting of the first and second Civil Wars of 1642-48, mainly because it was held for Parliament throughout. In fact the financial strain was greatly eased in 1642 when it was pointed out by the Committee for the Navy that no less than £6,919 was due to the Governor. The House of Commons ordered that £1,000 be paid forthwith and agreed to "take further consideration thereafter, of the remainder, what is fit to be done thereupon". Two payments, totalling £2,500, were made in July and then, in December, not only was a further £1,000 sent following a petition concerning "the Extremeties of the Soldiers of that Fort", but pay was also sanctioned "for 100 Soldiers drawn into Landguard by the Committee for the safety of the kingdom and for 40 Soldiers as a permanent garrison". In 1645 Parliament received intelligence that there was "some practice in hand against Landguard Fort" and, as a precautionary measure, they sent a Captain Hunter with fifty men to bolster the garrison. Captain Sussex Cammocke, the commandant, was briefly confined but, after his petition to the Committee of both Kingdoms, he was restored to his command for a few months.

Discovered too late for inclusion in Major Leslie's *History of Landguard Fort* but most fortunately noted for posterity by him in a letter of 21st October, 1898, to the *East Anglian Daily Times* is a report of a survey made on the fort on 5th November, 1647. This reveals that the combined onslaught of weather and sea, coupled with lack of maintenance, could damage a coastal fort to a far greater extent than any human enemy. The wall which had been advocated eleven years before does not appear to have been built, because it is here proposed to pile and plank the escarp "after the manner of a wharf". As for the sixteen-foot wall which is here suggested, this seems to be in the nature of a revetment of the unsatisfactorily turfed ramparts. Altogether this report gives some most valuable indications of the type of terrain surrounding the fort only twenty years before the momentous happenings of 1667:

"Landguard Fort . . . is raised to a point of land, shooting out from the main land about a mile; the main sea not being above 20 or 30 yards from the foot of the fort at low water and not above 12 yards at high water, the sea many times flowing on top of the bank without the mote, and of late hath made a breach there in, to the great danger of the Fort. The channel where the shipping must come into the Harbour, (excepting some small vessels at high water) is not above 60 or 70 yards from the Fort: the ground whereon the Fort is raised is all shingle and sand which will make no upright or steadfast work: but the best it can be brought unto will be so slope and oblique, that a man may easily run up it, with a musket on his shoulder, without the help of a hand: and at this present is much slip down into the mote, so that the graft, which was at first too shallow is much filled up: and the several defects, together with the charge of preparations, estimatively, are as follows . . .

"The bridge leading into the Fort containing 80 feet in length and 12 feet broad, being decayed is to be repaired with new planks and joists, which with altering the drawbridge, will cost per estimate £35. 0s. 0d.

"The sea breach into the mote, at the point of the King's Bulwark Southward must be filled with pieces of timber 10 feet long and 9 inches square, and planked at the top for preservation of the bank against the sea which is to be backed with beach for 14 rod in length, will cost per estimate £160.

"The mote round the Fort, being filled with shingle and sand especially upon the breach of the bank made by the sea, is to be digged three feet deeper and will cost per estimate £140.

"The foot of the work round about the Fort, within the mote for the sure maintaining of the wall that it may not be washed away with water, and so keep the bank from sliding into the mote, must be piled and planked, after the manner of a wharf, round about the works, containing 127 rods in length, and 7 feet high above the bottom of the said mote which will cost per estimate £460.

"If the face of the rampire or wall round about the Fort be made serviceable against a storm, their being no turf within two miles: and the substance of the whole work being sand or shingle, is so slipping, after it is dried with the heat of the sun, that it works through the joints, and so hollows it that in short time it slides down: besides the sand and shingle doth so much soak the moisture out of the turf that it soon makes it of its own mould and nature: therefore the works round about the Fort must be faced with a wall of brick (there being no stone to be had at so reasonable a charge), which will amount unto 122 rods in length, and 16 feet high, of five bricks thick at the bottom, and four ascendant, which to do and remove the earth slipped round about the Fort, to make way for the wall will cost per estimate £1700. 0s. 0d.

"To make a parapet of earth and turf upon the rampire round about the Fort, being 121 rods in length, and 6 feet high, with a foot bank and port holes for the guns, will cost per estimate £150.

"Also the platform of this Fort is much decayed which, is to be now laid with planks and timber, will cost per estimate £75.

"There hath formerly been allowed to the Fort two boats: which are utterly decayed, and of necessity must be supplied, which will much ease the charge of bringing materials to the work, there being two boatmen allowed by the establishment of the garrison, and these will cost per estimate £14.

"There is also much want of a store house for provisions of corn and victuals, for the soldiers of the garrison which is to be built of brick 30 feet long and 20 feet broad and one story and a half high, will cost per estimate £85.

"The total sum for this estimate is £2819. 0s. 0d."

In 1648 Henry Rich, Earl of Holland, who had served as the first Governor for twenty years, threw in his lot with an unsuccessful royalist rising and was taken prisoner at St Neots. In March of the next year he was executed in London, and meanwhile Colonel Thomas Ireton, brother of the Parliamentary general, Henry Ireton, had been appointed Governor in his stead. He gave his name to Ireton's Ditch, an arm of Walton Creek which made Landguard almost into an island at every high tide. King Charles was executed in 1649 and Cromwell ruled on in England.

The house debated certain information received concerning "a design" upon Landguard Fort in April, 1651. The matter was referred to the Council of State but, whatever it was, the plot came to nothing. Meanwhile relations with the Dutch had been steadily deteriorating, mainly because of the intense trade rivalry which stretched to distant parts of the world. There were also considerable disputes over the herring fishery[19] and about the rather curious but ancient claim that the sovereignty of the English crown extended from Norway to Cape Finisterre, in what were termed the British Seas. The ill-feeling which had never waned since the execution of some English planters at Amboyna in the Dutch East Indies in 1623 was finally brought to a head when Parliament passed the Navigation Act of 1651. This hit at the vastly expanding carrying trade of the Dutch because it decreed that all imports into England must come only in English vessels or in those of the country of origin. As soon as the English started to enforce this embargo the Dutch fitted out a considerable fleet to protect their merchantmen.

With the North Sea now an arena for the conflict, Harwich, Ipswich and the Suffolk coast towns became involved in the supply of sailcloth, other stores and crew replacements to the fleet. There was also at times a great influx of casualties who, it seems, had to manage as well as they could in the nearest town ashore. At Harwich a most efficient ship repair facility was set up by Major Nathaniel Bourne. The risk of actual coastal assault, however, did not develop despite the nearness of certain sea actions and the considerable passage of Dutch men-of-war towards the Channel. The latter was the scene in May, 1652, of the clash between Lieutenant-Admiral Maerten Harpertszoon Tromp and the English "General of the Sea" Robert Blake which finally precipitated both nations into the First Dutch War.

In August, 1652, Michiel Adriaenszoon de Ruyter, of whom much was to be heard in years to come, tangled with Sir George Ayscue near Plymouth and forced the latter to take shelter in that port. Then, nearer home for Harwich, there was a considerable battle on 28th September between Witte de With and De Ruyter on the one hand and Blake and Penn on the other near the Kentish

Knock. This was claimed as a severe defeat for the Dutch, but they had the better of it off Dungeness on 30th November when, by forcing Blake to retire to inshore waters, Tromp obtained temporary control of the Channel. Blake reversed this state of affairs in February, 1653, when he scored decisively in a three-day fight in the Channel, and thenceforth the course of the war turned in favour of England.

On 2nd June the English fleet under Monck and Deane, after lying at first off Yarmouth and then in Sole Bay, became involved in a great battle near the Gabbard, a shoal in the North Sea about thirty-five miles from Landguard. Deane was killed in this fight and Monck, who had been joined by Blake, returned to Sole Bay to land a multitude of casualties and prisoners. Blake himself was eventually landed at Walberswick "in a very weak condition full of pain in both his head and left side, which had put him into a fever". One can imagine the poor man tossing and turning in his uncomfortable

"The last Pass at Scheveningen", a drawing by Willem van de Velde the Elder, who was an eyewitness of this battle in 1653.

*The National Maritime Museum, London*

accommodation as this trouble with his wounds was "besides the anguish he endures by the gravel, insomuch that he has no rest night or day, but continues groaning very sadly". The Dutch lost at least sixteen ships in this gunfight off the Gabbard, the thunder of which must have been heard all along the Suffolk and Essex coast.

Then came the Battle of Scheveningen in July, 1653, so vividly pictured by the attending elder Van de Velde. In this encounter the famous Maerten Tromp was killed and the Dutch fleet mauled and forced temporarily back to port. Monck, the victor, was soon forced to return to Harwich to refit. Although there were considerable fleet movements thereafter, no further engagements ensued and peace with the Dutch, such as it was, came with the Treaty of Westminster in April, 1654.[20]

Meanwhile in 1653 the Council of State had ordered the two old forts at Harwich to be demolished by soldiers from Landguard "and the guns . . . removed unto the Fort called Langer Point", but that defence work itself could hardly have been in a position to resist attack during the First Dutch War. The

Council of State was informed in 1656 that it was "much decayed and ruined and that the company appoynted for Guard thereof are most of them quartered in the country for want of bedding". This report produced a payment of a mere £200 on account, and any hopes that the garrison would have better treatment after the Restoration of 1660 were soon shattered. In March, 1662, the pay of the garrison was more than fifteen months in arrear and, before the end of that year, Colonel Henry Farr felt obliged to tell the King:

> "That there is in this Garrison 12 Officers and 100 Soldiers whoe for many weekes past have lived upon Rye bread and the poorest sort of Suffolk Cheese, being for want of bedding (which they have not for above 20) forced to lye on the boards in the Court of Guard their hutts being so cold as not to be endured, and many of them are now thereby and by their great wante very sick and likely to perish, there being twelve months pay amounting to £1573 12 0 now in arreare to the said Garrison."

Not only does this petition appear to have completely failed, but the troubles of the garrison must have been increased by the arrival of a company of the King's Regiment of Guards from the Continent. In May, 1663, eighty-three men signed yet another petition to be brought to the King's notice and its heart-rending conclusion seems at last to have brought an assignment "out of the first Chimney Money":

> ". . . it is against humanity it selfe to perish by languishinge famine and the reall truth is if we have not a very speedy releife both Officers and Soldiers must quit the ffortt and cast our selves at his Majesties ffeette to receive his sentence of lyfe or death, the last of which will be farr more welcome to us than to perish one after another by the worst of death, Hunger."

In October, 1663, the company of Guards was transferred to Berwick and the Duke of Albemarle, alias George Monck, who had been elevated at the Restoration, issued orders for Landguard Fort to be dismantled. Very fortunately, as later events proved, Sir William Compton, Master General of the Ordnance, then forcibly objected to this "slighting". His wise counsel prevailed and in May, 1664, a memorial was presented to Charles II for the "better fortifying" of Landguard. Its armament was to be increased by six whole culverins, twelve demi-culverins, and two minions. In November Colonel Henry Farr was appointed Governor with an increased establishment of "one hundred soldiers besides Commission Officers" and there followed an issue of an additional thirty-six pikes, forty muskets and thirty beds. It was indeed lucky that things were at last on the upgrade at Landguard, for it was soon to face its severest test.

# CHAPTER FOUR

# The Terrible Thunder

DESPITE the treaty of friendship between England and the United Provinces in 1662 the deep-seated commercial antagonism which had been the main cause of the First Dutch War of 1652/53 still persisted. Such ill-feeling had been increased, moreover, by the continued refusal of the Dutch to hand back the spice island of Pulo Run, as they had agreed to do in 1654[21], and by the English renewal and strengthening of the Navigation Acts in 1660. It was the Dutch carrying trade, and sources of exotic cargoes for it, which brought great wealth and a rapid rise of power to the sleek burgher patriciate, but since this also adversely affected the pockets and trading aspirations of a prosperous and expansionary minded English merchant capitalism another outburst of violence could hardly be avoided. As George Cocke so succinctly put it to Pepys, "The trade of the world is too little for us two therefore one must down".

By 1664 an unofficial state of war existed in areas as far apart as the Indian Ocean, where the East India Company had suffered heavy losses from Dutch confiscations of their ships and cargoes, and Gambia and the Gold Coast, where the Royal Africa Company seized Dutch slaving bases with the assistance of three royal ships under Robert Holmes. In that year also the English took New Amsterdam, the modern Manhattan, as well as other Dutch footholds on Long Island. At the same time the English occupation of Queen Catherine's dowry port of Tangier remained a constant source of irritation to the Dutch in the Mediterranean. As if all this was not enough, the never ending scramble for the North Sea herring fishery brought further reason for dispute.

It is therefore remarkable that, as late as 26th September, 1664, the rival navies were still maintaining an air of surface cordiality. On that day Lieutenant Admiral Michiel de Ruyter and Vice Admirals Sir John Lawson and Thomas Allin happened to meet at sea when going their various ways. "De Ruyter", said Allin in his journal, "came under our sterne and asked how I did and saluted me with 7 gunnes and dranke to me and I dranke to him and answered him 7 he thanked me in 3 the which I answered". On 29th November

Lieutenant-Admiral Michiel Adriaenzoon de Ruyter, from a painting by K. Dujardin dated 1669. *Vereeniging Nederlandsch Historisch Scheepvaart Museum, Amsterdam* of this same year, not far from Cadiz, Allin and his squadron fell in with about thirty Dutch ships from Smyrna, convoyed by three frigates under the command of Captain Pieter van Brakel. The latter sailed towards Allin's flagship, firing a complimentary salute, but when the English guns replied it was with a whole broadside of shot. Van Brakel was killed in the ensuing engagement, an unfortunate happening for the English also as this spurred on Van Brakel's younger brother Jan[22] to take a truly poetic revenge less than three years later.

Even before the Cadiz engagement numerous Dutch prizes had been taken in waters nearer home and the States General, now thoroughly incensed, published their declaration of war on 14th January, 1665. The English, however, did not follow suit until 4th March. This inspired John Bradshaw, Rector of Cublington, to set out in awful doggerel "Some thoughts upon the Dutch Navies Demurr and upon the first squadron of the King's royall navy". For whatever misdeeds the Dutch had done he promised them an equally dreadful retribution:

"Th' *Norwich* will powre upon you without question
Vollies of Dumplings but hard of digestion".

Thus, for some who recollected Blake's ultimate triumph over Tromp in 1653, the rather tardy declaration of the Second Dutch War was a matter for jubilation. Nevertheless in Suffolk coastal towns there were stark memories of wounded men lying about in the streets. Southwold alone had done its best in 1653 to provide care for six hundred sick and wounded, and there were many more at Ipswich and Aldeburgh. They remembered, too, that the local fishery had suffered grievously and that the crews of smacks and merchantmen, who at first had volunteered readily for naval service, became later most unwilling and were nowhere safe from the Press Gang. Therefore, for the ordinary people, this second outbreak of hostilities brought great misgivings and a mental tension which built up remorselessly for more than two years.

When war seemed inevitable the two nations made great efforts to fit out and crew massive fleets and to hire all necessary auxiliaries. In January, 1665, a list was prepared of thirty-two Ipswich ships "fit for the King's service", twenty-seven of these being of 280 to 300 tons. At Harwich, Langley's ketch, a former packet boat, was to be armed with four small guns. On each side there were more than a hundred sizeable fighting vessels, including fireships, the most dreaded weapon of the day, and in consequence the war became entirely a struggle between navies. The first clash, known as the Battle of Lowestoft, took place about ten miles off Southwold on 3rd June, 1665. In this the chief Dutch admiral, Jacob baron van Wassenaer heer van Obdam, known as "Opdam" for short or "Foggy Obdam" by the British, was blown up with about four hundred of his men. His flagship, the *Eendracht,* had had the worst of

A portion of Captain G. Collins' North Sea chart showing the Dutch coast from the Scheldt to the Texel.

*Author's collection*

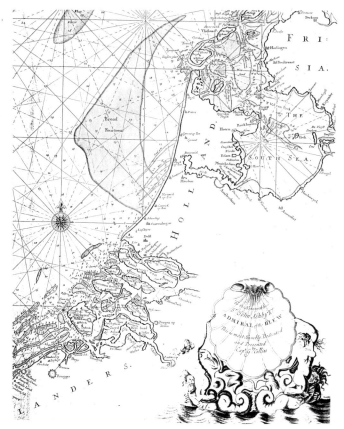

an encounter with the Duke of York in the *Royal Charles*. The Dutch lost eighteen ships by capture and fourteen more were sunk, as against the taking of the *Charity*, the solitary ship loss of any consequence on the English side.

Not only did Suffolk coast-dwellers hear once more the dreaded sound of gunfire but Sir George Downing[23], Envoy Extraordinary at The Hague, wrote of a "wonderful shooting with a continued terrible thunder" which rattled and blew open his casements and eventually "shooke the whole house and the very beds as if it had been a great earthquake". The danger for Admiral Jan Evertsen, who had taken over command after Obdam's death, was by no means ended even after his ships had reached home waters "miserably torn". Having landed at Hellevoetsluis he travelled across the island to Brielle where the populace, enraged at this decisive defeat, threw him into the harbour and he barely escaped with his life. He was, however, exonerated at the subsequent enquiry which publicly degraded some officers and shot a few more as a lesson to the others. The elder Van de Velde was present throughout this battle.

Some of his drawings, made in later years, show the ships manoeuvring before the struggle and also panoramic views of the whole action. He even included his own galliot moving under press of sail to a safer spot.

On 10th June the English were back in Solebay refitting their ships and landing wounded men and two thousand prisoners. Some of the latter were sent elsewhere in the county, resulting in a great scare at this time of the Plague. Six of one hundred and fifty prisoners at Hadleigh died at much the same time as two inhabitants of Ipswich. William Huggard, surgeon and Controller of Customs at Ipswich, ascribed the two deaths in that town to plague but two other experienced surgeons disagreed with him, it being said that Huggard had "a great hatred for the Corporation and would do anything against them". It was found, too, that there was no cause for plague suspicion concerning the other deaths in the marshall's house at Hadleigh.

Apparently Ipswich then had a bad name, but it was also said that "her present rulers were sober and disinterested". Colonel Legge's and Captain Darell's companies of the Lord High Admiral's Regiment (the original name for the Royal Marines) were quartered in the town and it was stated that the Captain, the future defender of Landguard Fort, had quarrelled with the bailiffs because they had not "waited on him at his lodging". Ipswich in fact felt itself overburdened "having 1600 sick and wounded, 300 Dutch prisoners, the two companies of foot and a concourse from the fleet, when it is at Harwich or in the roads". As for Harwich, fifteen enemy ships and 349 prisoners had been brought there after the battle but, because the port was already overcrowded and plague-ridden, the Dutchmen were sent to Colchester.

The Dutch fleet, having been badly mauled, was intensely occupied with repairs for the next two months. Meanwhile the English were on the lookout for De Ruyter, who was expected home from the West Indies. In July Vice Admiral Penn joined his ships to those left behind at Southwold but, although he took up station for a while near the Dogger Bank, De Ruyter managed to give him the slip and was home by the seventeenth. Then Lord Sandwich sailed with the fleet from Solebay towards Bergen where, on 2nd August, 1665, Sir Thomas Teddiman, who had been detached with a squadron of nineteen ships, attacked what was then a Danish harbour. His orders were to dispose of a number of Dutch merchantmen from the Mediterranean and the East Indies which were awaiting convoy home. Because of the spirited action by both shore defences and merchantmen, the difficulties caused by an off-shore wind and the fickleness of the governor of the fort, who had originally agreed with the English to withhold action and share in the spoils, the raid was unsuccessful.

The disappointed English fleet eventually came back to Solebay to land wounded and to victual ship. It went out to sea again on 28th August and was back by 11th September reporting the capture of twenty-one prizes, of which one, the 60-gun *Westfriesland*, is heard of later at Harwich. A Dutch fleet of eighty or ninety paid a flying visit to Solebay in October but found no English ships to fight. For two or three weeks they hovered about the mouth of the Thames but they had much sickness aboard and, with the onset of winter, the beginning of November saw them heading for home. During September, Johan de Witt and two other deputies of the States General had accompanied a Dutch fleet to Bergen and successfully brought back the merchantmen to Holland. William van de Velde the Elder was with them and made drawings of the event. Johan de Witt had also been active in the political field, arranging the demotion of Cornelis Tromp and the appointment of Michiel de Ruyter on 1st August, 1665, as commander-in-chief of the Dutch navy in his stead.

With the enemy barely out of sight of Suffolk, Treasurer Lord Southampton and Lord Ashley, safe in their sanctuary from the plague at Oxford, then delivered their own broadside against Landguard Fort. Information had been lodged by the Farmers of Excise of Suffolk "of considerable quantities of beer and ale being brewed at the Fort of which the officers had not suffered to take account". This enterprise of the sutler, however, seems to have been stoutly defended and entry refused to his premises. An official letter of 7th November, 1665, sternly said "Your fort must claim no exemption in this case"[24]. This dispute carried on until 29th July, 1668, when Alderman Bucknell, a co-farmer of the Excise, was told he could have a warrant to enter the fort "but he must not take from the soldiers; but that the Governor must certify what is exported"[25]. Apparently the sutler was selling beer outside the fort and sending it to sea.

In January, 1666, both France and Denmark declared war against England and the Dutch started cruising the East Coast as soon as Spring set in. Lowestoft, expecting trouble, had petitioned for four demi-culverins in February, and at Harwich there was a great increase in activity at the new shipyard. The old ship repair facilities, which had dealt with men-of-war in the sixteen-fifties, had been leased to the Navy Commissioners in 1665 and Anthony Deane, the famous master-shipwright, immediately started to build. His first launching in February, 1666, was the successful third-rate *Rupert* of 827 tons and 66 guns, and she was followed by two sixth-rates, the *Frances* and the *Roebuck*. In the same year two little sloops, the *Spy* and the *Fan-Fan*, were built at Harwich from the left-over timbers. They were said to have been built to the order of Charles II "to clear the Sands before this Harbour, then much infested with small Dutch Pickaroons".

Prince Rupert was sent down-Channel with a sizeable squadron towards the end of May in view of a supposed threat from the French. This splitting up of the English navy then led to the defeat of Albemarle and the rest of the fleet in the bitterly fought Four Days' Battle. The cannonade commenced some miles off Ostend on 1st June and raged back across the North Sea until at last on 4th June the Dutch "bore away to leeward". The English, as Allin thankfully put it, "glad to part soe", immediately stood over to the English shore. It had been a terrible battle, with the Dutch much superior in numbers. Even so, both sides were badly shattered, "almost beaten to pieces". Things would have been a great deal worse for the English had there not been a timely distant view of Prince Rupert's squadron returning from the Channel and a growing shortage of gunpowder on the Dutch side.

As it was the English lost about twenty ships sunk, burnt or captured, including the *Royal Prince*, "the finest ship in the British Navy". The spectacle of her ashore on the Galloper shoal provided a famous subject for Van de Velde. British casualties were horrific, and the victorious Dutch also suffered considerably in ship losses and men. On the authority of Pepys and Cooper it is known that the sound of firing was heard both in London and in Cambridge. The impact on Isaac Newton's eardrums in the latter place is also said to have produced a remarkable prediction. Newton, coming down from Trinity College observatory, told some of the Fellows that the English had just lost a great sea battle. This, according to Walter White's *Eastern England*, he had deduced from the intensity of the firing, which could only have come from two large fleets. Because the sound grew louder and louder, "he concluded that they drew near our coasts, and consequently that we had had the worst of it — which the event verified".

A notable English casualty was buried in old Harwich church and his handsome memorial tablet was later removed to the present church of St Nicholas. He was Sir William Clarke, Secretary-at-War to Charles II and also the Duke of Albemarle's secretary for twelve years. His harrowing experience during the great battle is described in Lindsey's translation of the extremely wordy Latin inscription:

". . . as he fought by the admiral's side, on the second day he lost his right leg by a cannon ball, on the fourth his life. Yet notwithstanding his wound, he would not suffer himself to be moved from the danger of the battle but whilst the rest of the wounded were carried ashore he remained in the ship which was shattered and exposed to the fire of the enemy, and with surprising constancy awaited the doubtful issue of the battle and his own life. His wounded body, having for several days been tossed on the sea, was at length cast into this haven, whilst his soul retired to its native heaven . . ."

Another casualty, which caused "great lamentation both of King and Duke" and all who knew him, was Captain Philip Bacon, second son of Nicholas Bacon, of Shrubland Hall, near Ipswich. His ship, the "Bristoll Frigott of 52 Gunns", was brought into Harwich with her masts and rigging

Portion of a line engraving by I. Ottens showing the Four Days' Battle of 1666.

*The Parker Gallery*

gone and no fewer than one hundred and eighty enemy shot in her hull. Ipswich Corporation, the town militia and the chief gentlemen of the county paid the greatest respect to the captain's body when it was brought upriver and the funeral itself took place in Coddenham Church, where a long memorial inscription is still to be seen.

It was during the Four Days' Battle that Rear Admiral Sir John Harman put up a particularly heroic fight. He brought his damaged ship into Harwich for repairs and set sail just one day later to rejoin the fleet. Two men from the *Royal Charles*, who had landed at Harwich on 3rd June, asked to see Pepys in London next day just as he was going home for dinner. The stark realities of a naval battle again come through in his diary description of one of them:- "his face black as a chimney and covered with dirt, pitch and tar and powder, and muffled with dirty clouts, and his right eye stopped with oakum". After the battle seventeen more disabled ships came into Harwich Harbour and such were the efforts made that they were ready for service within three weeks. Eight hundred of their crews deserted during the same period while, in the town itself, limbless wounded men were left lying in the streets and the plague raged unabated.

The Council of State, responding to the now definite threat of invasion, at last ordered the governors of all forts "to use all industry to have their works repaired, fortified and victualled for two months and to fill up the allotted number of soldiers". In particular "the Plateforms of Landguard Fort" were to be viewed and repaired and "pallisados from Ipswich or Harwich or anywhere else" were to be sent there with all convenient speed. As for bricks, they were

A drawing by Willem van de Velde the Younger of the surrender of the *Royal Prince* during the Four Days' Battle of 1666.                           *National Maritime Museum, London*

sent round from Gravesend. Soon Sir Charles Lyttelton's and Colonel Legge's companies of the Lord High Admiral's Regiment and the Earl of Oxford's troop of Horse arrived from Sudbury for duty at the fort. The Horse were ordered to encamp within two miles of the fort and, in all probability, they did so on the high ground of the nearby township of Walton.

The need for these moves was immediately apparent, for the Dutch fleet was sighted in great force off the Suffolk coast. Hoping that he could surprise the English before their fleet could be refitted, Johan de Witt set in motion his plan to end the war at a single stroke. With the backing of the States General he instructed De Ruyter to sail into the Thames estuary with a fleet of eighty-eight men-of-war, twenty-two fireships and the usual auxiliary craft. These carried no fewer than 20,000 seamen, 1,600 marines and 2,700 soldiers, but the operation, which appeared so feasible to those at The Hague, immediately ran into practical difficulties. "Not one pilot could be found who would dare take such a fleet or even one large ship into the river." Those with most experience of the Thames Estuary, having previously sailed there in small, light-draught craft, knew full well the dangers of a massive fireship attack launched against a States fleet crowding these very restricted waters.

Nevertheless, on 24th June, 1666, Vice Admirals De Liefde and Bankaert and Rear Admirals van Nes and Evertsen did sail into the Kings Deep to

40

reconnoitre the position. Having penetrated to a point where Colchester bore northwest-by-north they saw a ketch lying near the Middle Ground and she, most probably a Medway scout, immediately made sail. Then, looking further down the channel towards the Thames, the probing forces saw seventeen frigates "lying on guard". The latter signalled each other by firing guns and loosing their top-gallants, while "those on land answered them in equally good order". Then, as the frigates made off towards the English fleet lying off Queenborough, the Dutchmen reckoned they could see fifty large men-of-war and sixteen fireships. Further progress was clearly inadvisable, and the report of the admirals at a later council-of-war brought about an indefinite postponement of the plans for a Thames landing.

The idea of an alternative land assault on Harwich had been considered but that also was abandoned. "General" de Ruyter judged it foolhardy to risk the narrow entrance with the States ships because his commanders had reported sight of twenty-five ships there under "the Rear-Admiral with the white flag". The Dutch reckoned also that there were twenty-eight guns in Landguard Fort, a further two batteries of twelve guns each at Harwich and that the English "were well awake and in a position to put up a good defence". So, although the Dutch fleet remained to harry the East Coast, their great plan was back on the shelf. It was indeed a different kettle of fish in the next year when the English fleet was hardly in evidence.

Meanwhile the whole Suffolk coast was in a state of considerable alarm. On 2nd July Edward Suckley, a lieutenant at Landguard Fort, reported to James Hickes at the London Letter Office that about sixty sail of the Dutch fleet were anchored near the Gunfleet and that the garrison had fired "4 whole colveringe" at one of their scouts which had come within range while "running two (to) and againe". He supposed that she had been shot "thorough and thorough" and that she would certainly have been sunk had it not been dark. The *Spy* ventured out of Harwich Harbour the next day and it seems that she brought in this small vessel, whose crew of three abandoned ship and made for the shore. On 4th July Suckley said that since his last letter the Dutch had made an excursion to the southward and "ye Great Guns went off very Thick but the *vent* as yet is not knowne". The enemy soon returned to their anchorage with their number increased to about a hundred sail. A letter from Ipswich, of 5th July, stated that "30 of De Ruyter's men in his boat landed on the marshes about Bardsey[26] for fresh meat for their general but boat and men were all taken as was some wine going to him". Then, on 7th July, Suckley informed Mr Hickes that the Dutch fleet was still riding in sight of the coast and that the Earl of Suffolk had visited the fort. A survey had been made regarding necessary repairs "which will be sudingly done on Friday". He also said that Sir Charles Lyttelton had come to the fort "where he is ordered to remain until further order". The appearance of the Dutch had "put the whole

County into armes to attend their motion" and rumours came all the time that the English fleet would soon be putting in an appearance.

At Harwich the Earl of Oxford had ordered "both horse and foot for the security of these parts" and an alarm had been raised when Landguard Fort fired a gun to stop a vessel which was coming into the harbour during the night. She turned out to be an English ship bringing in pressed men for the *Rupert* and another man-of-war in the harbour. Then, on 10th July, a Dutch hoy and another vessel set ashore ninety English seamen "returned on exchange" from Holland. These prisoners had been taken in the last engagement and were all out of hospitals being "weak, old or children". No fewer than twenty of the latter were under twelve years of age, presumably powder monkeys from the English men-of-war.

A report from Southwold of 10th July spoke of nervousness occasioned by the discharge of two militia companies stationed in the town and the appearance of eleven enemy vessels off their coast. Other soldiers had been hurriedly sent to join the local troops but they had only nine good guns and barely enough ammunition for two hours' skirmish. Next day there were three Dutch men-of-war and a French sloop near Aldeburgh and a further eighty Dutch vessels "five leagues south-east". The people of the town feared it might be sacked as they had "only 35 ill-disciplined men of the trained band and 20 guns, but not enough to manage them".

On 14th July, having little else to offer, Suckley embarked on his oft-quoted description of an extraordinary maritime jaunt out of Harwich. Leslie's version of State Papers Domestic tidies up the text somewhat and transcribes what clearly seems to be the word "handed" as "hanged". Presumably he meant he would be roughly manhandled. So, for the truest view, it is preferable to keep to Suckley's unpunctuated and difficult to read wording and, even for those days, his execrable but often amusing spelling:

"The Dutch are still at Ancker and this morning Excersiceing theire men  Upon Monday or Tuesday oure English fleet intends to be with them the Lord give us Good Suckses  Upon Thursday last in the afternoone one of our Galote hoyes with a Great store of Company would needs goe to take a perfet vue of the Dutch fleet and when they were about a League & a halfe from them the Dutch faired a Gunn for a small vesell to chease ours who coming out and bareing to ours some of the English Gentlemens harts began to fayle  then they desired the Master to Make all his sayle he could from the Enymie but hee Refuseing and telling of them hee ought to be handed when he com backe they began to Mutinigh & told him they would cot his Throught but if he would by faire meanes they would Give him a peece of plate and told him theire lives were at a Greater value than his two of them being Knights which I sh (torn) feare nameing at present but they (torn) perseved theire promise to the master    they faired some Gunns Each at the other and the English vesell had brought her in had not the Gentlemens harts bein soe faynt."

With the enemy at such strength in the Gunfleet anchorage it was necessary that when the English came out of the Thames estuary they should do so in great force. It was also clear that any vessels which emerged from Harwich would be subject to piecemeal destruction. By 13th July most of the English ships in the Medway and the mouth of the Thames were ready to sail and, after waiting for a few more ships to be commissioned, they started to move north-east five days later. Navigational difficulties and the exceptional number of ships involved meant snail's pace progress down the Swin. Then on 19th July the wind came north and they were forced to anchor near the Middle Ground until the twenty-second, when the wind shifted somewhat to the west. Slowly spreading along Kings Deep came the most stupendous sight those waters had ever seen. "The Dutch who had two or three weeks lyen vapouring at the Gunfleet, were amazed to view it, and some of them said, they thought that every oak in England was grown into a ship since last battell." The enemy themselves were no mean sight, since by then they numbered ninety-eight men-of-war with twenty fireships and attenders, but the forest of masts now approaching them belonged to:

"90 men-of-war
17 fireships
50 or 60 attenders of the fleet
2 hospital ships
24 victualling ships
a fleet of merchantmen bound for Gothenberg and part of the
    Newcastle collier fleet"

The view from Beacon Cliff was so clear on this occasion that Taylor remarked that "the Flags of both were easily discerned without glasses". The Dutch wisely drew off to sea, leaving the Gunfleet and Sledway anchorages vacant for the English warships. The *Rupert* and the new-built *Fan-Fan* came out of Harwich to join them and the victualling ships, the colliers and the Baltic-bound merchant fleet went into the harbour "to stay there until the expected fight be over". By special order of the Duke of York any soldiers wanted by the fleet were withdrawn from Landguard Fort, there being a proviso that eighty men be left behind to defend it. During the afternoon of 22nd July Sir Charles Lyttelton's and Colonel Legge's companies and "40 of Colonel Farr's men" were embarked. The *Spy*, the other shoal-draught vessel recently built at Harwich, brought in a letter from Sir Thomas Clifford, written to Lord Arlington when the *Royal Charles* was near the Middle Ground. The sender did not sound very optimistic about its prompt delivery in

43

London, for he said "if the Postmasters neglect their duty and this comes late, will your lordships see one of them punish'd and the rest will amend".

The battle started between nine and ten in the morning of 25th July after the English fleet had weighed and come down upon the Dutch with a very light air from the north-east. The guns were heard over a very wide area, one man writing, "I do think our Fleet will bang the Dutch to some purpose, of which I pray God Almighty they may". A captain at sea off Yarmouth heard "very great shooting, which made his ship bounce as if struck aground". The St James's Day Fight, as it came to be called, slowly moved across the North Sea from near the North Foreland to Holland. It was a great victory for the English, its magnitude perhaps best appreciated from a statement which Pepys endorsed as having been read from the pulpit at Bow —

"July 29th 1666
The Dutch totally routed
14 ships taken
26 burnt and sunk
2 flagg ships taken and out of them 1200 men and what else they would and sunk them.
Taken in all 6000 men
Our Shipps have blocked up the Zealanders in Flushing and ride before them.
The Dutch fleets have got into the Texell, we ride before the same.
The Lord Mayor ordereth thanks to be given this forenoon throughout the city."

Harwich, of course, regarded this as a special deliverance and fired a victory salute "to show their sense of this mercy". At Ipswich, by order of the Earl of Suffolk, there were "bonfires, guns and bells". Harwich, however, had an extra reason to celebrate, for it was this St James's Day Fight which brought everlasting fame to a locally built ship.

On the second morning of the battle the pursuing English strove to catch up with the Dutch ships making for the sanctuary of their shoal waters. The wind was so light, however, that the two fleets just drifted along out of gunshot of each other, but this did not suit the *Fan-Fan's* crew. One of their number had been killed earlier in the action by a shot from *De Zeven Provincien*, and thus they felt they had a score to settle with De Ruyter's flagship. The casualty had occurred as the little sloop "lay behind" the *Royal Charles*, in all probability while she was in tow of this famous vessel. It was remarked at the time that the *Fan-Fan* had "been made the last week for Prince Rupert at Harwich" and he was on board the *Royal Charles* with the Duke of Albemarle as commander-in-chief.

So the little *Fan-Fan* set off "upon this extraordinary chase to be revenged" and, with both sides looking intently on, she "made up with her oares", brought her two small guns to one side and "for neare an houre continued plying broadside and broadside" against her enormous enemy. Clifford described it as "soe pleasant a sight, when noe ship could come near, there was soe little wind, that all ours fell into a laughter and I believe the Dutch into indignation to see their Admiral soe chased". Eventually *De Zeven Provincien* managed to score two or three hits "between wind and water" with her stern guns and the valiant attacker was forced to disengage.

There was much worse to come for the Dutch, however. Not only were they blockaded within their own harbours but also, on 8th August, Sir Robert Holmes made a devastating attack on merchant shipping at anchor in the Vlie, a channel between the islands of Vlieland and Terschelling. A Dutch traitor told of their whereabouts and "the Prince's Pleasure Boat", the scouting *Fan-Fan*, soon confirmed their presence. Of the one hundred and seventy ships in the roadstead, guarded by two small men-of-war only, a mere ten or eleven escaped the destruction of "Holmes's Bonfire" and this they did by going up a creek. Next day the village of West Terschelling was attacked and many dwellings and storehouses burnt. If they did not have it before, the Dutch most certainly now had a great desire for revenge. It is hardly surprising that many of them regarded the Fire of London in October as Heaven-sent retribution.

Lack of provisions forced the English fleet to return home by 17th August and, during that month, no fewer than a thousand sick seamen were landed at Southwold. Despite his terrible setback De Ruyter was at sea again on 26th August and manoeuvres took place to prevent joint action by the French and the Dutch. For three weeks Prince Rupert held the Straits of Dover, but the danger abated at the beginning of October when De Ruyter was invalided home from Dunkirk with a fever. In any case the weather did not then favour hostilities and the naval war for 1666 was at an end.

A view of Harwich from a yacht in the harbour which has all the appearance of the seventeenth-century scene; a water colour by an unknown artist.     *Felixstowe Town Council*

# CHAPTER FIVE

# The Mounting Tension

NOTWITHSTANDING the July victory there was still a great feeling of insecurity in Suffolk and Essex. On 15th August the Council of State issued orders "to cause Landguard Fort to be repaired where need arises, also a Redout to be raised in such a manner as shall be thought best for the defence and security of the said fort". Whether money was ever made available for this work remains questionable, but the troops at any rate had been brought up to strength by recruiting at Sudbury after the battle. Dutch prisoners of war had also been escorted to that town from whence, on 8th September, 1666, a company of the Lord High Admiral's Regiment, under Captain Nathaniel Darell, marched into Landguard Fort. Back in the time of Charles I Darell was known as "a man as well of great fidelity to his King, as bravery against the enemy", and both he and his company had served at sea during the St James's Day Fight. He was a son of a one-time Lieutenant-Governor of Guernsey.

Money for the English navy was now so short that a start had been made as early as 2nd October in taking the first and second line men-of-war out of service. This was to be expected in winter, but soon news began to filter through that the King had no intention of fitting them out in 1667. It would have been cold comfort, too, for the Harwich people when the Duke of York gave orders before 1666 ended to set up a battery of guns at Sheerness and a chain across the Medway channel near Gillingham to protect the laid-up ships. Since the pay of the Chatham shipyard workers eventually ran up to twelve months in arrear, and suppliers of materials were equally badly treated, many delays ensued and the work was never satisfactorily completed.

In December, 1666, the States General approved Johan de Witt's renewed plan to fit out a massive fleet and February, 1667, brought news of exceptional shipyard activity by the Dutch. On 6th March Pepys remarked that the few remaining active units of the English navy were to be dispersed at various ports in small squadrons. He also revealed that there was some fear of invasion and that even a blockade of the Thames was to be expected. As the Dutch public were still thoroughly stirred up over the St James's Day battle and particularly by the sack of poor people's dwellings on Terschelling, the outlook for the Essex

The Dutch in the Medway; a portion of a line engraving by Matthias de Sallieth after Kirk Langendyk, published in Rotterdam in 1782.
*The Parker Gallery*

and Suffolk coast dwellers was worse than ever. They must have regarded all their fears confirmed when the Duke of York visited Harwich from 20th to 22nd March to plan harbour defences with Sir Bernard de Gomme [27]. Both the Duke and the King had already been down to Sheerness where, around this time, the soldiers on the guardship were described as "poor silly lads and raw country fellows". On 24th March Pepys was present at a conference in London when the King and the Duke approved plans which envisaged Harwich being "entrenched quite round".

Concerning Landguard Fort, the Council of State had already ordered that the fortifications be "finished with brick and stone, and some out-works made there". Darell's company of marines had proceeded to Yarmouth by sea in January, 1667, and had been replaced by a company under Colonel Farr. In April, however, the two detachments exchanged stations and the Landguard garrison was increased by the arrival of a company under Captain Cartwright from Harwich. Four companies of the Lord High Admiral's Regiment remained at Harwich, these being commanded by Sir Chichester Wrey, Sir Charles Lyttelton, Colonel Legge and Captain Edward Roscarrack. On his second arrival at Landguard Captain Darell immediately assumed the governorship of the fort which had been temporarily held by Cartwright pending his arrival.

Towards the end of April a Dutch squadron under Lieutenant-Admiral van Ghent came out to sea to convoy some merchantmen northwards and to carry out a hit and run raid on the Firth of Forth. The latter was a diversionary tactic which caused little damage and the loss of only a few small vessels. Meanwhile De Ruyter had sailed with the squadron of the Maas to the Texel, where he was joined by the returning Van Ghent. Attempts had been made to secure pilotage services from prisoners of war and disaffected Englishmen and no fewer than four thousand Dutch soldiers and marines had been placed under the command of Thomas Dolman, one of the chief renegades. This time Johan de Witt remained at home, possibly because of the expected peace negotiations. In his stead his elder brother, Cornelis de Witt, was to accompany the fleet as overall commander with De Ruyter. Cornelis was Burgomaster of Dordrecht, a French communication also describing him as "Ruart et grand Drossart de Putten".

On 14th May the English peace delegates arrived at Breda and negotiations started on the twenty-fifth. The States General reckoned, however, that their fleet commanders were their "best plenipotentiaries for peace" and on 27th May De Ruyter left the Texel with detailed instructions from them to attack the Thames and Medway estuaries. He embarked some troops in the Maas on the 29th, took on more later when anchored in the Schoonveld [28] and finally sailed for England on 4th June. A letter of 31st May from The Hague mentions that there were nine flutes full of soldiers and four

Cornelis de Witt.
*Vereeniging Nederlandsch
Historisch Scheepvaart
Museum, Amsterdam*

CORNELIS de WIT .
Ruart *van* Putten &.

more loaded with entrenching tools and other materials for land operations. The Dutch ran into heavy weather near the North Foreland but De Ruyter regathered his fleet and took them into the Kings Deep, where the late-starting Friesland squadron joined them. Their next move must have been awaited with some trepidation by the people of Harwich, since their defence preparations were far from complete, but the immediate objective of the Dutch was not their harbour.

Following a council-of-war held on *De Zeven Provincien* on 8th June and resumed at four o'clock next morning, a small squadron under Lieutenant-Admiral van Ghent made an early start for the Thames. The 50-gun *Agatha* was used as temporary flagship and Cornelis de Witt accompanied Van Ghent. De Ruyter and the bulk of the fleet remained in the Kings Deep to protect the rear and a few ships under Vice-Admiral Schram were deployed to watch the Straits. The Thames raiders made progress until the ebb set in and forced them to anchor off Hole Haven. There they landed a few men who burned barns and houses and stole sheep on Canvey Island until the local militia drove them away. Next day De Witt discovered that some merchantmen, which he had intended to destroy in The Hope[29], had moved upriver. Then, being

49

uncertain about the strength of the Gravesend and Tilbury defences, he thought it best to proceed as soon as possible with the Medway attack.

At dawn on 10th June Admiral Spragge had sent ships to destroy the buoy of the Nore, but its absence did not delay the Dutch one whit. The dramatic scene as the enemy ships came out of the Thames and processed round the seaward tip of the Nore Sand, turning to approach the uncompleted Sheerness fort, cannot be better described than in Edward Gregory's own words. He, a "Clerk of the Cheque" at Chatham, saw it with his own eyes, for he was helping with those guns:

> "The last quarter ebbe the enemy plyes downe the other river where he wrought seamanlike with the danger visibly before him and, if he came on ground, a whole approaching tide to lift him. Being gott about the East End of the Nore, his headmost ships stood with us, and ahead of them a galliot hoy sounding as wee suppose, who came no sooner within shott of us, then wee obleidged him to a speady retreat, nor did the foremost man of war though a great ship care much for aproaching us, after wee had placed a shott or two in him; thus wee began with them much about 5 in the evening, when their admirall now having gott the length of the Buoy, hove out his bloody flag att topmast head, when immediately a ship of theirs (the same that afterwards boarded the *Unity* att the chaine) came boguing upon us and att her stern a fireship." [30]

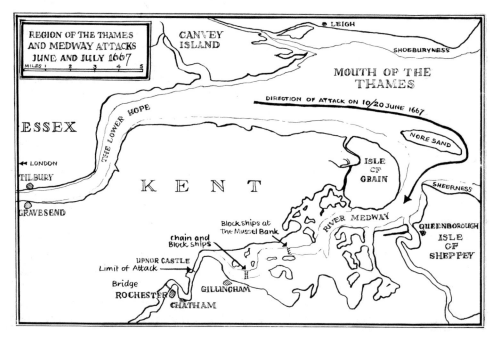

The ship which sailed into the Medway entrance, regardless of heavy fire, and also pressed ahead two days later at the Gillingham chain, was the *Vrede*. Her commander was Captain Jan van Brakel, the younger brother of the Van Brakel who had been killed in the fight with Allin's squadron off Cadiz in 1664, and he had most earnestly requested the honour of leading the attack.

After Van Brakel's bold entry, with the wind and the tide in his favour, the anchored guardship *Unity* fired one broadside, then cut her cable and retreated upriver followed by her fireships and her two ketches. It was left to the speedy royal yacht *Henrietta* to rescue the remnants of those who had gallantly served the inadequate and insecurely mounted battery which was overwhelmed once the rising tide enabled the enemy to bring his guns effectively to bear. Meanwhile Van Ghent's ships came crowding in, eight hundred of Dolman's troops landed on the Isle of Sheppey and the embryo dockyard at Sheerness, with all its stores and installations, was completely at the mercy of the Dutch. Queenborough was spared, because Henry Yevele's 14th century castle had been demolished in 1650, and looting and ill-treatment of the civilian population had been strictly prohibited. Van Brakel's crew stupidly violated the no-pillaging orders and their valiant captain himself languished in Dutch captivity aboard the *Agatha* until he was freed two days later when he gladly volunteered to attack the Gillingham chain.

During the next day, 11th June, the Dutch surveyed the channel as far as the Mussel Bank and then sent up a small squadron which worked through the night moving aside the blockships only just sunk. De Ruyter came down from the Middle Ground anchorage in response to an urgent message from De Witt and a small vessel took him up the Medway to confer about further operations. On Wednesday, 12th June, the Dutch sailed into Gillingham reach and up to the chain which had been reinforced with two cables and furnished with batteries at each end. It was guarded also by the *Unity*, the *Matthias* and the *Charles V* men-of-war and by fireships.

At this point there was a hitch in the attack until Captain van Brakel sailed boldly up in the *Vrede* and laid her alongside the *Unity*. He speedily boarded and captured her, suffering only three casualties in the process. This exploit gave the Dutch fireships a chance to attack. The first failed but the second broke through the chain without much trouble and she soon set the *Matthias* ablaze. The *Charles V* alone succeeded in sinking a Dutch fireship but was herself soon set afire by another. Van Brakel boarded her from a small craft and tried to save her as a prize, but eventually she blew up. Two fine men-of-war, in no state of defence, now lay ahead, most tempting prizes for the Dutch, but one of them, the *Monmouth*, managed to cut her cable and escape upstream. The other, the famous flagship *Royal Charles*, the renamed *Naseby* which had brought the King over from Holland to England at the Restoration, was immediately deserted by her skeleton crew. The joy of the

Dutch, who swarmed aboard, knew no bounds. Soon her British ensign and jack were both torn down and a trumpeter gleefully sounded the tune with appropriate name, "Joan's placket is torn".

Every English effort was now devoted towards fortifying the reaches which lead past Chatham to Rochester Bridge. The Dutch, according to Gregory, "spent the remainder of the day in much mirth, firing guns and sounding trumpets all that afternoone". Some of the three thousand Englishmen said to be serving on Dutch ships shouted to those on shore that they were most happy to "fight for Dollers" rather than for the much deferred payments under the impoverished Navy Office ticket system. They also enquired after and sent kind regards to mutual friends ashore. Apart from mopping up a few straggling Dutchmen, who had landed to loot, the six thousand or so horse and foot in the Gillingham district achieved nothing at all in the way of defence. Their own depredations on civilian properties in fact exceeded those of the Dutch.

On Thursday, 13th June, the enemy made their final attack with four men-of-war, three armed yachts and five fireships against English vessels moored, it had been thought, in a place of safety upriver. To do this they had to run the gauntlet in the much narrower Cockham Wood and Upnor reaches of the Medway, past Upnor Castle and some recently mounted batteries which included ten good field guns hurriedly sent down from the Tower. Nevertheless, with the loss of only one big ship, which they themselves blew up during the night, the Dutch succeeded in burning the *Royal James,* the *Loyal London* [31] and the *Royal Oak,* "three stately and glorious ships" as Edward Gregory described them. It speaks much for Dutch courage that, with everything possible being hurled against them in these narrow waters, both De Witt and De Ruyter coolly directed operations from rowed boats. Pepys said they "made no more of Upner Castle's shooting than a fly". This in itself was hardly surprising, for it was said afterwards that the fire of this particular battery "excited laughter and derision rather than alarm". Apparently the ball ammunition which had been collected did not fit the bore of the guns and some of the gun carriages were rotten. Some guns were honeycombed and the four which could be used were badly loaded. Lee, who had designed Upnor Castle in 1560, must have been turning in his grave.

The Dutch attempted no further hostilities on Friday, 14th June, and spent most of that day re-rigging the *Royal Charles,* which they were determined to take back to Holland. Saturday brought their main withdrawal downriver. Since the tides were then abating several ships went temporarily aground. Pepys said that they safely brought down the *Royal Charles* "at a time, both for tides and wind, when the best pilot in Chatham would not have undertaken it, they heeling her over to one side to make her draw little water". His sister, who lived at Leigh-on-Sea, saw the emergence of the big ship into the Thames estuary "and how they shot off their great guns for joy when they got her out of Chatham River".

Before leaving the Medway the Dutch levelled the Sheerness installations to the ground and then, while lying off Sheppey, held a council-of-war regarding further dispositions of their fleet. Van Ghent, with seventeen men-of-war and their attenders, was briefed to sail northwards to provide convoy for a fleet of merchantmen expected from the East Indies, and to attack English shipping at every opportunity. Vice-Admiral Cornelis Evertsen was to cruise between Harwich and the Straits of Dover and Rear-Admiral van der Zaan was to remain in the Harwich-Kings Deep area to give warning of any attack from the north. It was agreed also that the redoubtable Van Brakel should take the *Royal Charles* and the *Unity* to Holland, receiving initial convoy from Van Ghent. The very successful Medway operations were then rounded off with a Thanksgiving Service on Sunday, 16th June.

Harwich was in a turmoil days before news was received of the great disaster. On 7th June the Earl of Oxford, Lord Lieutenant of Essex, arrived, sent down by the King "to raise the country there". Lord Berkeley of Stratton, a Commissioner of Pepys's Navy Board, came also, having been hurriedly appointed Lieutenant-General of Militia in Suffolk, Cambridge and the Isle of Ely. He brought with him "a great many young Hectors", some of noble birth. Concerning these Pepys observed "but to little purpose I fear but to debauch the country women thereabouts". He was probably right, for there followed a marching of small detachments of militia hither and thither, dictated solely it would seem by fleeting panics at various places along the coast. Around 13th June it was decided that the defence headquarters should be at Harwich "as the properest place to receive news and intelligence".

London was kept well in touch with events by faithful correspondents who reported frequently to Lord Arlington, Secretary of State, usually through his own secretary, Joseph Williamson, or to Samuel Pepys at the Navy Office. Chief English contributors to the vivid picture of these three-century-old events were Silas Taylor, Storekeeper, and Captain Anthony Deane, Master Shipwright, of the Harwich Naval Yard, Richard Tyler, temporary purser of the prize *Westfriesland*, and Richard Browne, up the coast at Aldeburgh. Other reports came in from Southwold, Lowestoft, Yarmouth, Chelmsford and Norwich. Alarming accounts of the Medway débâcle speedily travelled throughout the land and everywhere the most extravagant rumours were rife.

Immediately after the Medway operations the Dutch fleet, still off Sheppey, was reinforced by the somewhat tardy arrival of Vice Admiral Banckaert with its last squadron from Zeeland. Then on 19th June, Van Ghent, Evertsen and Van der Zaan having sailed on their agreed missions the previous day, the main body of the Dutch fleet collected some sheep and other livestock from the island and set off down the Swin to take up anchorage again at the Buoy of the Gunfleet. These ship movements, as they slowly progressed with a contrary wind, spread alarm and despondency all along the coast.

On 18th June Silas Taylor reported no men-of-war in sight of Harwich, but he had heard of two Dutch ships aground near St Osyth. However, he had plenty of Dutchmen to contemplate before nightfall. On the same day two Deputy Lieutenants of Essex reported from Chelmsford that a great fleet, "discerned in three squadrons", had been seen from Southminster steeple. Two companies of foot had already been sent to Burnham, another two were protecting Bradwell and some horse militia had been hurriedly sent from Southminster to Manningtree. Richard Browne reported that Aldeburgh, Lowestoft, Southwold and Dunwich had been "left without forces which are all drawn towards Landguard Fort". People had carried most of their goods elsewhere since Aldeburgh might be burning "three or four hours before help could come". It was a misty morning so nothing could be seen in the Gunfleet anchorage, but a great Dutch man-of-war was standing southwards. At 7 a.m. on 20th June Browne wrote to say that the appearance of thirty Dutch men-of-war off Lowestoft had caused alarm and that fifty in the Gunfleet were expected to attack Harwich. Silas Taylor's effusion of the same day was written in instalments which not only give details of the frenzied preparations but

A drawing by Willem van de Velde the Younger of flutes getting under way in a light breeze.
*National Maritime Museum, London*

indications also of the degree of menace, which varied almost from hour to hour and was to continue so for ten more long days:

"Harwich June: 20: 1667

Sr. Last night just in the close of ye evening there came to ye Dutch Fleet in ye Gunfleet 6 or 7 sayle more from the Thames: who this morning sayled all out of ye Gunfleet wee beeing able to discerne them betwixt ye Longsand head & Bardsey sand; soe yt we by their trending conclude them gone home; and were judged by several att ye Beacon this morning to be not above 52 or 53 sayle great and small. Yesterday 2 of their small vessells went sounding below the fort; we had layd 7 colliers in length from the inside of Landguard fort a crosse ye Arme of our side Beacon & neare ye cliffe foot rocke the West-friesland a ship of above 60 Gunns soe yt by ye Altar[32] & these Shipps we should have puzzled them they haveing holes ready cutt to have been suncke had they attempted us; but in ye meane time there they rode with Jacks, Ensigne & pendant for that they appear'd to ye enemy like men of warre. My Lord of Oxford yesterday comanded severall companyes of the Militia to this Towne, & a Troop or 2 of Horse; & the like is at Landguard. This is all but to tell you I hope the Colliers at Newcastle are securd from ye Dutch for it is strange to me that they should not attempt them before they goe home or else Deale & the Downes parts. I am sr your humble servant Silas Taylor

One of our small vessels is goeing out to observe wch way the Dutch steer it is concluded by most they saile homeward   Since the makeing an end of my ltre I went out so had the sight of a great many of them about the Longsand; & also 2 great ones from ye Thames came cleare of ye Naze to our sight standing after ym.

Sr since the sealing up my letter I went out to view ye Dutch Fleet; who returned makeing for this Port by their standing about the west-rockes[33] & now they ply up and downe the foremost of them are now turned into the Sledway by Bardsey sand; the rest of their Fleet to my judgmnt are come into ye Gunfleet they being above 60 sayle.

It is sd a great ship of theirs is runne aground about the Shoe; and hath been aground 2 or 3 Tydes; but that is out of our sight; and we must expect a greater certainty of it

Yours Silas Taylor

For Joseph Williamson Esq"

Saturday, 22nd June was so hazy that it was not until evening that part of the Dutch fleet could be seen at anchor in the Sledway. At ten o'clock next morning Vice Admiral Sir Joseph Jordan, who commanded the light forces in Harwich Harbour, sailed out on a windward course to attack them. His little squadron consisted of the *Lennox*, an impressed privateer, the sixth-rate *Lily*, a galliot-hoy, of which much more is heard later, and two new fireships. It was a gallant attempt, for their adversaries consisted of thirty sail, great and small, with two admirals and a vice admiral among them. It was probably the sight of the fireships, however, which caused the Dutch ships to weigh anchor in a hurry. On his second board out of Harwich Jordan managed to get "within halfe shott' of one of the Dutch admirals and fire was exchanged. A frigate and two galliots, detached to attack the English, were forced back to their main body but the action was soon broken off because the favourable tide was spent. While they were offshore Jordan's ships saw many other Dutch vessels away to the south towards the Kentish Knock.

Next day Jordan sailed out again from Harwich with his maximum force. This time he had the *Lennox*, the *Lily*, the *Truelove* sixth-rate, the *Spy* and eight fireships to harass the enemy but, when he had penetrated through the mist to the Sledway, he found the enemy gone. Eventually the Dutch were seen far away to windward near Orfordness but Jordan could not reach them on that tide. On his return to Harwich he was told of a large Dutch ship which had gone ashore on the Middle Ground. She had been there for three or four days with two ships lying alongside to unrig her. The little *Spy* was then sent off to investigate. Next morning it was still somewhat hazy and no Dutch ships could be seen from Harwich.

Deane's shipyard pressed on with the fitting out of fireships and by 29th June eighteen were ready, these being the bulk of the twenty-six vessels impressed for service by an Order in Council of 16th June, thirteen belonging to Ipswich and one to Woodbridge. Meanwhile it was reported that Jordan was "very forward to attempt the enemy" but contrary winds prevented him leaving port and he was also plagued with crew trouble. A bare month before the Navy Board had been requested to cut expenses still further by reducing the crews of the fireships at Harwich and other places. Only enough men were to be left on board to weigh anchor and now, when they were so badly wanted, Deane sadly noted that out of eight hundred men originally on board the colliers not enough could be found to man eight fireships. On 21st June Pepys said that few seamen were standing by at Harwich "and those with much faintness". A correspondent of the day before had announced that the town was in a distracted condition "because of the enemy's continuing before the harbour".

Southwold also was in a distracted condition on 21st June because forty enemy ships were in sight and fears of a landing had increased. Guns had gone off all day and a French shallop cruising in the bay had boarded three Swedish vessels and taken clothes and provisions from them. Two of the Swedes promptly sailed into Yarmouth "for fear of five Dutch men-of-war off Orfordness". On the same day Yarmouth itself was "in a great fright", having seen thirty Dutch warships near the Barnard. Their trained bands had been sent inland to Newmarket "and none sent in their room". Two foot companies had been marched out of the town to, of all places, Ely; but two more were due to come in. As a precaution several Ostenders moored off the town quay were told to remove themselves nearer the haven mouth. Three days later at Yarmouth there was a fly-boat ready to be sunk "at the entrance of the boom" and considerable troop reinforcements had come into the town.

"The ranting Dutch have given some alarm to the Suffolk coasts", said a man named Corrie in a letter of 24th June from Norwich. He added that people were terrified "with everything which had canvas about it". On the same day at Harwich the Lord Lieutenant of Essex was much dissatisfied with the Colchester postmaster "for ill-mounting persons that come post in this important conjuncture, and neglecting to speed forward expresses and even ordinary letters". Off the coast below Aldeburgh nine Dutch men-of-war, including six with three tiers of guns, were stopping coastal traffic from the north towards London and Harwich. On the previous day, a Sunday, a Dutch boat was seen making towards the lighthouse at Orfordness but "a force goeing downe put them off from doeing any mischiefe". Sir John Rous had gone off to Southwold with his company of militia and Sir Henry Bacon's company had also departed for Lowestoft, but there were still three companies of foot and a troop of horse in Aldeburgh. Browne remarked about the enemy "certainly they intend some attempt these spring tides, the winds being very favourable unto them".

An order from Whitehall of 24th November, 1666, had only served to keep alive the widespread fears of internal disaffection. The King had commanded that all "Popish Recusants", and others within the Lieutenancy who refused to take the Oath of Supremacy and Allegiance, were to be forthwith disarmed "to remove all apprehensions of their possibility to disturb the publique peace". Even so, Browne reported in his letter of 24th June, 1667, that there were "very great reports of papists designes". Fifty were said to be "armed in a wood about Lowestofe" and several cases of pistols had been found in the house "of one Barker a papist about Framingham", also an abnormal quantity of provisions. The scare got to such a pitch that Sir Samuel Barnardiston, the richest man in Suffolk, wrote to the King and Council alleging that Captain Nathaniel Darell, Governor of Landguard Fort, was a Papist and that the seamen and soldiers under his command were at variance. Darell begged "justice against this malignity" in a letter of 29th June to Lord Arlington, and he enclosed a certificate from Ipswich worthies testifying to his good behaviour. A few days later the Council of State ordered Barnardiston to appear before them, and no more was heard of this matter.

The immediate threat to the Suffolk coast, however, was about to subside once more, if only for a short time. On 25th June Cornelis de Witt received a letter from the States General requesting him to take action against both

A seventeenth-century prospect of Harwich from Beacon Hill, by Francis Place.
*The Trustees, Cecil Higgins Art Gallery, Bedford, England*

Harwich and Gravesend, or even further up the Thames if that proved possible. On the next day De Ruyter fired a salute to mark the General Thanksgiving in Holland and afterwards his council-of-war decided that Lieutenant-Admiral Banckaert with fourteen men-of-war and two fireships should head for London River.

The raiding squadron sailed at dawn on 27th June and were at anchor a little downriver from Gravesend by early afternoon. There they were joined by De Ruyter, who had followed with some more ships, but it was soon decided to fall back to the mouth of the Thames because of sunken blockships ahead and the large number of guns mounted on the river banks. The enemy in fact came within "two shots" of Tilbury Blockhouse, which fired several rounds at them "with two brass guns that are now well mounted". Pepys noted that about eighty enemy vessels, great and small, came up the river that morning, "some of them to the upper end of the Hope". Forty-five of them were still in sight of Tilbury at four o'clock the next morning. With relief Pepys wrote on the 28th, "We hear the Dutch are gone down again; and thanks to God, the trouble they give us this second time is not very considerable". He reckoned that a chance had been missed to burn "a good ship of theirs" which went aground near Hole Haven.

John Evelyn saw De Ruyter's fleet anchored off Sheppey on 28th June, "as dread a spectacle as ever Englishman saw and a dishonour never to be wiped out". It was reported from Chatham that some Dutch vessels had "hovered about the Nore" and that two or three had even come "within the Ness" but

58

when Pepys came there on 30th June all the enemy were gone. Count van Hoorn had arrived from Holland with troop reinforcements and Harwich, although it did not yet know it, was in danger again. There the tension had abated somewhat, with growing optimism regarding the peace negotiations and the departure of the main enemy fleet down-coast three days before. Richard Browne, after speaking with a Swedish vessel, accurately reported from Aldeburgh that the enemy were "on some design, probably up the river as high as the Hope". All the time, however, there were up to twenty-five ships in the Gunfleet anchorage, or plying between there and the main fleet, but it was realised that they were there just for blockade and for fleet communications.

Defence preparations, it was thought, were going well at Harwich because a new battery had been built on Beacon Hill "to gall ships coming in, if the cannon in the fort should make them endeavour to enter on that side". On the other hand a company of soldiers had become "harassed with lying on the ground without the town" but the Lord Lieutenant had brought in his own militia to relieve it, with the exception of one company "which mutinied at Chatham and refused to march". The troublemakers were disposed of at Tilbury fort, which wanted men, but it was thought impossible to keep the rest together much longer "unless there be some provision for their Maintenance". In response to a cry from Wivenhoe a company of foot had been ordered to Mersea Island.

On 30th June Sir Joseph Jordan sailed out from Harwich when some Dutch vessels appeared in the offing, but the tide was "too far spent" and he returned to Landguard Fort. Then, as the afternoon progressed and more and more Dutch ships came along the Kings Deep, all previous anxieties returned to Harwich. By ten o'clock that evening no fewer than seventy enemy sail were in the Gunfleet anchorage and word came from the Navy Office that this time it was thought the Dutch would make an attack. There was a frantic last-minute rush to get guns mounted on some recently erected platforms and twelve hundred militia foot were said to be marching to defend the town. Not much love being lost between Deane and Taylor, the latter sneakily reported to Williamson that Deane had sent away most of his goods "to the discouragement of many who knew him no better".

Next morning the whole enemy fleet weighed anchor at dawn and headed northwards, as they would certainly do on the first leg of a course for Landguard Fort and Harwich. Their progress with a north-westerly wind and adverse tide was painfully slow, stretching jangled nerves ashore to limits heretofore unreached. Then, just as they were due to turn towards the harbour and a massive attack seemed inevitable, the enemy, every man Jack of them, sailed away up coast. At nightfall only a few tailenders could be seen away in the distance by Orfordness.

59

60

# CHAPTER SIX

# The Threat Materialises

IN view of the previous day's departure of the entire Dutch fleet from their offshore anchorage and their slow and halting passage up the coast, Tuesday, 2nd July, 1667, dawned for Harwich and Felixstowe people with a feeling of blessed relief. Silas Taylor confirmed the apparently diminished threat in his letter by the morning post out of Harwich:

> "Since my last by that expresse that went hence on Sunday, little hath occur'd; but what I guessed then I now believe the whole Dutch Fleet are come away from you: yesterday Morning they were seen at an Anchor (yett about to weigh) some of them in the Gunfleet & some in the Sledway; about 10 & 11 = of the clocke yesterday I saw them sayling Northerly with topp gallants sayles, inclining towards Orfordness & I counted by my glasse of them about 70 small and great off of Bawdsey = This Morning proves very hazy; yett they could from the Beacon discerne many of them at an Anchor where we left ym yesterday; about 9 & 10 of ye clocke this morning, the most of them were sayled out of our sight & only 4 or 5 seen in the Sledway, what course they will take I know not & this is all."

The view up-coast from Beacon Cliff, however, was somewhat limited and the post must have scarcely departed on its way before Taylor had reason to regret the sending of that note. At noon Joseph Quine wrote very hurriedly from Harwich on behalf of the Lord Lieutenant of Essex, who was understandably occupied at the time. His letter was endorsed "For his Mat'ies speciale service hast, hast hast JQ" and it was addressed "For Joseph Williamson esqr Secretary to the Right ho'ble the Lord Arlington, Principall Sectry of State at Whitehall". No doubt the post-boy who carried this express received it with the gravest enjoinders that it be promptly passed on at Colchester, Chelmsford and any other stages on the way.[34] Nevertheless, it seems that the postmaster at Harwich was unable to arrange for its dispatch until about two o'clock that afternoon.

> "My Ld Lieutenant hath commanded me (being to busie to write himself) to give my Ld Arlington notice by your hand; that the whole Bodie of the

The attack on Landguard Fort; the right-hand portion of Willem van de Velde the Elder's grisaille of 1669 with a stern-on view of Jan Roetering's ship *Het Huis te Oosterwijk*. Behind the other ships is the entrance to the River Deben.

*National Maritime Museum, London* 61

enemie is now standing in to this Towne, and their formost ships so near Landguard Fort that wee expect fire to be given on both sides everie moment. Yet wee are not certaine whether they will begin an attaque this tide or no, because the wind slackens on them, though what wind there is blowes faire for them: They come in close betweene the sands from the Suffolk coast, a way our great ships never usd to adventure, I need not tell you that my Lord is making the best Provision he can to receive them and how confident soever wee are of giving them a Repulse wee must expect the successe from the Highest Power."

As things turned out, Quine's faith in the Almighty was completely justified, but it was a letter written at Aldeburgh at seven o'clock that morning by Richard Browne which should have given the earliest and truest indication to those in London. It is astonishing that this correspondent should have missed the early morning post but, discovering this, he arranged around eight o'clock that his tidings should go by express. At the same time he thought it a good idea to enclose a private letter to his wife which, when it got to London, was to "be sent to the post house the very next post". Finally he added to his official letter the up-to-the-minute information that "just now Capt. Millesent Troope is come to our assistance haveing now 2 Troopes of horse and 3 companys of Foote". It must have been a considerable shock to him when someone informed him later that it was usual for the postmaster to pull off the express labels on such urgent communications and to send them on five or six hours later by ordinary mail. Whether this was the fate of his particular missive is not known, but it still survives in London and enables historians to fill in important details of the early hours of this momentous day:

"The Dutch fleet of about 80 saile with 9 flaggships came to anchor in our Bay about 2 miles out from shore. We did expect they would have Landed in the morning but about day Breake they all weighed, and stood nearer into the shoore, a little after that they stood to the Northward aboute an houre then they all tackt and stood to the Southe ward close by orfford light house and at this time are all past the nesse towards Harwich were we imagine they may attempt somewhat there, when they sett the watch last night they fired noe guns but made false fyers and so they did this morning when they weighed anchor. They have a Tide of ebb and but little wind."

It could be that the "false fyers" were misleading substitutes for the unlit lighthouse, but that they were some form of night signal for the Dutch fleet seems more likely. Whether the setting of the watch meant that the Dutch rowed night guard round their anchored fleet or whether it referred to the manning by the English of shore defences during the hours of darkness must also remain a riddle.

Around two o'clock that afternoon Silas Taylor sent off another letter to put his record straight. With De Ruyter actually knocking at the harbour door his earlier prediction now looked ridiculous and he obviously felt obliged to tear himself away from the intriguing view through his telescope from the top of Beacon Cliff. It was almost a mile back to his house in the shipyard and his agitation shows up in his disjointed phraseology:

"Sr, about 11 = of ye clocke after noone by the post not discovered till they appear'd come about Filstow alias Felixstow cliffe; and then I went up Beacon Hill where I have stayd till now I understood an expresse was sending away; wch I would not neglect; about one of ye clocke they came all to the backe of ye fort beeing about 47 sayle besides tenders, besides 5 that lay in the Sledway, they sent out 8 or 9 ships who came boldly into ye outer pt of ye Rowling = groundes & there just now came to an Anchor; and soe the rest that were without the Fort They have in my sight wch I could discerne by my glasse about Flixstow cliffe they have landed about 1000 men in about 50 small vessels & boats Flixstowe beacon was fired"

The Felixstowe beacon was situated in the now built-over Beacon Field, near the site of the present-day building which used to be the Cliff Hotel. The message of the smoke signal was very clear. A meeting of the Deputy Lieutenants of the County of Suffolk at Snape on 13th February, 1665, (OS) had decreed that "no Beacon neare the Costes shalbe fired but upon the appearance of a Considerable Fleete of an Enemye, and an attempt at landing souldiers from the said Shipps".[35] As for Felixstowe Cliff, it undoubtedly meant to Taylor and other contemporary eye-witnesses the extremity of Felixstowe Bay which now goes by the name of Cobbold's Point. It was there that their landward view of the coast was cut off and there, in fact, was the part of the cliffs nearest to the villagers of Old Felixstowe. In the middle distance, beyond the low-lying Landguard peninsula and stretching round the northern portion of the bay, there was largely tree-covered ground, the then quite undeveloped site of modern Felixstowe town.

Thus, since six in the morning, a truly awesome panorama had unfolded in the slow motion of those days. Strung out from the Rolling Ground, just outside the entrance to Harwich Harbour, throughout the whole of the Felixstowe anchorage and also stretching northwards beyond Felixstowe Cliff, was De Ruyter's fleet of nearly fifty men-of-war, transports and fireships with a fair number of faster sailing sloops and galliots in attendance. Further out, guarding the rear and keeping a particular eye on the entrance to the Kings Deep, were five great ships in the Sledway. Then, as those on shore anxiously watched, a flotilla of more than forty boats and barges rowed away from their mother craft and made for the Felixstowe shore. Van de Velde's picture shows galliots taking some of the landing craft in tow.

For those on the Suffolk and Essex shores (and for some historians afterwards) it seemed that the Dutch had employed a ruse to mislead the Harwich defences. Captain Anthony Deane thought that way for, in writing to Pepys, he said "I see theire intelligence so good as to return to us the next day most of our militia was departed in Souffoulke". Nevertheless, although it is true that by going up-coast the Dutch had drawn an entire militia regiment into the country between the Deben and the Alde, this was only a slice of luck which they made the most of later. Their clear intention had been to mount the attack on the previous day and it was an unfavourable change of wind which brought about the postponement and resumption on the following morning by an approach from Orfordness.

The scheme of attack had in fact been most carefully worked out. At sundown on Friday, 28th June, five transports had arrived from Holland to

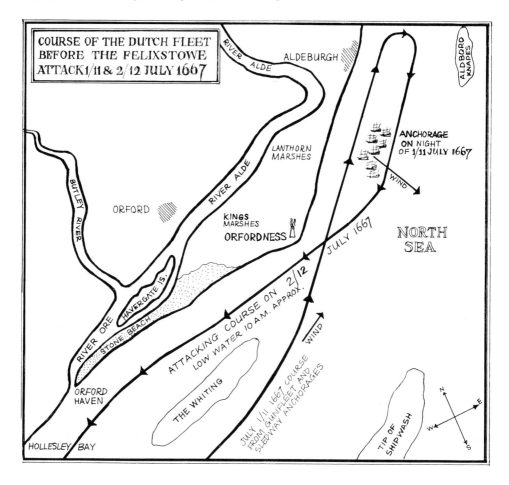

join De Ruyter's fleet as it lay off the coast of Kent by Sheppey. At that time the famous flagship *De Zeven Provincien* was anchored north-east of Queenborough. The newcomers carried Colonel the Count van Hoorn and eight companies of his regiment and they brought with them the strongest representations from Johan de Witt and the States General that, with the advent of these reinforcements, an important operation should immediately be undertaken. Moreover it was the opinion of the Deputies that "an exceptional service would be done for the State and considerable damage done to the enemy if the army and landing forces could become masters of the fort near Harwich by a determined attack by the ships on one side and the army on the other and with God's blessing the place be taken possession of."

It was considered of course that such a landing would greatly add to the alarm caused by the Medway attack and put further pressure on the English delegates at the peace conference in Breda. If successful, the main, and largely unmanned, reserve of English fireships, together with their supervising squadron of small and lightly armed warships, would be at the mercy of the Dutch, and so would the important naval yard at Harwich. Any commercial craft trapped in the harbour and lower reaches of the Orwell and Stour, like those in the Vlie, would be due for destruction. The chances of intervention by other units of the depleted English navy were very slight. Those in the Thames and Medway were sorely needed for local defence, and all other squadrons were more than a day's sail away.

No time was wasted by the Dutch. A conference of senior officers of the army and marines was held on board *De Zeven Provincien* at four o'clock next morning and Admiral De Ruyter, with the backing of Cornelis de Witt, put forward the amibitious proposal. Presumably any naval objections or difficulties were given an airing, but there was a unanimous decision on the part of the military to go ahead. It was then agreed that "fifteen or sixteen hundred of the army and marines should be organised" under various officers already listed for the action and that to them should be added four hundred sailors under Rear Admiral David Vlugh and Captains Adriaen Jacobsz Swart and Abraham Lus. Furthermore, "in each group of twelve, there should be four accomplished grenade throwers and some of them should carry scaling ladders and others should be armed with heavy axes, which would be used with lengths of rope to pull down and destroy any palisades that might be found". It seems that Van Hoorn and his officers had already given much thought to detail planning since it was also agreed that orders be sent forthwith "for the necessary division of the army" and such orders were to state "what boats had been designated to take the troops to the shore". All proposals were committed to writing in considerable detail for dispatch to the States General and a council-of-war for the army was called for noon on the same day. The members of the latter, who must have had a rather wet boat trip to the

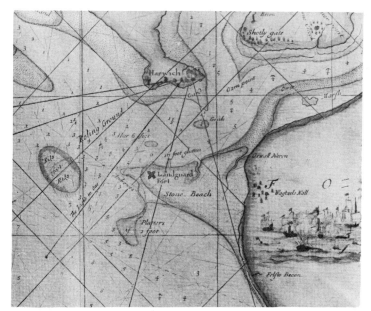

A portion of a chart of the Approaches to Harwich Harbour by Captain G. Collins, dedicated to Samuel Pepys.

*Author's collection*

ɪgship in the west-south-west wind "with hard squalls" then prevailing, were formed of the whole plan. A discussion took place as to how it could be best achieved and it was considered advisable to set sail for the waters off Harwich on the following morning.

At 5 a.m. on Sunday, 30th June, the wind was "fresh and cold" from the south-west. De Ruyter put up a white flag calling all captains for instructions and they were told to provide "12 good sailors in addition to the rowers" and these sailors were "to hold themselves in readiness to help the operation". In view of the earlier reference to four grenade throwers "in each group of twelve" it seems likely that these were the seamen who were to make up the total of four hundred needed in the landing force. At eight o'clock De Ruyter hoisted a blue flag for all ships to weigh anchor and they set out in the south-south-west topsail breeze then prevailing.

The placing of mark boats in the Kings Deep, which in all Dutch accounts meant both the East and West Swin, ensured trouble-free navigation for most. Only Captain de Wynbergen's ship and two water vessels went aground and they were successfully refloated when the flood came, with the assistance of two galliots under Captain Nannick who had been sent by De Ruyter. The fleet passed the Middle Ground at noon and finally brought up between five and six o'clock in the Gunfleet anchorage and in waters stretching north-eastwards towards the Sledway. Awaiting them were the squadrons of Vice Admiral Enno Doedes Star and Vice Admiral Cornelis Evertsen.

When all were anchored for the night De Ruyter held conferences for both senior and junior naval captains and the following instructions were given to Vice Admiral Cornelis Evertsen and Rear Admiral Jan van Nes:

"... the captains noted below with the States ships under their command shall sail into the entrance of Basil[36] in the morning with the first of the flood, wind and weather permitting, keeping out of range of the fort at Harwich while the troops commanded to attack are being landed; and as soon as he sees that they have begun to advance to the fort, the vice-admiral with the ships under his command will get nearer to the fort and open heavy fire on it. And when our troops begin to storm the fort then the vice-admiral with all the boats well manned and armed and provided with grenades will use all their endeavours to aid the attackers and to breach the fort ..."

| *Officers* | *Ships* |
|---|---|
| Vice-Admiral Evertsen | Zierikzee |
| Rear-Admiral van Nes | Delft |
| Capt. Dirck Schey | Spiegel |
| Jan de Haen | Calandtsoog |
| Jacob van Meeuwen | Comeetstar |
| Hendrik Adriaensz | Woerden |
| Nicholas Naelhout | Harderwijk |
| Pieter Jacobszn. Nanning | Gorinchem |
| Cornelis Evertsen | Middelburg |
| Jan Pieterzn. Vinkelbosch | Windhond |
| Roelof Ketelaer | Stad en Lande |
| Dirck de Munnick | Fama |
| Willem Meerman | Hoop |
| Willem Gerritzen Alberlandt | — — |

Of these fourteen ships the first eleven were men-of-war, the *Fama* was an advice-vessel and the *Hoop* and the unnamed vessel were fireships. The honour of inclusion among the ships to be most closely engaged in the action seems to have been deliberately spread among all the Dutch admiralties, these being the colleges of Amsterdam, Maas, North Quarter, Friesland and Zeeland. The squadron was divided, but it is difficult to reconcile the exact numbers of the two divisions with contemporary accounts. From Silas Taylor's reference to eight ships in the Rolling Ground it may be that Van Nes was to sail into the harbour with five men-of-war, the two fireships and the advice-vessel. The *Delft*, flagship of Van Nes, and the *Woerden*, with a Danish marine named Hans Svendsen on board, were certainly in this division and, probably, either the *Harderwijk* or the *Gorinchem* from Rotterdam. Such a disposition would have left Evertsen with his flagship, the *Zierikzee*, and five other ships for his bombardment from the north-east. Brandt, writing twenty years later, leaves out the *Middelburg* of Cornelis Evertsen the Youngest (otherwise known as "Little Cornelis the Devil") but includes instead *De Kaleb* under Captain Jan Mauw.

So passed that very busy Sunday, with over forty miles of fleet movement and much planning. That evening, as the anchored ships lay "outside the banks" within sight of Harwich, those on board the *Deventer* reckoned that the town lay three miles northwest by north of them, but this no doubt was an understatement. They could see several English ships, probably the fake men-of-war moored as potential blockships in the harbour entrance. Meanwhile aboard all Dutch ships orders had been given to get their "boats and barges in a state of readiness" and afterwards they lay all night keeping a watchful eye on the wind which blew fairly strongly at first from the south-south-west and later from the west.

At dawn next morning, Monday, 1st July, it was found that the fresh breeze had veered still further to west-north-west. The sun was due over the horizon just before four o'clock and it was at that hour that De Ruyter displayed a green flag at his mizzen-topmasthead to call all senior officers of the army to the flagship for a conference. At seven o'clock the whole fleet got under way and, since it was about half-ebb, the tide was favourable for the first leg of their course, sailing roughly north-eastwards behind the West Rocks and the Cork complex of sands. Five ships under Vice Admiral Enno Doedes Star and Captains Cornelis de Liefde, Jan Vizelar, Wytze Beyma and Joost Michielzoon Kuik were given orders not to come inshore with the other ships but to stay cruising in the sea area "before the King's Deep". The men-of-war of this rearguard were the *Groningen*, the *Wassenaer*, the *Oostergo*, the *Westergo* and the *Prinses Albertina*.

Before long the wind changed to south-west-by-south, and this was unfavourable for an approach to Felixstowe Road from near Orfordness. "All against us sailing inside the sands", recorded De Ruyter, and he therefore ordered the fleet to anchor at about noon. *De Zeven Provincien* brought up at "about the height of Orfordness" and she soon signalled for all officers and captains to come on board. The previous day's orders for the attack were postponed and further detailed recommendations were made as to its execution. At the same time it was agreed to send Captains Frans van Nijdeck and Gerrit Boos to the Texel "to fetch some victuallers and fireships". During the afternoon letters came to the flagship from Holland in "the galliot of Pundt" and three ships under Captain Goskens joined the fleet, also from the Maas. The *Deventer,* which had first anchored in twelve fathoms, with Orfordness bearing northwest-by-north two miles away, shifted with the coming of the ebb at about half past four to a position in ten fathoms only half a mile east of the point. The *Hollandia*, 82-gun flagship of Rear Admiral

Willem van der Zaan with young Engel de Ruyter aboard, originally anchored at one o'clock within two miles south-southeast of Orfordness. She got under way again at five o'clock and finally brought up at seven with the Ness bearing west-northwest a mile away. The weather had been good all day and in the evening there was just a light breeze from the northwest.

At dawn on Tuesday, 2nd July, the flagship signalled the fleet to make sail, the wind then being "NWbyN a fresh breeze". Some units further up the coast, nearer Aldeburgh, may have moved towards Orfordness during the night since Engel de Ruyter wrote of the ships being under way "between one and three o'clock". He is not altogether reliable as a diarist, and all times quoted can only be approximate [37], but the flood tide would then have been favourable for a shift. This is possibly the explanation of the flare signals which Browne saw from Aldeburgh since, with the number of ships remaining at anchor, the risk of collision would have been high.

A course was then set "to get inside Orfordness, between the Whiting sand and the land", such navigation no doubt being helped by two English pilots who, as a Swede reported later, were aboard De Ruyter's flagship. The next records show that at about six o'clock the ships were "inside the lighthouse close to the shore at Orfordness", the word *vurrboet* being here used for the fire-light structure. The long, largely shingle spit, which forms the seaward bank of the river at Orford, is nowadays locally referred to as "the island" but it is called the *vurrbank* (firebank) in old Dutch sailing directions.

Having sailed through the mile-wide gap between the head of the Whiting and the mainland, the Dutch were enabled to sail south-westwards, skirting the shore of Hollesley Bay. Such a course would have hidden all or most of the fleet from watchers on Beacon Cliff at Harwich, an element of surprise which brought about the comment in Joseph Quine's letter. They were, however, in full view of those on the Suffolk coast and much galloping of message carriers to the inland areas must have resulted. Nearer the mouth of the Deben the course would have been laid rather more offshore since the southern end of Hollesley Bay is complicated by the Cutler shoal. This, according to Greenvil Collins in 1686, stood only one-third of an English mile from a projecting area of the beach. There was, moreover, only two fathoms at low water in the inside channel. It is only twelve miles as the crow flies from Orfordness to Cobbold's Point, but the progress of the Dutch fleet would have been slow until around ten o'clock when the flood set in.

As the enemy ships "stood close aboard the shore and sailed towards Harwich . . . they spied Sir Philip Parker's regiment of the white fferrying over Woodbridge water to follow theire motion". Captain Anthony Deane mentioned this in his narrative to Pepys and there is no doubt that these troops would have been clearly visible to the Dutch as they made their vain attempt to get back over the Deben in time to prevent a landing. Even before they had a view into the mouth of the estuary the Dutch would have seen the bustle on the way to the ferry because, in those days, long before the building of "The Manor", the road ran along Bawdsey Cliff. Then, as now, the transference of small batches of soldiers in rowing or sailing boats across the narrow neck of the swift-running tideway would have been a lengthy and chancy business. Apart from natural difficulties the Dutch soon took aggressive action to prevent it. They detached four ships which "went with their boats and a galliot in that direction, getting as near as possible, and then opened fire on those who were being shipped over". According to Deane the Dutch boats had "gunns in the head of them", a most unpleasant surprise for some of the cavalrymen who, as reported by Dutch militia captain Castillego, "were towing over their horses made fast to the vessels". The rest of the horsemen, Deane said, "weare forced to ride to Woodbridge which was 16 milles to come to the place" and the great clatter of this cavalry as they rode through the narrow Woodbridge Thoroughfare is a lively subject for the imagination. This surely must have been the most irritating day for the Horse Militia and Fencible Cavalry since 1661, when at Wangford "a Knight, a Colonel and a Captain of a Troop were much mangled by a thunderbolt which came in at the top of the house . . . where they had met on 1st August to make merry with March beer". As for the infantry, the Dutch thought that several hundred had already crossed but they reckoned that "the greater part remained on the other side of the river and they could not be shipped over for fear of our guns". The foot soldiers, so delayed until after four o'clock when the fierce ebb probably forced the Dutch boats to move, were the White battalion of the militia, raised in South Suffolk.

Meanwhile, back in Felixstowe and obeying their orders to the letter, five companies of the Yellow regiment, under Major Holland, marched to Landguard Fort. On the assumption that the regimental colours were the same as later recorded in Dutch William's days, these troops would have been raised in West Suffolk "about Clare"[38]. Deane said that they happened to be "just where the Dutch landed" but, in view of their instructions, "did not attempte a shote one the enimy". Since there is no mention whatever in any of the Dutch reports of a force of this size near the landing place, it can only be assumed that, if such a force was in fact exercising in the vicinity of the beach, these troops were purposely kept out of sight and that they afterwards approached the fort by a roundabout route not easily visible from the sea. It is clear that the large number of defenders at Landguard was eventually a great surprise for the Dutch. Possibly Major Holland marched his troops back to the camp at Walton and then proceeded by way of Peewit Hill.[39] This would have taken him across the marshes, which would have been easily passable in high summer, but where, and how, the troops crossed the old Walton Creek[40] is a matter for conjecture. Also obscure are the whereabouts of the sixth company

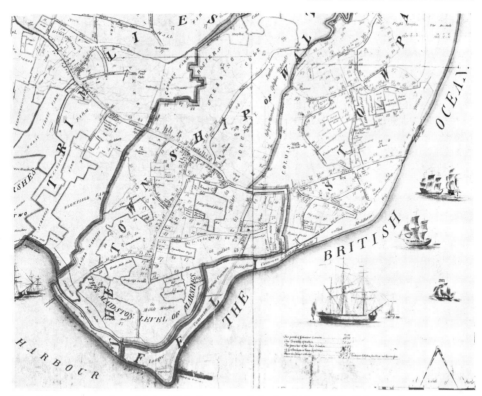

The Felixstowe portion of John Kirby's survey of the lordships of Sir John Barker in 1740-41, showing the now-eroded common between the cliffs and the beach. It also provides a useful guide to the road system of the previous century.     *Suffolk Record Office, Ipswich (A 53/1)*

of the Yellow regiment and their troop of cavalry, but perhaps they remained to reconnoitre the land near the cliffs and to guard the camp? In a letter of five years later Sir Charles Lyttelton said that there was also a troop of horse from Cambridgeshire and they, too, were probably in the vicinity. The commander in the field of all militia stationed in the county was forty-eight-year-old James Howard, Earl of Suffolk, Lord Lieutenant and former Governor of Landguard Fort, but there is no specific mention of his headquarters. This may be because the Earl himself was under the direction of Lord Berkeley, the new Lieutenant-General of Militia, recently installed at Harwich.

Both Deane and Taylor reported that the foremost units of the Dutch fleet were in sight off Felixstowe Cliff by eleven o'clock and soon most, if not all, were anchored. "About midday", Castillego wrote, "all the ships from which our men were to be disembarked put a jack on the bowsprit, that being the sign that all was ready; after that Admiral de Ruyter put up a red flag at the fore and . . . they all rowed for the shore." Conditions must have been ideal for such an operation since Admiral Sweers noted that "at 11 o'clock it fell flat calm and was very hot". Deane, reporting afterwards from Harwich, reckoned they "saw about 45 boates goe ffrom them".

If anything, this estimate of landing craft numbers seems to be on the low side. Specific orders were given to four admirals and fifteen captains to provide thirty-five boats and barges, also a galliot, to transport the troops of Count van Hoorn alone. Maybe included with these would have been the batches of twelve seamen, additional to the rowers, who were to assist with the beach landing and shore operations generally. Also to be set ashore were Lieutenant-Colonel Palm's 396 marines with their officers. Some of these at any rate were to be accommodated in two boats and a barge provided by Admiral Sweer's flagship, *De Witte Olifant*. The orders concerning Van Hoorn's men suggest that, in addition to rowers and any additional seamen, a barge and a boat between them were expected to carry a platoon of up to forty-eight men with its officer or officers.

The use of a shuttle service for the initial landing seems unlikely. Engel de Ruyter said "our men all landed at once" and no other report suggests that the operation was a piecemeal business. Rear Admiral Vlugh and Captains Swart and Lus were jointly in charge of the beach landing and also of the sailors engaged on shore. Presumably they kept tabs, too, on the interesting supply arrangements. Galliot master Arien Jansz Rootie was to collect Commissioner Tusschen and the engineer du Blois from De Brouwer's ammunition flute. He was also to carry ashore, for the use of the landing force, "the fascines, 100 large axes, the available grenades, 100 pickaxes, 100 choppers, 2 bundles of fuses, 6 butter boxes filled with powder". Another galliot, appointed by Rear Admiral van Nes, was to convey "Mr Johan Harlingh, surgeon-general, with six surgeons and appropriate medical stores . . . for the assistance of the ships in which the men are landing". Finally, and doubtless an essential in the ruling hot weather, a note was made "to send another galliot with beer".

Concerning the total of Dutchmen landed, there is a bewildering variety of figures but some of these can be ruled out forthwith. Silas Taylor reckoned that a thousand had landed by one o'clock and put the total at "above 2,000 men". Both Deane and Tyler told Pepys "about 3,000 men", a figure which the *London Gazette* adopted, but there must have been a deliberate or subconscious tendency not to minimise what was considered to be an English victory. An intercepted letter, from an English exile in Holland who was present at the attack, said "We landed 1,200 brave fellows under the command of the noble Dolman", presumably ignoring the four hundred seamen. Engel de Ruyter wrote in one diary "about 1,800 strong" but raised this to 3,800 in another version. Captain Adriaen de Haese reckoned "about

2,000 men" and Admiral Sweers, in his very matter-of-fact record, said "about 1,500 men were embarked and landed in good order by Felixstowe cliff".

For the most reliable figures it seems best to look to De Witt's, De Ruyter's and Castillego's records. In all probability Castillego faithfully copies from the original written orders which he had retained and, in quoting from another copy, it is likely that De Witt's hurried report to the States General inadvertently understated by six the number of musketeers in Captain Ruys' platoon. De Ruyter's records give the detailed boat arrangements, so providing a useful check, but he does not give the platoon numbers.

The particular snag for the historian, moreover, is that where the troop numbers are definitely stated some sections do not add up to the totals stated. In consequence Castillego's "total landed including soldiers, marines and sailors — 1,474" is suspect. The trouble arises with Van Hoorn's troops. In Castillego's summary not only are the 106 men of the two colonels' companies entirely excluded from the totals but also thirty-six of the other musketeers. Officers, presumably, should be included in the grand total and while this is in the long run not very material it does seem that the 1,474 quoted by Brandt, and by those who followed him, should be amended to "somewhat in excess of 1,650".

### TROOPS UNDER COMMAND OF COLONEL DOLMAN AND COUNT VAN HOORN [41]

| | | |
|---|---:|---:|
| 18 platoons — musketeers (amended total) | | 594 |
| — pikemen (amended total) | | 228 |
| Commanders and named officers | | 20 |
| | | 842 |

### TROOPS UNDER COMMAND OF LIEUT-COLONEL PALM

| | | |
|---|---:|---:|
| 11 platoons — firelocks | 396 | |
| Commanders and named officers | 12 | 408 |

### SEAMEN UNDER COMMAND OF REAR-ADMIRAL VLUGH AND CAPTAINS SWART AND LUS

| | |
|---|---:|
| | 400 |

| | |
|---|---:|
| TOTAL BASED ON CAPTAIN CASTILLEGO'S LIST | 1650 |

OTHER OFFICERS named in De Ruyter's landing orders, etc. (Guicherie, Brederode, Limburg, De Clarges, Assendfeldt, Paul)     6

NAVAL OFFICERS, DOCTORS, ENGINEERS AND OTHERS     ?

The stretch of beach used for the landing is confirmed by several accounts as being at, by or about Felixstowe Cliff, the more prominent forerunner of the modern Cobbold's Point where the promenade ends. Deane placed it as being "about 2 mille from Landguard Fort" and "not above 2 mille" from the Deben ferry. Therefore, as the troop landing was fully in sight of those on Beacon Cliff at Harwich, the shore immediately downcoast of Cobbold's Point is indicated. Here there is a break in the cliff formation for about three furlongs and the high ground is considerably set back, with banks of varying steepness descending haphazardly to sea level. Nowadays this rather exclusive section of the beach has its own short length of seafront road, entirely separate from that of the rest of the resort. This is overlooked from above by a convalescent home, embracing the remains of a martello tower, and some sizeable residences. There is also an hotel and one or two houses on the road itself, but in 1667 the scene was vastly different.

Where road, promenade and beach now stand the widest part of Felixstowe Common then projected towards the sea. This fairly level area, of greatly varying width, covered with rough grass and seaside vegetation, stretched along the shore for more than one and a half miles from a point well beyond Felixstowe Cliff (below the site of the now-demolished twentieth-century Brackenbury Fort) to Bulls Cliff where the old lane to Landguard Fort once descended. It was alternatively known as Middleton Way and, at its south-western end, it merged with Wadgate Common and Landguard Common which, with adjoining marshlands, made up the low ground which stretched a mile further to the fort and Harwich Harbour.

For centuries the common, immediately down-coast from Felixstowe Cliff, was protected from the fierce scour of the north-east gales by a massive ledge of septaria which stretched out underwater from the point, and this probably assisted the landing operation of 1667. The head of the beach, then as now, was probably shingle but at low water it is likely that many septaria rocks, with patches of sand in between, would have been revealed. The scene changed dramatically after 1812 when some 200,000 tons of septaria were dredged up from this area alone for use in the cement trade at Harwich. By 1842 this part of the common had almost disappeared and Captain John Washington of the Hydrographic Department of the Admiralty reported "a large slice of Felixstow Cliff has gone into the sea, two mortella towers and a small battery, only built in 1808, have been swept away and the beach at Landguard Point has grown out . . . to the extent of 500 yards".

The place of landing appears to have been well chosen, because the effectiveness of musket fire from the high ground would have been greatly diminished at over 200 yards range. Also reduced was the risk of a flanking attack from the common to the northeast round the point, because there was no way down to the low ground before it tailed away under steep cliff.[42]

Two tracks, however, came down to the landing area itself, these being the forerunners of the present day Brook and Maybush lanes. The seaward section of the former, from Fosgrave (now Foxgrove) Lane downwards, used to be known as Middleton Lane and it provided access to that part of the beach from the High Road for those who lived in the township of Walton. The other road, Maybush Lane, was formerly called Wynyard or Vineyard Lane. It also descended from the highway which led to Walton and Ipswich and it was the way to the sea for the villagers of Old Felixstowe. Had there been any opposition on the beach itself, or any emergence of defence forces from these lanes, it would probably have been conclusively dealt with by fire from the shallow-draught galliots and from guns in the bows of some of the barges but, as it happened, the landing was completely unopposed. Once ashore, it is likely that these access lanes would have been immediately shut off by advancing picquets. This was a particular necessity because any troops which had managed to get back over the Deben would be marching not much more than a quarter of a mile away. Strict orders to report back to the Earl of Suffolk on the high ground nearer Walton are the probable reason there was no early assault by the White militia down Vineyard Lane, their nearest route to the grounded boats.

First ashore was Lieutenant-Colonel Palm, commander of the marines, who was identified to his troops by a blue pendant in the stern of his barge. His platoons "of 36 soldiers each led by a captain, a lieutenant or ensign with two sergeants" formed up on the beach in two bodies with "a distance of 150 paces between them". The second marine detachment was commanded by Lieutenant-Colonel "Monsieur" de la Guicherie. The Count van Hoorn, commander of the other troops, flew a white pendant in his barge. As soon as his men had landed in boats which had collected them from the flutes *Jongen Drost, Postilion, Gouda, Glasemaker, Den Harder* and other vessels they formed up in battle order 100 paces to the right of the marines. Two hundred of Van Hoorn's musketeers "and their appropriate officers", stationed nearest to the marines, were under orders to link up with the latter eventually for the assault on Landguard Fort. For that purpose they were to be commanded by Lieutenant-Colonel van Rheede. Where exactly the four hundred sailors assembled is not clear.

By two o'clock the landing, marshalling and handing out of assault equipment had probably been completed. Then, as Captain Castillego reported, they "marched for about half an hour with our troops divided into three battalions". Once past what is now called Bath Hill they came under the cliffs which now front the modern town of Felixstowe and there the low ground narrowed. In confirmation of this, Castillego's account says "the shore along which our troops were marching being 20 or 30 rods with high hilly ground on the right hand side, where at once and several times afterwards the enemy

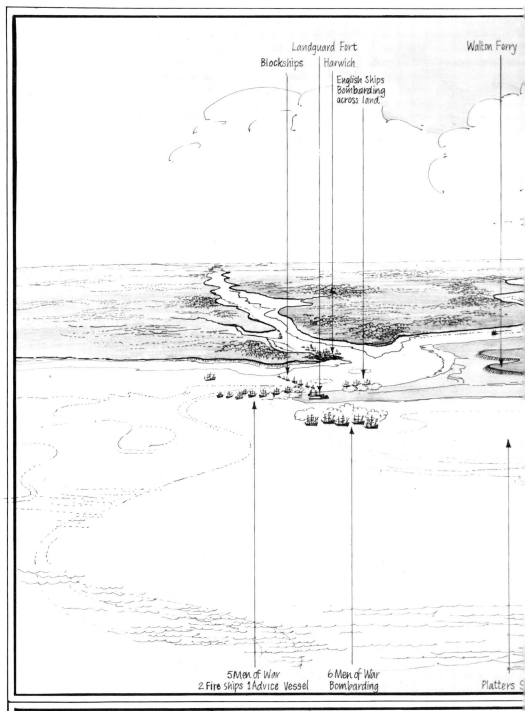

Landguard Fort

Blockships

Harwich

Walton Ferry

English Ships
Bombarding
across land

5 Men of War
2 Fire Ships 1 Advice Vessel

6 Men of War
Bombarding

Platters S

A View of the Action
up to 12 P.M. (approx) on 2/12 July 1667

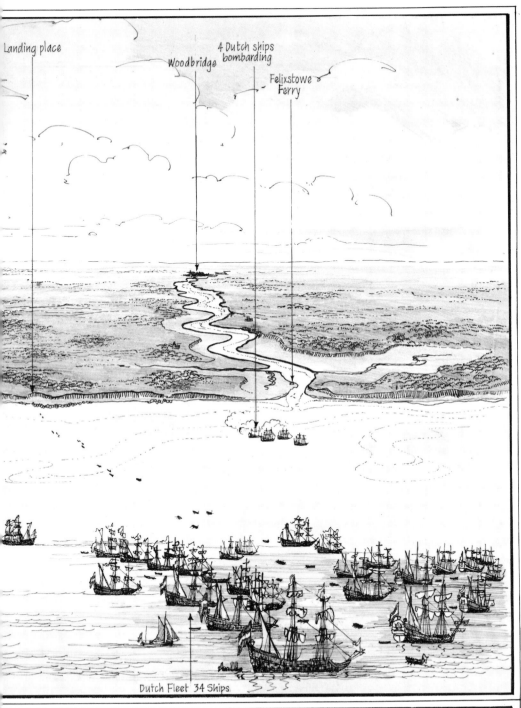

Landing place

Woodbridge

4 Dutch ships
bombarding

Felixstowe
Ferry

Dutch Fleet 34 Ships

Wind North by North West at first but Dying away,
Weather hot and apparently dry. High Water 4~4·30 P.M.

appeared". The width of the low ground there was thus about 100 yards, since the Rhineland rod approximates to twelve feet. A little less than half an hour's march would have brought the Dutch to Bulls Cliff where the high ground turned inland. There, Castillego said, "a halt was made and it was found that there was a considerable pass which it was judged should be occupied. This the Count van Hoorn did and remained there with four or five hundred soldiers".

"In the meanwhile", Castillego continued, "some five hundred marines and soldiers under Colonel Dolman marched on to the fort, together with the 400 sailors." In using the words "a considerable pass" it seems likely that Castillego was referring not so much to the narrow Fort Lane coming down Bulls Cliff as to the valley of sorts which later accommodated the railway and the extension of the modern Garrison Lane.

Deane, in his report, mentioned not only the marshalling of the enemy forces and the eventual detachment of the Count van Hoorn's troops but also some Dutch activity on the high ground. He said that the invaders landed "at the bottom of Fillstow Cliffte in a plaine wheare they drew themselves in a boddy with a good stand of pikes".

"When they weare in this order", he continued, "they did with a good company get up the hill and lined the hedges and made good the way to the south end of the hill and at the bottom kept a reserve of about 600 men." The latter were the previously mentioned rearguard for the assault force, and the inference seems to be that a fair-sized scouting party had been detached immediately after the landing to ascend the high ground near the present-day Bath Hill, where smoke from the beacon would have been rising. The first objectives, presumably, would have been to command not only the common running south-westwards for just over a mile from the beached boats to Bulls Cliff, where the old Fort Lane descended, but also every route to the cliff top from the High Road which would have enabled the English to overlook the advancing troops. Fort Lane came from the outskirts of Walton in a meandering fashion and, almost certainly, was the road which Deane described as "the way to the south end of the hill". It followed the course of the present-day Garrison Lane as far as Hustings Way (now Mill Lane) corner and then turned abruptly left until it could resume its southward trend along roughly the line of today's Princes Road. Then, as tradition has it, it sloped steeply down to Wadgate Common from the site of the present "Q Tower" residence.

The Dutch skirmishers on the cliff top took three or four prisoners, possibly the beacon watchers, but one at any rate was "a brave officer". These were sent down below for interrogation and brought before the renegade Colonel Dolman "and other English" who threatened them with death if they did not tell the truth. They were forced to show the Dutch "the wayes and tell them of the strength of the contrey which they did not believe to be so good".

This was known in Harwich later, because one of the prisoners escaped during the night, and other information came from a Swede from Hamburg who had spent the day on De Ruyter's flagship and had talked with an officer. This Swede and his ship had been detained for eight or nine days for security reasons. Some of the prisoners under interrogation told the absolute truth, maintaining stoutly that there were sixty guns and eight or nine hundred men in Landguard Fort against the Dutch assertion that there were "but 10 or 12 guns and 100 men". They were called "lying English rogues" for their pains, but there is a hint of much local amusement in a remark in a letter to Pepys that the Dutch "found it too trew for them before night".

In his grisaille of 1669 Willem van de Velde the Elder gives a distant view of a landing operation with boats and barges making for the shore, some in tow of accompanying galliots. Nearer at hand, to the right of the picture, a boat with armed men aboard has just left two moored men-of-war, another boat is alongside, presumably loading up, and there are other oared craft and galliots among a whole bevy of warships on the extreme left. The apparent beaching point of the small craft in the picture is nearer the fort than seems to have happened at Felixstowe, but perhaps this is an understandable licence taken for artistic balance. It is probable that this grisaille was commissioned by Captain Jan Roetering a year or so after the action with a request to show his comely man-of-war *Het Huis te Oosterwijk*, clearly identified by the large painting of a country mansion on her stern, as the most prominent feature. Such a patron is bound to have asked also for a satisfactory impression of the sea action which surrounded his vessel on that day. So we have, suitably grouped with other men-of-war, the flagship of his commander, the famous De Ruyter. In common with many old ship pictures, the grisaille shows the vessels in rather closer proximity than was likely to have been the case. A fort under attack on the left point of the shore, rigging of ships in the waters behind it, a range of cliffs and an estuary entrance on the extreme right provide sufficient identity with the view from the anchorage known as Felixstowe Road.

Van de Velde was a master of ship detail, and he never made mistakes in seamanship, so his showing of a drifting sail, a *drijver*, rigged from the furled mizzen of *Het Huis te Oosterwijk*, together with her mizzen topsail laid aback, may be to give some idea of the great skill necessary in the restricted searoom of the Felixstowe operation. The artist could only have been working from hearsay, since there is no evidence that he was present at either this or the earlier raid on the Thames and Medway. Here Van de Velde provides an interesting example of the compression of both space and time by the early ship painters in creating an overall impression of an extensive action. Somehow these old masters managed to incorporate a series of incidents into one satisfying picture, leaving it to the viewers to disregard any maritime

Willem van de Velde the Elder's grisaille of 1669 showing the Dutch attack on Landguard Fort two years earlier. Behind the fort can be seen the rigging of the English ships in Harwich Harbour.                                        *National Maritime Museum, London*

incongruities, such as the run of the tide here, and to sort out the whole as a moving picture in their own minds.

The position at about half past two on this hot summer's afternoon was that the bulk of a Suffolk militia regiment was still on the Bawdsey side of the Deben ferry, tied down there by belligerent Dutchmen in the river mouth with fearsome cannon in their little boats. On Felixstowe cliffs, meanwhile, other Dutchmen lay by the hedgerows waiting for the English who would not be arriving in force for two more hours. Ready for a call for assistance from their advance parties above, the rearguard troops of Count van Hoorn rested on the common as other soldiers, marines and sailors under the renegade Dolman made their slow way over beach and benthills towards Landguard Fort. At sea, forty or more ships, which had been involved in the troop landing, were spread out at anchor in Felixstowe Road and five others could be seen brought up in the Sledway. Eight more warships, which had sailed to the outer part of the Rolling Ground outside the entrance to Harwich Harbour, had dropped anchor and furled their sails. To the northeast of Landguard Point, on the far side of the Platters shoal, a few more Dutch warships were already "in ffight with the fforte". Truly the stage was set for a lively afternoon and tension was at its highest in Harwich where a crowd had gathered to watch from Beacon Cliff.

# CHAPTER SEVEN

# The Assault on the Fort

VICE ADMIRAL Cornelis Evertsen and Rear Admiral Jan van Nes were due to start their run in towards Landguard Point as soon as the land forces began their advance. The wind had fallen light but the flood tide would be in their favour for about two more hours and they had, at the most, only three or four miles to go. Their first task, as Silas Taylor neatly put it, was for Evertsen's ships "to lie near the Platters and to play on the fort from that side" and for those of Van Nes to "play upon the fort on t'other side", that is from the Rolling Ground and further in. Never was anything more easily said than done!

Among the main armament of the Dutch warships was the culverin, a gun of over nine feet in length and weighing in excess of 4,000 pounds. It fired an 18-pound solid iron ball and its range, quoted at the time of the English Civil War (1642/49), was 460 yards at "point blank" and 2,650 yards at ten degrees elevation. Such a shot would have little penetrative power after one and a half mile's flight, but at six hundred yards it was said to be capable of piercing the thickest of ship timbers. Nevertheless earthworks, such as those at Landguard, were able to absorb impacts which could demolish ships and even the old castles built of stone, and this was a fact well known to the Dutch who were themselves experts in the fortification field. Therefore their plan in 1667, as the journal of Admiral Sweers reveals, was to bombard if possible from musket shot range. This was a mere 200 yards and, as they soon found out, would only have been possible from within the estuary. Such a holocaust would have been likely to overwhelm the garrison, and there would also have been little distance for the Dutch seamen to cover in their planned second landing to aid Dolman's troops in the final assault.

To give them their due, the Dutch naval commanders had all along stressed the difficulties and dangers of operating in these restricted East Coast waters. In 1666 De Ruyter's opinion that it would be foolhardy to attempt to sail into Harwich Harbour had prevailed. This time the parlous state of the English navy and the desire to influence the peace negotiations had greatly increased the political pressures and those "who fought from afar on cushions" ruled the roost. Faced with the alternatives of attacking Landguard or mounting another operation in even more restricted and well defended waters up the Thames, De Ruyter had opted for what he no doubt considered to be

81

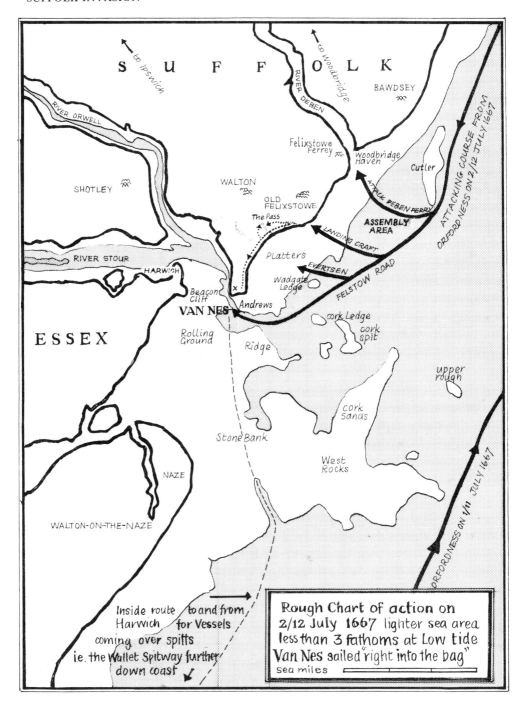

Rough Chart of action on 2/12 July 1667 lighter sea area less than 3 fathoms at Low tide Van Nes sailed "right into the bag"

the lesser of two evils. If he had had available an accurate chart of the Harwich approaches it is extremely doubtful whether he would have made the attempt.

It is clear that the Dutch did not even know the full extent and exact location of the Platters Shoal, despite soundings made from two of their small craft only twelve days or so before. Adrien de Haese, captain of the *Veere*, when writing to his brother in India on 8th July, 1667, said, "We could not get near to the fort on account of the sandbanks and no-one knew about them". There were certainly charts in existence, such as that of Waghenaer, published in 1588, but they were far too crude for such a delicate operation. In fact the first local survey of any accuracy was that made by Captain Greenvil Collins round about 1683 and published three years later. In 1732 I. P. Desmaretz made a most useful chart of Harwich Harbour but it was not until 1804 that Graeme Spence, a maritime surveyor of Ipswich, plumbed the crucial outside waters right in to the Felixstowe beach. There had long been slight seabed changes due to local erosion but Carlyon-Hughes, in his *History of Harwich Harbour,* states that "before 1812 the loss had been gradual and not very large so far as is known". So Spence's survey, although made 137 years afterwards, gives a valuable indication of the shallows in Felixstowe Bay at the time of the Dutch attack. His three-fathom contour, surely the limit of prudence in rapidly shoaling waters, shows the impossibility of men-of-war approaching within a mile of the shore until the Rolling Ground is reached. At one point the fairway was only half a mile wide and it was barely 250 yards at the Rolling Ground entrance. Greenvil Collins was not so prolific with his soundings but he clearly shows the latter hazard.

As the English had wisely removed all navigation marks, both divisions of Evertsen's squadron were soon in difficulties. Things became much worse when Van Nes himself went aground, an ignominious occurrence involving a decisive time loss which Cornelis de Witt adroitly skated around in his otherwise adequate report sent to their "High Mightinesses" the States General on the following day:

"... We saw that the ships under Vice Admiral Evertsen, who were to engage the fort from the sea side, were lying far from the shore; and that those under the rear-admiral had not sailed inside the entrance. We decided with Lieut.-Admiral de Ruyter that we should be put on board these ships to get them closer in and inside the entrance. On coming to those under Evertsen, it was found that they could not get nearer to the shore on account of the shallowness of the water, so that their shots could scarcely reach the fort. And on rowing to the rear-admiral, the pilot who had been given to the rear-admiral [he was a lieutenant of Lieut.-Admiral de Ruyter's called Marten Ros, who had sailed for a long time into Harwich and was well acquainted with the harbour] declared that all the marks and even the withies (boomen) there had been cut down, so that he could not find the entrance, which was very narrow. And so we decided to look for the channels with the barges and take soundings. But in the meanwhile it being the top of the tide, it was impossible to sound in the entrance or to sail there on account of the lack of wind. As there was no other way, we were forced to decide that the ships should get as close to the shore as possible. What the barges had found out was that the ships could not float any closer to the fort than a half cannon shot. With all these ships, none could make any impression on the fort. The ships that were in position fired on the fort as far as they could and they received a similar greeting from the fort . . ."

At this stage of the action, however, it is likely that Captain Darell, the fort commander, was conserving his ammunition. Deane, writing to Pepys the next day, said "the ffort spent littell more powder than to annoy them" and "The want of ammunition and provision in our forts" was No. 12 of the "Heads of Miscarriages of the late Warr" which were laid before the Committee of Parliament on 1st November, 1667. Andrew Marvell made much of it in his unkind poem which heaped blame for the national disaster on Peter Pett, the Navy Commissioner at Chatham:

> Who did advise no navy out to set?
> And all the forts left unprepared? *Pett*
> Who to supply with powder did forget
> Landguard, Sheerness, Gravesend and Upnor? *Pett*

Others in their journals and letters added to the Felixstowe picture and did not forget to say that the admiral had gone aground. Deane, for one, passed on the information which he had obtained from the Swede who had spoken to De Ruyter's lieutenant:

". . . the Reare admirall of the 9 shipps which came into the Rowling Grounds came on ground on the reidge and lay an howre and a halfe, and no ffiership of ours could get neare them being all to leaward; so soon as de Rutter see the ship on grownd he ffired a gunn and called a counsell of warr and altered the designe and sent his owne boate away with a white antient, and ordered the rearadmerall that he should not venture in but com to an ancker with his ships and ply the fforte to effect the designe of storming the fforte . . ."

The most interesting item in this report, apart from the confirmation of the decisive time loss, is that Deane reckoned the place of the admiral's stranding to be on the outlying Ridge shoal, rather than on the tip of the Andrews on the landward side of the narrow entrance to the Rolling Ground. Hans Svendsen, a Danish marine who was on board the *Woerden* of the Van

Nes division, said, "Our commander ran aground but was got off again with the help of the boats and barges of the other ships". Admiral Sweers merely remarked that "The admiral himself was stuck on a bank lying off the point". De Ruyter, who personally investigated the stranding of the *Delft*, said:

> "Vice Admiral Evertsen lay with seven ships on the north-east side but he could not get within a 'goteling' shot. Rear-Admiral van Nes was to bombard on the north-(west?) side of the fort. He went aground on the reef that lay off the point."

So the oft-quoted Silas Taylor who, in his letter of 4th July, 1667, referred to the "Vice-Admiral that ran on ground the Andrews", may after all have been wrong. He is likely to have known less about sea matters than Deane, who was his superior in the shipyard. It seems more probable that Marten Ros, with his long-standing knowledge of the harbour entrance, would have been particularly careful to avoid his Scylla on the starboard and landward side and that, in overdoing it, he fell into the grasp of the local Charybdis to port.

The thought of the senior naval commander, another high-ranking admiral and an important representative of the government calling a hurried meeting in the middle of a sea action and then themselves embarking on a trouble-shooting expedition is intriguing enough, but there are other items to whet the imagination. De Ruyter, noted for his forceful initiative, had to bottle up his feelings while being rowed from *De Zeven Provincien* to the *Zieriksee* and he must have boarded Evertsen's ship like a ball of fire. Such was the effect of his personal appearance, not to mention that of De Witt and Van Aylva, that the bombarding vessels even resorted to Captain Plumleighe's expedient of 1629[43]. It was Admiral Sweers who said, "at last with warping they got to a small shot distance away and then opened a brisk fire". The range of a 2½-inch calibre falcon, at ten degrees elevation, was said to be just over 1,900 yards. Discounting this somewhat, and assuming that the ships ventured over the flats at high water, it is possible that the distance was reduced to something less than a mile. Regarding the shooting, Admiral Sweers added, "this was not as effective as if, as was expected, the ships could have got within musket shot and so could not have missed". Young Engel de Ruyter said in his journal, "Our appointed ships fired on the castle but they were lying too far off".

"From there", Sweers said, "they went to Rear Admiral van Nes, whose squadron was in the wrong place and could not find the right passage at all." On board the *Delft* De Ruyter and his colleagues had words with her luckless pilot Marten Ros, who, as is clear from De Witt's report, had no lack of excuses for the stranding. Opinions are divided, however, over the translation of the Dutch word *boomen* as withies, which are rough tree branches or whole saplings stuck into sandbanks as marks of danger. In its usual sense the Dutch word means growing trees, so whether or not the famous Pain Tree [44] and other tree landmarks were sacrificed is a moot question. There is, it should be noted, no mention of such a drastic measure in the reports of the Harwich people, and a drawing of the town and its surroundings by Francis Place not many years later shows no sign of such a depredation. The Pain Tree is shown as a landmark for the Stone Bank, a hazard on the shallow water "inside" route to Harwich, in the Greenvil Collins chart which was made about 1683. In all probability it was the removal of the Harwich lighthouses, installed as recently as 1665, which got Marten Ros into trouble since by keeping them "in one" a safe course between the Ridge and the Andrews was normally assured. As distinct from the fire-room and lower lighthouse described by Silas Taylor in 1676, those of 1667 were probably temporary structures erected on the same bearing as earlier unlighted beacons and, if so, their removal could have been easily accomplished. A seventeenth-century fortification plan of Harwich shows simple bascule fire-basket or lanthorn lights on top of the town gate and on a hut-like base in the lower position. Regarding their removal, it is worth recording that a later Dutch threat during the reign of James II caused Pepys to order the lower lighthouse "to be removed and set up in another place". This proving difficult, the local people devised a substitute plan to blow up the structure and erect a wood and canvas replica to mislead the enemy. [45]

The arrival of De Ruyter, De Witt and Van Aylva alongside the *Delft* and what happened afterwards was viewed by Hans Svendsen from the *Woerden* not far away:

> "While our commander was aground de Ruyter rowed to us in his barge. He had a silk Orange flag flying at the stern and he wished to go on board our commander; and when he arrived the English fired a whole salvo at his barge from the castle, but caused no damage except that one man who was sitting forward in the barge was killed. When de Ruyter got on board it was decided that when our commander hoisted a white pendant, our five ships should stop firing. De Ruyter then left our commander's ship and when he got into his barge the English opened fire again. We lay with our five ships in the roads each astern of the other, and opened fire also, and we could see big pieces of the castle flying off and when a shot hit the earth, it flew up a man's height in the air. Then the English began firing at our five ships, but it caused little damage except to a Rotterdam ship that lay close under the castle; this ship received so much damage that she began to list."

Why De Ruyter's barge should be wearing "a silk Orange flag" during the "stadhouderless" period presents a puzzle for Dutch historians, since the House of Orange was not then playing any part in the Dutch government and Cornelis de Witt was himself an important member of the anti-Orange party.

Deane, on the other hand, described it as a "white antient", but it is not thought that the House of Orange arms would have been displayed on a white ground. This arouses suspicions that someone may have been colour-blind but, from museum specimens, it is known that these old silk flags were of very open weave, so maybe their colour was not easily discernible at a distance. Whatever the nature of the flag, it certainly attracted the attention of Darell's

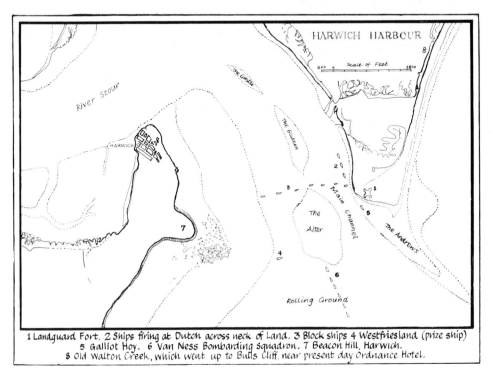

1 Landguard Fort. 2 Ships firing at Dutch across neck of Land. 3 Block ships 4 Westfriesland (prize ship) 5 Galliot Hoy. 6 Van Ness Bombarding squadron. 7 Beacon Hill, Harwich. 8 Old Walton Creek, which went up to Bulls Cliff, near present day Ordnance Hotel.

gunners who, as Sir Charles Lyttelton revealed later, were assisted by "100 brave seamen which ye Towne of Ipswich sent him".

It is likely that the leading ship of the Van Nes division finally dropped anchor at the landward end of the Rolling Ground since it was only there that the Dutch barges, as De Witt said, could have rowed to within half a cannon shot range. This would place her at about one thousand yards from Landguard Fort, somewhere near the narrow entrance to the harbour. Sweers said that "orders were given for boats to look for the opening but in the meanwhile the wind dropped and it was the top of the tide so that, although the squadron was able to lie there, it was not in the right position." The efficacy of the blockships was therefore never tested, but Deane thought they would have been of little use. He said as much when he took credit for the empty threat posed by his inactive and, as it later turned out, poorly prepared fireships in the harbour:

> ". . . itt is the ffierships this boute hath preserved us and nothing else hindered the Dutch coming in to this place, ffor all other things could not have prevented, though ships weare sunke and five more ordered, yett they coulld not a quarter stop the channell and that they knew as well as oursellves."

Silas Taylor, writing on 4th July, said that the Dutch "were much troubled by our ships that lay across the entrance, not knowing whether they were men-of-war or fire-ships but wondered more to see some of them sunk". Nevertheless the brave show of the colliers, with their men-of-war jacks, ensigns and pendants, is unlikely to have deceived the Dutch. Abraham de Wicquefort, a French diplomat and historian writing from The Hague, mentioned a communication from the Dutch fleet, dated 29th June, which reported a reconnaisance of the "Bay of Harwich" by the vice-admiral of Zeeland. Cornelis Evertsen the Young [46] had seen eighteen or twenty sail which at first sight appeared to be "armes en guerre" but turned out to be only coal ships which had come from Scotland. Whether this is a reference to the blockships and, perhaps, some fireships behind them is not clear but, at any

A drawing by Willem van de Velde the Younger of a council-of-war in the Dutch fleet.
*National Maritime Museum, London*

rate, it is their flags and rigging immediately behind the fort in Van de Velde's picture which so long afterwards help to identify it. De Witt, it seems, was glad enough to mention them in a postscript to his report of 3rd July as a further reason for calling off the operation:

"P.S. The enemy had sunk four ships in the entrance to Harwich to prevent the States ships getting in and we did not consider it right to attempt any further attack on the fort."

While English delight still prevailed at the providential grounding of the *Delft* and its consequences, De Witt and his colleagues determined to make the best of a bad job:

"As we could not be of any further service there, it was agreed with Lieut.-Admiral de Ruyter that we should go in the barges to join the troops which we found drawn up in battle order waiting for the men-of-war to sail inside the harbour. We reported to them that the ships were not able to sail inside the fort and it was decided that without further loss of time the soldiers, the marines and the sailors should attack the fort by land. The senior officers thought it advisable to leave a good number of foot at a certain pass for the protection of the boats and barges, and also so that no horse would attack our men from the rear. When orders had been given for this the troops marched off in good order to the fort. With de Ruyter we followed the troops until we were less than a musket shot away."

The notabilities probably landed some time after four o'clock within a mile of Landguard Fort. Had they done otherwise it would have necessitated a very long row from the Rolling Ground and a time-consuming trudge back over beach and rough terrain, and this would hardly fit in with the time of the first attack. Somewhere near the site of the present-day Regal Restaurant may be as good a guess as any.

Hans Svendsen, describing his grandstand view from the *Woerden*, said, "After we had exchanged fire with the castle for some time, our people came marching along the shore, the sailors with the hand-grenades in the lead and 1,500 men behind them". He was, however, inclined to exaggerate because the assault troops and their officers totalled only about six hundred, apart from the four hundred sailors. The grenadiers among the seamen would have been easily identifiable as each was provided with a canvas bag to carry his four missiles, hollow cast-iron or glass spheres weighing about two pounds and containing a bursting charge of four or five ounces of powder. They were already in common use as a close-quarters combat weapon, no fewer than thirty-six thousand having been used by the Spanish against the French at Valenciennes in 1656.

There was little cover on Landguard Common so, instead of approaching the fort on a broad front, the assault parties marched out of sight of the defenders below the steep-to banks of sand and shingle which steadily curved round that end of Felixstowe Bay. They advanced "under ffavor of the sea bancke", Deane said, and it was Silas Taylor who added that they came "in the smoke that ye shipps from the Rowling = groundes had made". Taylor said later that "It was judged that the 8 Dutch shipps who sent such cloudes of smoake upon the Fort out of ye Rowling = Groundes were meerly for that purpose", thereby leading some to believe mistakenly that the smoke screen was intentional. The clinging gunsmoke, however, could only have been wafted by a quite unpredictable air from the south-west, a fluke of the prevailing hot weather. By "that purpose" Taylor probably meant "for the purpose of bombardment", as distinct from the originally expected attack by these ships from within the harbour.

The original intention of the Dutch was to launch a three-pronged attack against the north, east and south sides of the fort, each assault group consisting of about two hundred musketeers and a proportion of seamen. Lieut.-Colonel Palm, Lieut.-Colonel de la Guicherie and Lieut.-Colonel Rheede were the group commanders. They were to be assisted by Sergeants Major Brederode and Limburgh and each group was to have "the same proportion of ladders, fascines and grenades". There was, however, a distinct element of precaution in the arrangements because De Ruyter noted, "We shall reconnoitre the fort before an attack is made and after that proceed as we think fit". The possibility of an early retirement had even been considered during the preliminary discussions when the fleet was off Queenborough.

"Finally, when the advance to the fort is made and the drums of the pikemen begin to beat the 'Boeren Palsrock' so all the platoons will turn right and right again and march to the barges and boats without any confusion."

On 2nd July, however, things did not work out as planned. All the pikemen had already been left with the rearguard and there was no chance of a tidy deployment of the assault troops across the common, with the ordained six paces between the platoons, who were supposed "to advance steadily on the fort as they fire". Instead it seems that a general fusilade broke out as soon as the defenders, whose attention had been somewhat diverted by the ship bombardment, eventually saw movement on the nearby beach. Taylor related that the enemy:

"made up to Landguard Fort with scaling ladders painted of about 20 long or more = hand = granadoes &c: they came briskly up with their cutleaxes drawne upon their armes; & their musketts; & came up close to ye fort: whose reception to them when discovered was as briske."

Hans Svendsen's diary records the cease-fire of the ships' bombardment:

"When they got nearer to the castle the English began to fire on them, but our people were not hit and they began themselves to fire their muskets at the castle and when our commander saw this he ordered the white pendant to be hoisted, otherwise we would have caused our people damage."

Deane reckoned that the Dutch were given "a warm entertainment" and Taylor scathingly remarked that their reply from the shelter of the sea bank was "rather against the Firmament than the Fort". That the Dutch rank and file were most unwilling to budge from their position while a storm of shot flew above them is well brought out in Deane's narrative:

"[The assault troops] got neare the fforte within pistoll shot, and when they had gott soe neare as they could they fired estreamely with theire small shott one the forte ffor halfe an howre, but neaver came over the banke at all, though about 4 of theire officers did do it and much urged theire ffollowing them up to the fforte wall, yett they would not haveing a goode banke to ffrind . . ."

Since the sea actually breached the counterscarp of the ditch in 1647, the nearness of the leading section of the long Dutch column was no exaggeration. Silas Taylor said that they were heard calling out "Peace, peace!" in a derisory manner and this may link with a statement by De Ruyter that "the surrender of the fort was demanded in vain". "Nonetheless our men made several charges against the fort", said Castillego, so a few brave men were eventually aroused to action. Engel de Ruyter noted that some of the attackers had penetrated as far as the palisades "where one of our men was wounded and he died on the 13th." On the whole, however, a stalemate position seems to have resulted until a little English galliot hoy sailed close to the fort to take a hand.

Nine years later Silas Taylor was still sufficiently impressed to emphasise the part played by this small sailing craft when writing in the quaint italics and capitals of his manuscript history of Harwich. He said that the Dutch "were put to Fright and Flight by two or three small Guns out of a little *Galliot* firing amongst the Shingle (which covered them from the Sight of the *Fort*) scattering the Pebbles amongst them". Deane, while admitting that the galliot was among the ships which "ffiered at theire men and galled them", was at pains to point out that he did not consider this the reason for the eventual retreat:

"It was not as simple people imagine that our *Spie* or the gallioate hoy who shott about 8 shote and them att randum which maid the ffoot to retreate for they killed not one man with great shot; noe, it was the militia whose collers displayed on Phillstow Clifte near where they landed, and not knowing but that the whoulle millitia was come they therefore retreated."

Nevertheless, the reason for the ultimate withdrawal from the fort was two-fold, as will soon appear, and it seems that the galliot, on enemy testimony alone, was a main contributor to the earlier demoralisation of the assault groups. It was De Witt himself who said:

". . . on coming close to the fort the sailors advanced with their scaling ladders and their weapons. But the enemy fired on them with much grapeshot, chiefly from a galliot which was inside the entrance, which upset our people, principally the sailors who threw down their ladders and lay behind a rising."

Castillego reported much the same:

"The enemy had no lack of means to answer us, both with guns and muskets, and chiefly from a galliot which sailed up on the far side and bravely fired at our troops and caused them damage, we suffering some casualties both dead and wounded."

Svendsen wrote of "two English ships lying close to the castle which were causing our people a lot of damage". Admiral Sweers confirmed that the grapeshot came "particularly from a galliot which was lying inside the harbour" and he added, "this brought most of our men into confusion because they had no cover and little or no help from the ships". So it seems that this was a successful attempt to enfilade the enemy by the brave crew of a light-draught vessel brought up only a few yards from the beach in full view of the Dutchmen. Anchoring would not only have aided their shooting but also have prevented them from being swept out to sea by the ebb tide. They could hardly have achieved the considerable effect they did with their small guns from any other position within the harbour. While earlier on the Dutch clearly lacked the absent Van Brakel and his crew in this action, it seems at any rate that there were a few Englishmen of comparable mettle.

It is clear that the fort guns could not range effectively on the sea bank, which was at first a help and then a danger to the enemy. One of the first tasks of the garrison after the action was to clear away shingle to improve their field of fire, but in any case the need to preserve palisades as an obstacle would have had a limiting effect. On the other hand the galliot, once she had threaded her way past the blockships, would have been able to range over the whole blunt head of Landguard beach, then vastly different at high tide from the attenuated point of the present day. The early charts indicate a great mass of sand and shingle stretching some five hundred yards eastward from the harbour entrance and fronting the entire southern face of the fort. On a calm

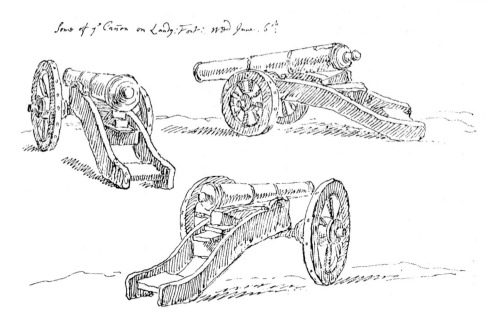

*Some of y^e Cañon on Landg: Fort: wᵈᵈ June. 6ᵗʰ*

James Thornhill's diary sketch of guns at Landguard Fort in 1711.
*Victoria and Albert Museum (L.1280. 1961)*

day there would have been at least a hundred yards of shingle between the fort and the nearest seaward high water mark, and there it continued submerged to form the Andrews shoal. It would have been a different story at the height of winter gales, with spray and flying shingle covering much of the area but, on this hot and almost windless afternoon, it would have been easy for the Dutch, as Taylor said, to lodge themselves "within Carbine Shot on two sides of the Fort". Since the beach turned away at right-angles along the way the Dutch had come, the eastern face of the fort, or most of it, was already covered by their advance. Thomas Major's print of Gainsborough's view over Landguard Common in 1753 gives a good idea of the approach to the fort in 1667, but the ramparts then faced differently (see page 100).

The first attempt to storm the fort seems to have taken place around five o'clock, since the order to modify the sea attack was apparently given at about four. According to Taylor this first action lasted for about three-quarters of an hour. An hour later there was another and much weaker assault lasting about fifteen minutes and this, for some of the Dutch troops, finished in precipitate retreat. About twenty storming ladders, "their hand = grenadoes & a case of very handsome pistols" were left behind, apart from a few fatal casualties who remained where they fell or were dragged a short distance. A twenty-two rung ladder, eighteen and a half feet in length, was kept as a trophy by the Darell family for well over two hundred years. It is surely one of the strangest quirks of history that this should be destroyed in August, 1944, when a flying-bomb demolished the church at Little Chart in Kent.

Other English ships contributed some gunfire to the action, but not very effectively it seems. At first because of the head wind and later because of the calm it had been found impossible to use those of the eighteen fireships which had been able to find crews, but there was air enough, apparently, to get the smaller and handier vessels moving. The ships mentioned in various people's correspondence, apart from the galliot hoy, were the sixth-rate *Truelove* of 12 guns and seventy men, the sixth-rate *Lily* of eight guns and forty men, the *Lennox* privateer which belonged to the Governor of Dover Castle, and the little reconnaissance craft *Spy* which was said to be the sister ship of the famous *Fan-Fan*. When the height of the tide served these vessels could have fired shots at the enemy across the low neck of Landguard Common but, for those upriver of the blockships, the fort itself would have greatly limited their field of fire. It is likely that it was only the galliot which got herself into a really advantageous position.

The Dutch prize *Westfriesland*, originally a fourth-rate of 50 guns and 180 men, did not take an active part. She was anchored near the Cliff Foot Rocks, presumably to deter the Dutch ships from attempting the southern channel of the harbour entrance. Letters from her purser, Richard Tyler, suggest that some of her guns had already been moved to augment the Harwich shore defences.

A perspective view of Landguard Fort as it appeared in 1667, showing the very low profile of the defences.

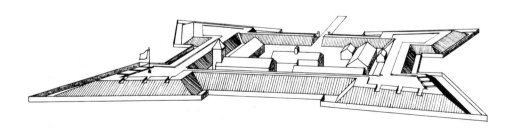

The Dutch senior officers, meanwhile, had completed their far from encouraging survey of the fort. Castillego said that the Regent of Putten (Cornelis de Witt) and Lieutenant-Admiral de Ruyter "came within musket shot of the fort, where they could see and have the full benefit of the officers' observations". They found that the fort was constructed as follows:

"Firstly, it appeared to be fortified with four good bastions or bulwarks, partly with earth and the rest with masonry with a good ditch.

"Secondly, it was fortified with a good covered way and counterscarp, leaving those standing behind it in safety. The covered way was filled with men, who were well disciplined and alert and were faithfully keeping a lookout for us.

"On recognising this, Colonel Dolman called all the senior officers and captains to a council of war to consider whether it was possible to take such a well organised fort; and it was unanimously agreed that it was impossible and just not practicable, all the more so because they saw that the Count van Hoorn's troops were being attacked."

De Witt himself said to the States General that "the army officers, after they had taken a closer look at the fort, came to the conclusion that there was no likelihood of being able to take it, so that the army and the sailors decided to withdraw and they marched off in good order." He also gave these additional details:

"The fort at Harwich had been fortified more strongly than we had been informed, there being inside the walls a 'fausse-braye' on the side we were: and although the water in the ditches was not deep, there was a masonry base built up ten or twelve feet high, which dampened the morale and courage of our men, which had been exceptionally high before they came upon it."

Thus the wall which had been so earnestly suggested as far back as 1636 had at last been built, although exactly when this happened is not clear. Adriaen de Haese summed it all up in his letter to his brother: "It would have been impossible to capture a place so strong without a formal siege being undertaken." The moat, with its vertical wall on its inner side, would certainly have been a great obstacle entirely covered by defensive fire. The "Workmeister" in 1626 had announced his intention of making it sixty feet broad and twelve foot deep, and Hans Svendsen referred to "a ditch in front of the castle which our people could not get over".

Engel de Ruyter also noted that there was a fausse-braye and said, rather obscurely, that the castle "hadt 2 laegh schuttren waren wel 600 soldaten daerin". This Old Dutch can be doubtfully translated as either "two low fences" or "two rows of guns with a good 600 soldiers therein", and one explanation is that young Engel may have been thinking of musket fire coming both from the ramparts and from the fausse-braye below. The latter, by then a rather outmoded form of defence, consisted in its usual form of a low parapet and fire-step at the top of the escarp, the inside wall of the ditch. At Landguard, however, it appears from a subsequent drawing, as well as from the absence of an earthen bank behind the topmost section of the wall and the sandy nature of the soil, that the brickwork wall was built mainly to provide a satisfactory escarp rather than as a deliberate fausse-braye construction. It was the space behind it, running back to the base of the bastions and curtains, which constituted the "covered way", a path to afford easy movement of the troops around the fort. This arrangement, however, differed from many existing forts and castles which presented a more or less sheer climb from the bottom of the ditch to the top of the ramparts. The latest practice in 1667, moreover, was to push out the defences by building a low rampart and covered way at the very top of the "glacis", a cleared area providing a field of fire on the "country" side of the moat. This was not so at Landguard since the state of the moat was observed by the Dutch, an impossibility had there been such a fortification full of troops in their way. As Castillego said that the troops "advanced right up to the counterscarp outside the fort" and De Ruyter noted in his journal that "there were some of the sailors who reached the palisades", it would appear that the latter were mounted at the top of the counterscarp. A peep through palings was the best the Dutch could manage, it seems!

Only one of the fort garrison was killed, and their four wounded included the Governor and commander, Captain Darell, who was hit by a musket ball in the shoulder, but not dangerously. A notice on the ladder trophy, previously mentioned, said that Darell drove off the Dutch under Admiral de Ruyter in a sally from the fort, but whether some of the garrison did emerge in this way is unconfirmed. The only naval casualties on the English side resulted from return fire against the small ships. Strangely enough these were two Dutchmen who were hurt by one shot on board the *Lily* and they, according to Deane, were "very ffearful". All that could be said concerning Dutch losses up to this time was "about the fforte 8 dead and wounded unknowne".

So ended this phase of the action, but there was a good deal of relief in what Anthony Deane told Samuel Pepys about it:

> "I am glad of the allteration of theire designe, ffor had they come in and bin masters of the river they would have pusshed hard ffor the fforte especially if their foot had come over the bancke and got into the trenches with granarders would have soone put our men from the brickwall which is all the strength of that place, and bettween your honer and myselfe could not have missed it, the fforce within the forte weare all but 2 companys, green men of the mellitia, and of them you may guess at."

# CHAPTER EIGHT

# The Brave Withdrawal

WHEN the retreating Dutchmen made their way back from the fort towards Bulls Cliff some of them came into view of the English men-of-war in Harwich Harbour. Silas Taylor reported gleefully that "as the shipps saw them within the Fort in the Salt-road, they bestowed upon them a bullett welcome". The range, however, was likely to have been in excess of 750 yards, too far for musket fire and somewhat long for the effective use of small cannon. Taylor's mention of the Salt-road, too, leaves some room for argument because, for easier marching, the Dutch may have been using the rough track which paralleled the beach along Landguard Dry Common. On balance, however, the term seems more likely to refer to the location of the English ships in the estuary anchorage, which was then usually known as Orwell Haven.

Meanwhile action had commenced on the Felixstowe high ground where the Count van Hoorn's forward troops were stationed in "a covered position", and it was rapidly becoming clear that it was only the timely decision to leave a strong force to guard the way back to the boats which would save the Dutch from disaster at the end of that day. The alarm was raised even before the attack on the fort. "On the way", Castillego said, "information was received of a serious situation. It was that the enemy foot and horse were massing and in quite a number and one had to be on one's guard." He followed this with his reference to English troops being shipped over from Bawdsey, and an intercepted letter from Holland also revealed that the Dutch "were designed to be cut off by a party of horse, which skulked as it were in ambush".

That the Count van Hoorn was a seasoned campaigner and his troops skilfully deployed seems evident from Castillego's journal:

"When our troops had done all the damage they could they withdrew in good order to help the troops of the Count van Hoorn. These in the meanwhile had not been idle in this encounter, for the skirmishing had scarcely begun near the fort when the enemy appeared in the pass with foot and horse where the Count van Hoorn's troops were occupying it. They began with a furious fire upon them, trying to break through the pass and so to attack us from the front and rear and then wipe us out. Our men were in no great need of help but performed their duty courageously. There was much skirmishing and firing lasting for two hours, until the enemy began to withdraw, pursued immediately by our men but they soon returned to their posts as further pursuit was dangerous."

Concerning the English troops delayed on the far side of the Deben, Anthony Deane reported that "the ffoote by 6 a clocke in the afternoone gott over by which time the horsse meet them and on Fillstow Cliffte geathered together about 1500 ffoot and 3 troups off horse". It was the display of militia colours "on Phillstowe Clifte near where they landed", he said, which influenced the Dutch retreat from the fort. Although these seem to be particular references to the cliff above the point, rather than to the Felixstowe high ground generally, they are rather puzzling. The action at "the pass" took place a mile away and, in those days, the only road from Felixstowe Ferry turned inland to pass through Old Felixstowe village. However, it may be that the troops from across the Deben marched along the cliffs after they had traversed the stretch of low ground from the Ferry and then boldly planted their colours both as a rallying point and as a ploy to intimidate the Dutch. If they did so on Felixstowe Cliff itself they certainly made no serious attack on the landing craft below and they must have departed by an inland route for the Fort Lane area.

Taylor, from his vantage point at Harwich, reckoned that "the Suffolke forces came to them in inclosures about 4 of ye clocke or 5". By that Major Leslie [47] thought he meant a close formation attack. From Deane's mention of fifteen hundred foot, it would seem that infantry other than the White regiment of militia were involved. The sixth company of the Yellow regiment, which apparently did not go to the fort, were probably available but there is no evidence that any portion of the Red regiment, raised round about Hoxne, or the Blue, from around Beccles, was present at Felixstowe that day. The three troops of horse, normally about 180 men in all, were presumably those

A drawing by Willem van de Velde the Younger of a States yacht and Dutch ships before a light breeze. *National Maritime Museum, London*

attached to the White and Yellow regiments together with the troop from Cambridgeshire. Engel de Ruyter said that the Count van Hoorn was "on a hill with 300 horse against him" but one cannot swallow a statement by Hans Svendsen that those retreating from the fort "were pursued by eight squadrons of cavalry who were fighting fiercely". If such a sally was made from Landguard by a small body of horsemen it is very strange that it brought no remark whatever from the onlookers at Harwich.

Deane's hearsay was that "one part of the Dutch made good a way downe to the ffort but affter some time with the losse of about 12 of our men they put them also to the boates and there in a body they continued till dark". Castillego confirmed that there was a pause in the retreat of the assault party. He said that "the troops that had withdrawn from the fort came back to join the troops of the Count van Hoorn staying with them for some time and then made a good and orderly withdrawal". Taylor, in turn, gave indications that meanwhile there had indeed been a dour struggle:

> "They spar'd about 4 or 500, reliev'd from ye main body (yt stood neare the place they landed with a strong body of Pikes which I plainly saw) to assault the forces above on the Hill, & with them 2 or 3 drakes, wth wch they maintain'd the lanes and hedges; soe that the Earle of Suffolke gott his ground of them in a manner but by inches, because his horse were excluded from the service."

From a Harwich point of view "near the place they landed" might refer to anywhere on the common between Bulls Cliff and the present day Cobbold's Point. There at all costs it was necessary for the Dutch to delay the English forces from getting down to the area where the boats were grounded and in consequence the Dutch grip on the high ground near the cliffs must have been very tenacious. The drakes, which proved so effective, were small guns known as saker drakes and it seems that these were of a particularly portable character. Hans Svendsen said four men carried "two small metal pieces that could fire a three pound shot" and he also mentioned that they were used to fire grapeshot against the English cavalry. It was customary in those days to name cannon after various birds. In this case it was the saker falcon of which the drake is the male and the smaller of the species. Since grapeshot was fired it seems hardly likely that these pieces would have been the diminutive mortars devised by Menno van Coehoorn during the seventeenth century. These projected grenades accurately up to about 160 yards and could easily be carried by two men.

It is probable that the Dutch on the cliff top were hard pressed enough to call for assistance from their reserves below, but whether there was any great degree of reinforcement from the anchored fleet is very doubtful. The proposed second landing of seamen, which was to follow a successful bombardment from within the estuary, had obviously fallen through, but perhaps a few boatloads of men, including one from the *Woerden*, were sent ashore to aid the evacuation. It may be this which prompted Hans Svendsen to say in his embroidered account: "The English were too strong for our people. Then each ship had to send a boatload ashore to help them and we were a good 500 men who went to help our people". However no other contemporary writing, English or Dutch, supports his statement.

Castillego said that some of the English dead were plundered and left naked and Engel de Ruyter also had this to say about looting:

The terrain over which the advance to the fort was made is shown, somewhat foreshortened, in T. R. Major's print of 1753 after the oil painting by Thomas Gainsborough.

*Author's collection*

"There were some sailors who had some silk clothes and coats as booty. Father's trumpeter was with three soldiers in a house, where there were 40 horse, who shot all five of the sailors, who had been plundering but when they heard the trumpet sounding they fled and the trumpeter and the soldiers took with them the booty the dead sailors left."

A quick death at the hands of the English horsemen may, however, have been somewhat preferable to survival for the seamen. Only two weeks earlier some Dutchmen who had defied the no-looting order during a foraging expedition on the Isle of Sheppey had been immediately tried by court-martial and sentenced to be dropped three times from the yard, with one hundred and fifty lashes in addition.

Further details of this interesting evening are unfortunately lacking, but it is clear that there was much firing between five and seven o'clock, by which time the Suffolk militia had had enough. De Ruyter said "our position was so well defended that the English withdrew after sundown". Admiral Sweers also confirmed that the English were unable to dislodge the Count van Hoorn "from his favourable position". Presumably the Suffolk militia did their best to regroup and, if necessary, to remedy any shortage of ammunition, but no doubt most of them were extremely tired after all their marching in hot weather. In any case further operations would have been a matter of Blind Man's Buff and on very awkward ground at that. Allowing for the thirteen days of change from the Old Style Calendar, sunset on 2nd July, 1667, would have been at about a quarter to eight. Taylor, too, confirmed the lull in fighting soon afterwards:

"About 9 of the clock all was silent and they drawn to their body about Filstow Cliff, their boats being on ground which caused them to stand their ground longer".

Writing of the period which followed the English withdrawal from "the Pass", the subsequent movement of all Dutch troops towards the boats and the ultimate evacuation, Castillego said:

"The enemy made some alarms for us afterwards, but fighting was not so fierce as before. Nevertheless shooting continued until the evening at about 9.30, when we re-embarked . . . At about ten o'clock in the evening all were re-embarked and rowed out to the ships in the barges and the boats, leaving in the withdrawal not a single dead man nor a wounded one, although the operation was carried out in sight of the enemy, who was on our tail to the last. And the Lord be praised, all got back safely on board, some of them having booty."

Admiral Sweers also noted that the land forces "got on board the ships at about ten o'clock" and he added thankfully, "of my men there was not one dead, wounded or missing". Thus the evacuation, as De Witt happily reported, was accomplished "without any hindrance" from the English.

In addition to the comparatively small losses at Landguard Fort the final stages of the day's action produced some casualties, but by no means in the numbers with which Hans Svendsen sought to impress his readers. "When we went on shore with our five hundred men", he said, "a galliot lay close to the shore and picked up 200 wounded." He added that next day "a list was drawn up of how many people we lost on shore" and that "in the whole fleet we lost 1,200 dead and 300 wounded". According to Deane the Swedish captain who came into Harwich said, "They lost 33 men out of de Rutters ship" and that they carried off some of the dead men. Taylor told Pepys that "several boats laden with dead men were seen by several to put off from the shore" but here again the suggestion of quantity is probably the product of rumour. As well as Deane's mention of a dozen English casualties "near the way down to the fort" Castillego had this to say:

> "In this position we suffered several casualties in dead and wounded, in particular Captain Steenlandt van der Val, who was severely wounded; it is reported that he died two or three days later, having been taken back to Briel. The Lieutenant of Lieut.-Admiral Aert van Nes was shot dead in his boat. The enemy had their share of losses, among whom were several persons of quality."

Engel de Ruyter noted that a gentleman named Terburgh, a gunner (bosschieter) and a soldier were killed and two or three wounded. The order to the galliot master Pieter Harmessan to collect the wounded Captain van der Val from the *Justina van Nassau* and take him to the Maas is among those recorded in Admiral de Ruyter's papers. Captain Adrien de Haese said that seven dead and thirty wounded "were left" but there is no mention of the abandonment of any wounded in the English accounts. As for Dutch prisoners, Deane mentioned that the militia had taken some but he did not know how many. It is surprising that there is not a single contemporary record in or from Suffolk which concerns the land action or even the disposal of the dead. Truly, as Taylor said, "the particulars of ye losse on both sides is very uncertaine".

It cannot be doubted that the evacuation proper was completed well before midnight, much of it accomplished on a falling tide. So, if there was any Dutch movement ashore thereafter, it can only have concerned a few stragglers and perhaps the recovery of a stranded boat or two which could not be refloated earlier. It is probable that the flood set in at about half past ten and that high water was between four and five next morning. Meanwhile in the darkness confusion seems to have reigned among the defenders of Felixstowe and wild rumour was rife in Harwich.

Uniforms of musketeer and officer of The Lord High Admiral's Regiment at the time of the Landguard action.

*Royal Marines Museum Archives*

28ᵗʰ October 1664 'The Admiral 2.st'

At ten o'clock that night, when most Dutchmen were safely afloat, Richard Tyler sent a message to Pepys by the late London mail. "Their is of them about 2000 still on shore in the marshes and we are now sending 500 men over to joyne the trayn'd bands to fall upon them this night before flood." Nevertheless these tardy reinforcements under Major Legge of the Lord High Admiral's Regiment were dispatched by Lord Oxford only after some persuasion from Deane. The difficulties of keeping pace with events taking place over a wide arc only two to four miles distant over the water were stressed by Taylor in his letter next day:

"The designment of action in soe many places at once by ye Dutch hath rendred the whole account confused; and certainly had it been but 6 or 7 miles off we might have had a clearer account to have communicated than now we have as spectators of one action at the same time haveing dependence upon several other."

103

From Deane's and Taylor's vague accounts of the later stages of the action it would seem that nothing whatever materialised in the way of a night attack. It is not even certain that there was some desultory musket fire after ten o'clock against the phantom Dutch. Perhaps Taylor means "as" where he wrote "at" in the following letter and by "that" meant the actual process of evacuation, which in fact took place earlier than he states:

"[The Dutch] being pressed by ye Earle of Suffolke had a much to doe to keep themselves from disorder; especially could the Horse but have come at them at (*sic*) that began in the woodes above the cliffe about 11 = of ye clocke at night & lasted till about 2 in the morning; at what time the water floating theire boates they gott off to their shipps."

Deane, in his "NARRATIVE of the late transaction of the Dutch and us, July the 2nd. 1667", made no bones about the hesitancy of the English troops during that night at Felixstowe:

"seeing theire gaurd and our millitia ffier at each other one the hill, which made them all draw into the bottom and theire drew into battallia and stood whille darke night, ffor I veryly beleave they dare not take to theire boates for feare of our hors would breake in amongst them, but they need not have feared that for on discours with Sir Phillip parker tould me under the rose that the hors would have the ffoot goe on and the foot weare all disordered the horse went not which I dare say is trew."

Hans Svendsen made it clear that his landing party had a rough time and the conclusion of his account certainly strikes a human note. At least it must be admitted that he had a good tale to take back to Denmark. He was in Copenhagen by 8th October following his demobilisation on 30th August, 1667.

"When we got ashore we were 42 strong in our boat of whom only 22 got back on board uninjured. And so we came by night each to his own ship with what was left of our people and a party of wounded in tow."

At eleven o'clock that night, with vivid memories of musket fire in the darkness from Felixstowe cliffs and while thousands of Dutchmen remained in their ships at anchor only a mile or two away, Silas Taylor sat down to write his third report on the day's events. He had penned his previous letter at two o'clock in the afternoon when Van Nes had brought the eight ships of his division into the outer part of the Rolling Ground, but these ships soon advanced towards the harbour entrance with the results already narrated. First-hand information about the attack on the fort had been brought over to Harwich from Landguard by Major Holland of the militia but rumours of losses inflicted on the Dutch in the darkness since were rather wild. Even at this anxiety-ridden time Taylor's efforts to curry favour were undiminished and he seems also to have been rankled by somebody's curtailment or direction of his actions contrary to his inclinations. Possibly he had in mind the Lord Lieutenant of Essex and his officers, but he was in any case subordinate to his non-relative Captain John Taylor, the Commissioner in charge of the ship-yard, and to Captain Anthony Deane, the Master Shipwright.

"Sr since my writing of those this day of wch I sent one by the post & another by an expresse that went by 2 of the clocke this afternoone this succeeded viz = That about eight of the Dutch fleet came in to ye Rowling = groundes & fired very many gunnes at the fort & pt at those shipps yt we had placed for ye security of the harbour to be suncke; but some suncke & I know nott why the rest were not = however I must tell you that about Filstow cliffe severall of ye Dutch being landed to ye number as we judged of them of 2 or 3000 wth a very great stand of Pikes; some party of them attacqued the Fort of Landguard; where wth the death of one & wounding of two they were forced to retreat after 2 assaults, the first assault was long & tedious enduring about the space of 3 quarters of an houre; the 2d about 7 of ye clocke lasted about a quarter; they came up boldly but were as boldly & resolutely answered to their prejudice, what losse they had in both these assaults wee know not only it is reported that 150 were lost on their side since the sunne went downe; I saw much firing from Filstow cliffe by the militia of the Country; the Major of wch Regiment beeing in the fort during this assault sayes (comeing over the water this evening) that there hath been a great skirmish betwixt them & ye Dutch & in truth I saw the fire of them; it hath been a sharp bout; but the 2d attacque was not soe violent as the first; we dispayre not of secureing his Matyes concernes in this place; However I shall doe my endeavour though I want both friends & power; too morrow will manifest more: they [the Dutch] lye as close to our shore as they can: they have gott noe ground of us; we are hearty and well; they are about 47 or 48 sayle besides the five in ye Sledway. we expect too morrow's action; had I been in those predicaments as my place &c.: had priveledg'd mee to I should have done my endeavour & given you a more particular notice wch you may expect by ye next from yr most humble servt Silas Taylor."

Gerard Brandt, De Ruyter's biographer, summing up the events of this remarkable day twenty years later, may have understated the casualties, but most people will agree with his sentiments:

"Thus the well led attack came to nothing with little loss: for in the whole fleet there were not more than seven killed and thirty-five wounded and the honour of the brave withdrawal sweetened the sorrow at the failure of their expectations."

# CHAPTER NINE

# The Aftermath

THE anchored Dutch fleet waited only a few hours in darkness after re-embarking the troops. Sunrise on Wednesday, 3rd July, 1667, was at almost four o'clock and two hours later all the Dutch vessels were under sail with the exception of "five great ships still riding in the Sledway". These, presumably, were Vice Admiral Star's squadron under orders to watch the Kings Deep. The rest of the fleet then drifted up-coast on the ebb with the lightest of airs and by eleven o'clock they were in Hollesley Bay, shut off from the sight of Harwich people by Felixstowe Cliff. Three vessels went aground on the Whiting shoal and the others anchored until the flood refloated their colleagues. Progress up-coast thereafter was very slow and when evening came the enemy had anchored in force off Aldeburgh, only about two miles distant from the town. During the morning a Dutch galliot had put about forty men into a boat near the lighthouse at Orfordness. According to Richard Browne "about 10 Landed, peeped up and run aboard againe".

This second approach to their waters in two days caused a considerable stir among the Aldeburgh people. Browne thought that the enemy would have attempted a landing during the night of July 3rd or after dawn next morning. At least, he reckoned, they would "have given us some Broadsides". Others thought so too, and such was the grass roots reaction to this further threat of invasion that that night "the Country came down in great Companys both with Horse and foote wth Holberds sithes and what weapons they could gitt". As these forces were in addition to the four companies of foot and two troops of horse already in the town, Sir Robert Brooke, who was in command, would certainly have "well approved him selfe if the enemy durst have landed". Sir Robert, a Member of Parliament for Aldeburgh, was also a lieutenant-colonel under Sir John Rous. According to a minute of a Deputy Lieutenants' meeting at Sir Henry Felton's house at Playford on 4th July, 1666, the militia regiment commanded by Sir John was to rendezvous at either Beccles or Blythburgh. At least it seems that the message of the Felixstowe beacon had spread far and wide and raised the dust in many a Suffolk lane with galloping troopers and marching musketeers. "In case of invasion" the men of the other militia regiment were to make their first rendezvous at Halesworth.

These events on the Suffolk coast, however, came to an anti-climax. When Browne sat down to write his London letter at five o'clock in the morning of 4th July the Dutch had already weighed anchor and were two leagues away. Browne said that they were sailing southwards, bound, he thought, "either for the Gunfleet or Buoy of the Nore". He had heard "noe true news from ffilsto where the Dutch landed" and he hoped that Williamson would have it from other hands. So ended the biggest scare, and perhaps the liveliest night, in the history of Crabbe's "Borough".

First off the mark with the London post from Harwich was the Lord Lieutenant of Essex. While his opposite number across the estuary must still have been counting the casualties of the "great Skirmish", Lord Oxford dispatched the following note to Secretary of State Lord Arlington. It was dated "Harwich, July 3, 9 in the morning":

"My Lord, This night with the young flood, the enemy shipped the remainder of their beaten party, and this morning the fleet have turned their backs, and are driving away as fast as the dead calm will suffer them. I thought it necessary to inform your lordship of it, though I have nothing else to say but that. In case the fleet go quite off the coast, I hope his Majesty will give me leave to do so too, and attend him in London.

"This harbour (with the fortification and manning of the fort at Landguard, and this town), adding our fire-ships, is not now an enterprise for Dutch courages, and truly the disreputation that must follow such an enterprise as their first appearance seemed to promise, does a little moderate my trouble for our loss at Chatham.

"Pray God send all the King's enemies so base an end."

Although he seems anxious to have been first in line for the King's personal congratulations, Lord Oxford did not in fact get away from Harwich until 17th August. As it happened, the view in royal circles was by no means as optimistic as his own and the Duke of York, who knew the weaknesses of the district from his earlier visit, spent most of the night of 3/4 July travelling down to Harwich. He was there by seven in the morning and was soon looking at the Dutch fleet through a telescope, some elements of it, including three flagships, having reappeared in the Gunfleet and the Sledway. Taylor reported that the Duke would be staying and dining in Harwich before going over to Landguard, also that the royal presence "much comforted the people". This was a most timely boost for local morale since Deane wrote of "the corridge and willingness which is so lost in most men" that he was almost ashamed to speak of it.

On 6th July Taylor said that the Duke was visiting Landguard Fort but would return to Harwich if he found that the Dutch had landed at Aldeburgh. This last remark derived from a rumour of gunfire up the coast and a report from a newly-arrived sea captain that he had seen the Southwold and Aldeburgh beacons afire during the previous night. On 6th July, also, Taylor confirmed that the chief surgeon had distributed the £3 ordered to be paid out to the wounded seamen, who had received it "with many thanks and prayers".

Over in Felixstowe the Duke of York, accompanied by the Earl of Oxford and other gentlemen, inspected the whole scene of battle and listened to the reasons given for the comparatively unmolested evacuation by the Dutch. Deane, who had received Sir Philip Parker's "under the rose" thoughts regarding the lack of action, said "Yett to the Duke they make apolligies if they would have gott downe the hill they would have don it, and to see whether it be soe the Duke himself hath veiwed every place and found ways they could have gon and they must needs know the country as well as himself". The future King of England kept his own counsel, however, for Deane said "but littell the Duke says to it whatever he thinks". Thus the old Fort Lane, as well as any predecessors of Bent Hill, Bath Hill and the shore ends of Brook and Maybush lanes, must have come in for thorough royal scrutiny. Little did the Duke know that the present Beach House property, between the ends of Brook and Maybush lanes, would in time be the temporary residence of the future wife of the abdicated Edward VIII.

This immediate inquiry into their actions no doubt caused much heart-burning among the Suffolk militia. Without artillery they had been at a great disadvantage against better armed and more experienced adversaries, faced immediately after exhausting rides and marches in hot weather. Unlike the Essex troops based on Harwich, they had also suffered casualties in the brunt of fierce fighting. There was certainly ill-feeling over their generalship. Deane said on 13th July, "The head officers of Souffoullke of the mellitia are wholley disgusted at my Lord Berkely's power over them, and this Sir Checester Wray last night toulld me, at this time I was sorry to heare, and that they would not obey him." Brown, writing from Aldeburgh on 23rd July, said that there was some difference among the militia officers "upon some alteration". He had heard a report that Sir Robert Brooke [48] had been "committed to the Tower for speaking against Papists" but he conceived such items to have arisen from "seditious spirits".

The Duke of York remained in Harwich until ten in the morning of 10th July, being then recalled by an express letter which said that he should return to London where, presumably, he was needed to discuss the draft peace treaty. It seems that some drastic moves resulted from his short visit. Browne said on 11th July that the Earl of Suffolk had dismissed all the horse and foot and that the Aldeburgh people were much disheartened by the withdrawal of the soldiers. This was not without reason, for a Dutch vice admiral and five men-of-war were at anchor nearby and Browne was of opinion that "two shallops laden with men might destroy the town". The Dutch had put out a white flag but its significance is not clear since peace was still some way off. On the same day Deane reported from Harwich that the horse-militia had been discharged "and new troops come and some ould". He thought about five troops in all. Some of the militia foot had also gone home, but four companies in Landguard Fort were to continue there with forty horse.

Military risks seem to have been taken because two days later, with many of the Dutch fleet again in sight of Harwich, Deane said, "The militia of Souffoullke is all dismissed and as yet my Lord Arlington's nor Sir Allin Aspley's regiments is not come; this night they are expected". Whether these were some of the recently recruited royal troops which Pepys forecast "Parliament and Kingdom would never bear" is not clear but in any case the troop dispositions then made did not last long. "Yesterday on the Suffolke syde and heer in Essex the new raysed horse and foot were disbanded, and their arms dillivered into his Majestes stoares", said Richard Tyler on 17th August. Troop movements had been widespread since the Landguard attack. At Yarmouth on 6th July Sir John Holland's and Sir William Doyley's regiments had been replaced by Lord Townshend's new-raised regiment commanded by Sir Ralph Hare. At Harwich, however, Lord Oxford still kept his own regiment of Essex militia.

Meanwhile improvements to the Harwich defences continued. When telling Williamson on 11th July that two of the blockships were afloat again "and the other two buoying-up", Joseph Quine revealed that "that expedient of defence, being judged useless will be practised no more". He also said that Harwich had received "an addition of strength, both in its lines and batteries, from the Duke's presence". On the same day, in connection with the removal of the remainder of the *Westfriesland's* guns, Tyler said to Pepys, "The west syde of this towne is now allso a fortifying, every man's yard being a safeguard to himselfe and towne". It is evident that the Dutch assault across the low ground at Felixstowe had sadly shaken the centuries-old faith in the natural defence provided by the ooze of the later-called Bathside Creek and the ditches of Harwich Marsh.

As for the Dutch fleet, in spite of continued rumours from Breda as to the imminence of peace, it had very soon returned to menace the entire coast. The movements of the Dutch ships were uncertain. Sometimes they were reported before Aldeburgh and sometimes Southwold, and there was a good deal of anxiety about a London-bound fleet of colliers, temporarily brought up at Yarmouth because they dare not venture further south. The main traffic in and out of the Thames was blockaded by Rear Admiral van der Zaan in the Orfordness-Sledway-Gunfleet area and by other squadrons near the North Foreland under Vice Admirals Evertsen and Enno Doedes Star, thus leaving the way clear for the rest of the fleet to cruise around to their best advantage. The Thames blockade was very effective, raising the price of coal in London from 25s. per chaldron to £6 10s. within three weeks, and many bakers had to stop production.

Sneak passages, however, were possible provided there were no Dutch ships between the Middle Ground and the Nore. By 6th July the *Roebuck*[49] had arrived at Harwich from London "over the Spitts and found all clear from the river". On 9th July the *Spy* went out of Harwich "ass decoy to 2 Sweads laden with timber and deals for London". She was back two days later reporting that she had found the coast clear of enemy and had been to Sheerness "for intelligence". There her crew noted that rebuilding of the smashed-up fort had already started.[50] Nevertheless, on the very day of the *Spy's* return, watchers from Beacon Hill could see over a dozen enemy sail "on the backsyde of the West Rocks".

Elsewhere it is very clear that other Dutch ships and phantom fears of them kept up the pressure. On 9th July an enemy fleet was reported off Dover, presumably the force with De Ruyter and De Witt aboard bound west, but they did not fire a single shot and went on their way down Channel. On 2nd July the States General had dispatched an order to Cornelis de Witt to split the main body of the fleet into two portions, one of which under Lieutenant-Admiral Aert van Nes was to continue operations in the Thames Estuary. Then on 11th July there was a complete fiasco far away in Wales at Milford Haven where the arrival of thirty-eight sail in the offing caused great alarm. "The deputy-lieutenants caused the militia to arm, and a great number of men to draw to the waterside to defend the county. Sir Erasmus Phillipps troop and the county troop, with many young men riding as volunteers, were also ready". This fleet, when it anchored in the haven, was found to consist only of cow carriers bound for Ireland. Reports that the Dutch were lately at Portsmouth, at Plymouth, at Dartmouth poured into the Navy Board; so many, in fact, that old Admiral Sir William Batten finally lost his composure and declared with some emphasis "By God! I do believe the Devil shits Dutchmen."

By 13th July the position again looked very serious for Harwich. Browne reported from Aldeburgh that a Dutch fleet had anchored during the previous day near "Bardsey Sands" and that six great men-of-war had been in sight for eight or ten days off Orfordness. On the same day Taylor wrote from Harwich saying that the fourteen Dutch vessels which were "about Bardsey Sands" had been joined by more and that the total then was about sixty. Local opinion was that the Dutch "meant to regain their honour", which must have been a somewhat tiresome prospect since the weather was "exceedingly hot and the grass burnt up". Deane's report of that day was that about seventy sail of the Dutch fleet were in sight, spread about the sea with about eighteen of them in the Sledway, "most of them very ffaire for our harbour, as if they intended us another attack". Nothing materialised, however, and on 16th July Taylor was hoping that "Landguard Passage" was well guarded because the Dutch still had "an aching tooth against Harwich". There was a stiff breeze which prevented the English fireships from going out and Taylor remarked that the

Dutch "about the Sledway and off Barsey Sands dare not budge from their anchors for the wind, and are quiet neighbours".

The Dutch remained as a threat to Harwich until Sunday, 21st July. In the afternoon of that day six men-of-war came from the north to reinforce those near the Gunfleet, and later on four Norwegian vessels homeward bound from London were intercepted and their masters presumably interrogated. Then, as the flood set in during the evening of the next day, the whole enemy fleet weighed anchor and stood up to the buoy of the Middle Ground. They sailed with a westerly wind as long as the tide favoured them, brought up for the night and departed out of sight at dawn under a breeze from the north-north-east. An incoming smack told the Harwich people that the enemy had gone into the Thames and up to the Hope.

Once more it was a deliverance for the town and harbour of Harwich, so much so that Deane declared, "The people of this place are lulled into a peace". Then, by way of a knock at the military authorities, he said that he did not think the enemy could do much harm elsewhere "unless they have lefte theire secureing the harbours as they do with us ffor some time". Philosophically he continued "but wee shall at some time be convinced of this common securitie". He thought that this latest move of the Dutch resulted from a wish to stop the daily traffic through the Spitway. It was soon clear, however, that the enemy had gone down coast for a final fling in the Thames. They were no doubt unaware that a peace treaty had already been signed, subject to ratification, at Breda on 21st July, because two days later came the astonishing sight of Dutch and English men-of-war and fireships fiercely

A fireship attack is shown in this lithographed copy of a Van de Velde painting of the burning of the *Royal James* in the Sole Bay Battle, 28th May, 1672. The fireship crew row for safety in the foreground. *Suffolk Record Office, Ipswich (S Southwold 9)*

fighting it out well up the estuary in the confined waters of the Hope. At the same time a considerable number of Dutch ships lay at anchor near the Nore to safeguard the way of retreat. Upriver the Dutch were opposed by a squadron under Sir Edward Spragge and, during the seven hours of the action, no fewer than twelve English and five Dutch fireships were consumed. At least one enemy man-of-war was burnt and another blown up. It was, however, the sequel to this engagement which involved the so far largely inactive fireships at Harwich.

When the Dutch arrived in the Thames on 22nd July the possibility of catching a sizeable enemy fleet between two fires occurred to the Court tacticians and secret orders were sent off to Sir Joseph Jordan to come down-coast from Harwich with his little fleet. So secret was this project, apparently, that neither the Navy Board nor Admiral Spragge, the defender of London River, knew about it. On the other hand Dutch intelligence was so good that Lieutenant-Admiral Aert van Nes was aware of the plan a day or two before the actual encounter. The scheme, according to Pepys, was actually mentioned to a captured English fisherman who was released on the day preceding the action. Afterwards, William Liddall, a pilot aboard a Dantziger, reported to the Admiralty that it was subsequent to receiving information in a packet from Leigh that the Dutch intercepted the English fleet of fireships which had come from Harwich.

Vice Admiral Sir Joseph Jordan had called in his seamen and left the harbour during the evening of 23rd July. He had only the *Truelove*, the *Lily* and two other little frigates, which were probably the *Roebuck* and the *Lennox*, to shepherd his flock and it was only with the greatest difficulty that he had been able to find crews for sixteen of the eighteen fireships available to him. Pepys noted that "they were commanded by some idle fellows such as they could of a sudden gather up at Harwich". It was said also that when they were called for duty "ye 4th. part of our best men tooke ye opportunity of theire heeles and deserted". In consequence at least two of the sixteen ships were late in leaving port and had to catch up with the rest on the following day. Furthermore two of those which did sail were quite unsuitable for a sea attack. They were "small one decke yauchts" fitted out for harbour security and their real purpose was to tow fireships towards any enemy vessel which chanced to ground in the harbour. Another difficulty, which had yet to appear, was that Deane's arrangements for combustion were not very effective. It was said that the materials consisted only of broom and resin, with a few shavings and brimstone, and that there was a deficiency of fireballs to fire the train. Such was the forlorn hope which emerged from up-coast into the mouth of the Thames on 26th July. There was a strong north-easterly wind and a flood tide to urge them on.

Far from concerting action with Spragge, Jordan mistook that admiral's

Admiral Sir Joseph
Jordan, from an oil
painting by Sir Peter
Lely.
*National Maritime
Museum, London*

squadron in the Sea Reach distance for enemy ships and he proceeded to attack some Dutch men-of-war at anchor nearer at hand. Some said afterwards that he would have done better to wait for the ebb to slow down the speed of his attack but, as it happened, he immediately sent off the fireships in line to lay aboard the Dutch. Seeing some of them beginning to waver, Captain Jenifer of the *Lily* opened fire to make them hold course "for their lives" but this did not stop fourteen of the fireships from suddenly turning into the wind, leaving only the two unsuitable little ships to go bravely ahead. It was William Liddall who said afterwards that their approach was so resolute that the hearts of the Dutch "all fayled them". The enemy were so daunted, he continued, "that they could not open their mouthes one to another, and all ye men in ye Fregats which our Fireships laid on board, skipped overboard except fourty".[51]

This breathtaking attack at speed by the two little ships from Harwich was unfortunately of no avail. Having come upon the enemy to leeward, instead of "athwart their hawse", the grapplings did not hold and such combustion as there was blew away from the target ship. Because of this the Dutch were able to cut away the broken bowsprits and tangled rigging and

113

push their tiny assailants adrift. One of them, originally the seventh in the line of attack, was so small that "his maine yard was not 3 foot higher than the ship's side he layed aboard". The bravery of her crew seems to have been recognised by the enemy for, as they escaped in their small boat, they were quite unmolested by four boatloads of "Duch redie men" who had come to save those who had jumped overboard. These Harwich heroes even scraped down the side of an enemy flagship without harm.

The rest of the action was an inglorious confusion. Jordan's little frigates were chased off by bigger Dutch frigates, two of the fireships' crews deserted when there was a risk of being captured by Dutchmen in approaching boats and yet another fireship, set alight and abandoned by her crew, was subsequently saved by an English fisherman who took her into Faversham. Several of the others also suffered an ignominious fate and the matter was summed up by an eye-witness who said, "Wee were in hopes to see Bonfires made of the Dutch fleet in return to those they made of ours too lately but our Expectations were wholly frustrate". Eventually the whole Dutch fleet weighed anchor and with great skill, in view of the prevailing north-east wind, extricated themselves down-Swin to a more peaceful anchorage near the Middle Ground. Such an impressive feat, as the Duke of York declared in disgust, "never was nor would have been undertaken by ourselfs".

During the night of 30th July the *Lennox* and the *Spy* came into Harwich with a message from Sir Joseph Jordan that he and his ships were only two leagues away. Presumably the remnants of his fleet had followed the Dutch down the Swin and the two little ships had managed to get in over the Spitway ahead of the rest. Harwich was soon agog with news of the action and the valiant crews of the smallest fireships were given "greate credit by the people". Deane reported that the men from the other fourteen were "under a strange clamour". He also said that he had heard other excuses and impeachings but they were too long to repeat. This was putting it mildly, for the authorities were most wrathful that what seemed to be the best chance so far to hurt the enemy had been thrown away. Pepys, too, reckoned that there never was "such opportunity of destroying so many good ships". Subsequently the delinquent fireship masters were brought to trial and disgraced but one named How, who was actually condemned to death, seems to have been reprieved.

In spite of the signing of the treaty at Breda on 21st July, the *Spy*, out to sea on 6th August, found "19 sail of the Dutch at anchor in Bardsey sand and five between Orfordness and Aldeburgh". It was not until 14th August that the peace terms were finally ratified and a further five days elapsed before their proclamation throughout Holland. In England the official notification appeared in the *London Gazette* of 26th August, which was the day appointed for the cessation of hostilities in the Channel and the North Sea. There were later days for distant waters.

Meanwhile the enterprising Cornelis de Witt and Michiel de Ruyter had appeared with their squadron off Plymouth on 15th July and proceeded to attack merchant shipping in Torbay. This lasted until 30th July when two English colonels rowed out and announced, a little prematurely it seems, that peace had come about. These emissaries were delightfully entertained on board *De Zeven Provincien* with drinks and a collation of sweetened fruits, and they later sent out a most generous gift of foodstuffs to De Ruyter. As they left the Dutch flagship the colonels were complimented by a gun salute to which the Plymouth fort replied when they reached the shore. All this is reminiscent of the meeting between Allin and De Ruyter way back in 1664, but the Cowes official correspondent soon provided a jingoistic contrast. On 10th August, in reporting the passing of ninety Dutch ships, he said that had any hostilities been attempted, "a breakfast of cannon shot, interlined with horse and foot, was provided for them". These vessels were thought to be merchantmen homeward bound.

It was on 10th August also that Silas Taylor reported that the *Lennox*, although just discharged from naval service, had been out with the galliot hoy

Colliers off Harwich, a wash drawing by F. Swaine dated 1756. The background shows Harwich and the entrance to the harbour as it would have appeared in the previous century.

*National Maritime Museum, London*

in an unsuccessful attempt to find and capture an English-built pink which had been stationed to intercept small vessels proceeding between Orford and Woodbridge Haven. Through the mist, on the other side of the Whiting and Bawdsey sands, they had seen at least two dozen Dutch men-of-war. To all intents and purposes, however, the war against the Harwich coast had already been terminated in pleasantly dramatic fashion on Sunday, 28th July. On the morning of that day twelve Hollanders approached from the north and later altered course to sail down coast. Richard Tyler, who had already carried out a reconnaissance in a smack the previous day, was sent out again to watch the "ennemyes motion".

At seven o'clock that evening, after he had sailed as far as "the Beacon Stumpe of the Gunfleet", he saw fifty sail of the enemy just coming to anchor on the other side of the sand. They were mostly smacks, hoys and fly-boats, presumably an advance contingent of Lieutenant-Admiral Aert van Nes's fleet which had been anchored for the last two days near the Middle Ground.

Next day a large pink, laden with clapboard from Danzig, sailed into Harwich and it was her pilot, William Little of Yarmouth (doubtless the William Liddall already mentioned), who gave the reason for the Dutch withdrawal. He said that he had been stopped from going to London by the "Admirall of Holland" but he had, nevertheless, been most civilly treated on board the flagship throughout the previous day. When the twelve ships from Holland approached it was seen that one of them was wearing "white vanes". Then, Little said, "The men on decke the Admiral stampt for the ship's company to come up and shouted for peace". Thus it was that cheers of great thankfulness rang out across the desolate waters of an anchorage amid the sands which fringe the Essex coast. Purser Richard Tyler, who was still in Harwich, must have been no less happy to report to Pepys that "the letters from these 12 confirmed a peace to them and that their predecants alias parsons had thanked God in publike for it".

"This day", he said, "our late reputed enemy the Dutch weigh'd, the wind at W from the Gunfleete, and are gonn to the E wards; we judge hear (per the discourse of the peace) are gonn home".

# CHAPTER TEN

# The King's Visit

CHIEF among those who stood to lose by the outcome of the Felixstowe battle were the King, his brother James, Duke of York, and numerous hangers-on at Court. The Medway disaster, the blockading of the Thames and the harassment of a considerable length of coast had seriously unsettled the whole nation and should the Dutch have obtained even a temporary foothold in Suffolk, such ill-tidings could conceivably have provided the last straw. "It is high time for us to have peace", declared Pepys on 11th July, 1667, and there is no doubt that the aggressive attitude of the Dutch speeded the final negotiation at Breda. Pepys said furthermore that nobody had a good opinion of the King and his Council. At this time, of all other times in the reign, the future of the monarchy was perhaps most in doubt.

If, instead of grounding on either the Ridge or the Andrews Shoal, Jan van Nes had entered Harwich Harbour with his squadron towards the top of the tide the consequences could have been wholly disastrous. The effects of a high-water, point-blank bombardment of Landguard Fort, with its perimeter and largely unprotected interior over-full of raw militia, hardly bear contemplation. Such an onslaught from the water could conceivably have brought about a commotion which nullified the efforts of the comparatively few experienced defenders. After a barrage of round shot and grape against the lightly fortified *fausse-braye* and the gunners on the ramparts above, the following land assault, backed by portable cannon, would be likely to be just a *coup de grâce*.

Students of military history will be better able to assess the odds, but to the coast dwellers of the time it must have seemed that, once the enemy had sailed within the beach-end of the point, only those guns on the western side of the fort could have been effectively engaged. Totalling two dozen pieces at the most, they would have been outnumbered by the broadsides of just two men-of-war, not to mention the likely shortage of ammunition within the fort. No doubt Landguard would have proved a much tougher nut to crack than either the Sheerness battery or Upnor Castle, but the results of the comparatively small ship assault on the guns of both those places could not have led to British optimism.

At more than a mile range the Harwich guns, too, would hardly have been effective and any over-shooting on their part would have seriously hurt

117

A seventeenth-century drawing of King Charles II at Newmarket by Jan Wyck.
*Henry E. Huntington Library and Art Gallery, San Marino, California, U.S.A.*

their own side. The blockships can be dismissed as they were admitted by Deane to be ineffective, and he also said that the only real defence lay in the fireships which at no time could get to windward of the enemy. It is true that one or two could have been towed into action by the oar-driven harbour tenders but their combustion potential was poor and the quality and sufficiency of their crews remains a matter of grave doubt. On the other hand their Dutch counterparts could have drifted in so long as the tide was favourable and then made threatening progress against any anchored craft in the Stour. Gunfire from the fort and from the light forces in the harbour might initially have accounted for a few of the enemy ships but, with the fort subdued, the Dutch could have reigned over the great expanse of Harwich Harbour as easily as they did previously in the Medway for the best part of a week. Tide timing and wind strength and direction were key factors and failure to complete before the ebb, mainly because of the admiral's grounding, caused the ambitious plan to fail.

Once installed on Landguard Point, and throughout the common bounded by Walton Creek and the sea, the Dutch would have been able to keep at bay the meagre and untried Suffolk forces for several days. With no naval threat in the offing, only a shortage of provisions or the deployment of heavy artillery at Felixstowe would have forced a retreat. Meanwhile, in spite of all the efforts of the Essex shore-based artillery, the town and shipyard of Harwich would have been wide open to devastation by gunfire from within the harbour. Cutting-out expeditions against the Dutch could have been attempted but, in view of the enemy's proven skill with their many light-draught vessels, such manoeuvres would have stood little chance of success. The impotence of even large land forces without effective and mobile artillery was so clearly demonstrated in the Medway. Furthermore, if Landguard Fort had fallen, it would have been entirely disadvantageous to the English that the harbour entrance was situated so close to the Suffolk shore. Enemy men-of-war, anchored in Orwell Haven, would have commanded much of the low ground at Felixstowe with only moderate risk of damage from the Harwich batteries. Anthony Deane visualised some such sorry outcome and his thankfulness at the failure of the Dutch to enter the harbour was soundly based.

Therefore the royal visit of 1668 to Landguard Fort and Harwich, although characteristically combined with the King's two great interests of horse racing and sailing, might also have been something of a pilgrimage of personal thanksgiving. The trip finished with a sail up the coast past Orfordness which would certainly have completed the King's understanding of the previous year's action. This, most probably, was its main purpose, since a long ride back to Ipswich was undertaken immediately after the royal disembarkation at Aldeburgh next morning. Accompanying the King were the Earl of Oxford and the Duke of Monmouth, who must have witnessed the fight in 1667, and also the Duke of York, who had come down to Harwich immediately afterwards. Among others in the royal party were the Dukes of Buckingham and Richmond, Lord Cornwallis and the Marquis of Blanquefort. The latter was a naturalised Frenchman who was Colonel of the Duke of York's troop of Guards; he later became Lord Faversham. Also at Harwich was Sir Bernard de Gomme, the eminent military engineer of Dutch extraction who had worked at Harwich in 1667 and was still engaged on the port defences.

The King arrived at Landguard Fort on Saturday, 3rd October, 1668, having come over from Newmarket with his party by way of Ipswich. The final stage of his route would have provided a chance to view the greater part of the previous year's battlefield, but whether the royal visitors made a short diversion to inspect the actual place of landing and re-embarkation is unfortunately not stated. Darell, promoted Major on 15th April, 1668, was still at the fort with his company of the Lord High Admiral's Regiment but, despite their brave showing in 1667, they had been sorely neglected. So lax had been their treatment that Darell was glad to take the opportunity to present a petition while the King was at Harwich. This stated that "his Company of his Royall Highness the Duke of York's regiment in ye said fort doe only fall sick for want of Bedds, Blanketts, & other accomodation wch he humbly prayed may be forthwith provided". The King and his brother could hardly do otherwise than order that the requirements of the fort "bee immediately sent and delivered".

Awaiting the royal party were the yachts *Henrietta* and *Anne* which had been ordered round to Harwich Harbour with a kitchen boat in attendance. Silas Taylor had no boats or barge "fit to receive" the King so he had a stage built out into deeper water specially for the occasion. Charles II stepped on to it at three o'clock that Saturday afternoon and proud Silas was there to kiss his hand. Ashore at Harwich a Guard of Honour was provided by Sir Charles Lyttelton's two companies of the Lord High Admiral's Regiment and the Mayor and Aldermen presented their maces and keys which the King touched as he rendered thanks. Then the King asked to see the Naval Yard which had built the *Resolution* and the *Rupert*, and both he and the Duke of York praised the layout of the slipway. Among other things they inspected the cranes, one of which, together with the shipyard bell, survives to the present day. Then, having ascended the defence works, the King circuited the greater part of the town before returning to the Storekeeper's House in the yard.

It delighted Silas Taylor that the King reckoned his residence "a cheap pennyworth". It had cost £300 and had "4 rooms on a floor". Later, when the Duke of York joined the King in the parlour, the latter said, "Brother, this house is my house and it is a pretty one". Then, having refused a drink "because it was supper time" King Charles boarded a boat at the stairs nearby and was rowed out to the *Henrietta* before darkness set in. Later that evening the Duke of Monmouth was sent ashore to lodge with Silas Taylor and there also came "cooks and others to make ready his dinner against the morrow".

It was probably a watermen by the name of John Dickson who rowed the King out to his yacht, because the Harwich Chamberlain's accounts show ten shillings paid for Dickson's wherry "when the King was at town". The Mayor himself charged one shilling for when he "went aboard the King's great pleasure boat" and also five shillings for "a basket of quinces and a nother (*sic*) of grapes for the King's cook". "The town is not to pay so dear for his grapes and quinces which he presented to the King's cook" was the eventual written judgment of the local auditors, and they disallowed the other item, too, on the ground that the Mayor incurred the expense while "going to take his pleasure". The King's movements of the next day are best described in Silas Taylor's own words:

"He landed alone the next day, Sunday, at 6 o'clock, and he was waited upon by Sir Charles Lyttelton and Sir Bernard de Gomme; he went on foot out of the town, viewing all the places in relation to fortifications, and examining some drafts offered by Sir Bernard, which he rectified in the field at 2 or 3 stations, with his own hand, by black lead pen and ruler. After a 5 miles walk over high stiles and ploughgrounds, His Royal Highness found him out, and after some discourse and pacing the ground, returned. The King then went to 'his house' (as he called it 5 or 6 times that morning), and drank some chocolate, but his Royal Highness

Willem van de Velde the Younger's oil painting of the *Cleveland* yacht in a breeze, signed and dated 1678. The appearance of the *Henrietta* and the *Anne* as they sailed to Aldeburgh would have been very similar.          *Collection of M. S. Robinson, from the Ingram Collection*

and others drank Canary, and then to church, as well attended and accommodated as the little town could; his chaplain, Dr Tully preached. He returned to his house for dinner, the King and his Royal Highness dining in the great parlour, the Dukes of Monmouth and Buckingham in the Duke's lodging chamber, the other nobles dining in the little parlour, and the waiters in the Hall.

"After dinner, the Earl of Oxford presented a petition from the two prisoners that had stolen junk from the hulk. The King pardoned them as to their lives, but ordered them a sound whipping and to be released. I was busy just then in the yard with Mr Wren, but the King sent for me, and declared his royal pleasure to me. The King and most of the lords sailed that evening for Aldborough, and the next day rode by land thence to Ipswich, dined with Viscount Hereford[52]; and returned in the evening to Audley End."

With the departure of the yachts that Sunday evening the brief periods of glory and royal favour at Landguard Fort were over, but it nevertheless had a most interesting history over the next three hundred years, as will be presently seen. Also, thanks to King Charles II and his brother, the twin vantage points of Landguard and Beacon Hill had witnessed the opening scene of a pleasure-boat connection which was to provide the very stuff of yachting history itself. In 1668 the yachts *Henrietta* and *Anne* would certainly have caused a stir among local seagoers, second only to that arising from the presence of royal personages. With their lavish carving and gilding they would have provided a glamorous sight among the drab workaday vessels in the harbour, and the long chain of events which brought them there is vastly intriguing.

Twenty-two years earlier, after his father's defeat at Naseby, the sixteen-year-old Prince Charles had taken a spell at the helm of the *Proud Black Eagle* when escaping to the Channel Islands. There, in exile, he and his brother James cultivated their taste for sailing in a two-masted boat bought from St Malo. Five years later, after his inland adventures which followed the Battle of Worcester, Prince Charles made his second flight by sea from Brighton in the smack *Surprise*. After the Restoration he sought her out in gratitude, made a yacht of her and called her the *Royal Escape*. Before the glorification of this work boat, however, the Dutch had presented the King with the *Mary*, first of the royal yachts proper. She had been so named after the King's sister, mother of the future King William III. Despite the fact that these decorated craft had provided an alternative to the state coach in Holland for more than fifty years, such elaborate and convenient vessels had not previously appeared in Britain. Soon the word "yacht", with a great many other spellings, of which there had been rare examples in England at least since 1643/44, was firmly established in the language.

The *Mary*, drawing only three foot of water and having leeboards like a Thames barge, was not the most suitable craft for all weathers in the boisterous North Sea and the English Channel. In consequence the King, who appreciated the *Mary's* fine accommodation and smooth-water sailing qualities, requested Peter Pett of Deptford to design another pleasure boat of deeper draught. Pett was to outdo the *Mary* "for the honour of his country" and this spurred on the Duke of York to commission Peter Pett's brother Christopher, of Woolwich, to build a rival. Everything of the best was put into both yachts, each having sails of Holland duck, but when it came to races on the Thames the Duke's yacht, possibly because she was slightly the larger, proved somewhat the better sailer, particularly on a windward stretch. She was named the *Anne*, after the Duchess of York, and she was already seven years old when she came to Harwich in 1668. The *Anne* had a useful career thenceforth and was not sold out of the Navy until 1686, after which for many years she was used by the London Customs.

The yacht which Peter Pett had built for the King was named *Katherine* but, while undoubtedly a very fine vessel, she had proved a disappointment as a racer. Matters obviously could not be left as they were, so Christopher Pett was given an order in 1663 to build another yacht for the King, who himself took the greatest interest in her design. She was called the *Henrietta* and she pleased her royal owner mightily, remaining his favourite yacht until the end of her days. However it was the speed, handy working and seaworthiness of these yachts which became more of note than their glamorous appearance. In 1662, after a heavy Channel gale in which passage-making royal yachts were involved, Pepys felt constrained to remark, "but it all ends in the honour of the pleasure boats, which had they not been very good boats would never have endured the sea as they did". The sail up-coast from Harwich in 1668 would certainly have given the *Henrietta* a chance to show her paces against the *Anne*, but it was her duties as a fleet auxiliary in earlier and succeeding years which brought out her real usefulness.

On Sunday, 9th June, 1667, Vice Admiral Sir Edward Spragge, the later defender of Tilbury and Gravesend, boarded the *Henrietta* at Sheerness. She immediately proceeded to sea with an easterly wind and from near the Black Tayle at four o'clock her topmasthead lookout spied the Dutch fleet. After sailing on "for a glasse and a halfe" those on board could plainly see "nigh 30 saile, amongst them three flaggs, and attending on them, sundry galliotts and scutes". It was this arrival of the enemy "within our Buoyes" which brought the first inkling of the Medway disaster and the *Henrietta*, having confirmed her sighting with "our owne two ketches which had bene upon the scout", immediately bore up for Sheerness. There Spragge gave orders to "the guardship, fireships, etc." and sent grim warnings upriver.

Next evening those on board the *Henrietta* saw the whole unhappy business at Sheerness and, managing to steer clear of trouble themselves, they eventually picked up a few men who had been forced by dismountings, casualties and desertions to abandon the shore battery. Edward Gregory wrote of the yacht "standing too and fro upon the tide, whilest the enemy spent his shott liberally att the Nesse, and he ceased not firing till 9 att night, about which time we stood up the river". Where she found sanctuary Gregory did not mention, but she was possibly one of two royal yachts which, with masts lowered, took shelter under the arches of Rochester Bridge.[53] Wherever it was, her crew had a pretty tale to tell the King when he was aboard the yacht in Harwich Harbour next year.

The end for the splendid *Henrietta* came not while pleasuring with the King and his boon companions but during the Third Dutch War in 1673 when she was engaged with the English fleet in the Battle of the Texel. Willem van de Velde the Elder drew a panorama of the fight which shows the *Henrietta* going down by the head. It is better, however, to remember her taking part in a very pleasant scene of the previous year, since this raises the human spirit above the gore and destruction of Sole Bay and the other sea conflicts. On 5th July, 1672, Williamson wrote to Clifford describing the wartime passage of two ambassadors on a mission of peace. The Duke of Buckingham was in the *Katherine* and the Earl of Arlington was in the *Henrietta*, both yachts having left the Nore at two o'clock that morning. There was little breeze at first but they made good progress after ten o'clock when the wind came brisk from the south-west:

> "about 7 in the evening wee spyed the Dutch Fleet to weather of us about 3 leagues off Dombourg in Zeeland about 4 or 5 leagues W. and by S.; wee reckoned about 70 or 75 sayle in all. Three of their scouts came up with us our yachts carrying out the Union Flaggs in the top masts, and each a white flagg in the poupe. Each yacht made a shot to leeward in token we were friends and they answered and struck their topsayles. The captain of the biggest came on board and paid his civilityes to the ambassadors and then going off they all three saluted with neare all their guns. And so we lay a little by night, and at three in the morning we were in sight of Goeree land, and so stood to the Maes, where we arrived about nine."

On many occasions during the first seventy years of the next century those at Landguard Fort saw the gilded yachts providing a comparatively luxurious passage service for royalty and other notabilities. From the mid-century onwards, there came the beginnings of pleasure sailing for the ordinary man of the counties. Thus, during the 1750-65 period, little pleasure boats circled around their elaborately decorated visitors in much the same way as a few surviving yachtsmen of the early twentieth century still joyfully remember Harwich Sunday. Then, once a year, often after a blustery sail from their local river, they would gaze in wonder at "The Big Class" in the harbour.

In time the hazards from the King's enemies became so great that the royal yachts stopped coming to Harwich and most of the yachting took place in or just outside the estuaries. Despite the risks from prowling privateers, not to mention the many fierce gangs of smugglers, there came a very steady spread of small yacht sailing. This is evidenced by eighteenth-century advertisements concerning pleasure boats at Harwich, Ipswich, Woodbridge, Bourne Bridge, Freston, Walton Creek, Ramsey, Stutton, Mistley, Felixstowe, Bawdsey, Hollesley, Boyton and Orford. Thus the stage was gradually being set for the great yachting spectacles seen from Landguard Fort and Harwich in the nineteenth and twentieth centuries. First, however, the North Sea needed Trafalgar and Waterloo to bring it peace.

The rise of the yacht clubs and the big regattas is another story in which royal patronage played no small part. Suffice it to say here that most of what were then the best of British yachts made annual, if brief, appearances at Harwich Regatta and, from 1870 onwards, a succession of America's Cup challengers greatly heightened the interest. Whit Monday, 3rd June, 1895, stands out in particular in the annals of the Royal Harwich Yacht Club. Not only did it mark the start of the Jubilee Regatta to celebrate the fifty-year holding of the royal prefix but also the Duke of York, later King George V, was about to take over the commodoreship from the Duke of Hamilton. This he held until 1910, and graciously followed it with royal patronage until his death in 1937. His father, Edward Prince of Wales, travelled down by train to take part in the races, and like Charles II he slept aboard his yacht in the harbour. To the delight of the visiting multitude the famous *Britannia* triumphed in her race against the greatly favoured new yacht *Ailsa* and John Moore, the Ipswich artist, most fittingly captured the scene as the two great yachts ran down from Landguard Point towards the finishing line. Afterwards the Prince of Wales, accompanied by Lord Dunraven and another gentleman, chartered Robert Capon's cab from the old Felixstowe pier. At the original Post Office they alighted and took a walk, at first along the cliffs and then past the Bath Hotel to Mr Felix Cobbold's house where, in the words of a reporter, "they again cabbed".[54] Thus another heir to the throne visited the Dutch landing place of over two hundred years before.

125

The big J Class came to Harwich Regatta until 1936 and the Twelve Metres until 1939, but it was 1921 which brought an event comparable with the royal sail of 1668. Sailing along the channels used by De Ruyter and his fleet so long ago, the great yachts *Britannia*, *White Heather* and *Nyria* raced down-Swin from the Thames to Harwich. A light and fickle air made it a slow procession along the Kings Channel but a brisk breeze eventually came from the westward to give them a romp home. As *Britannia* rounded the old Cork lightship, with a bone in her teeth, her crew and all the guests, five admirals included, tailed on behind each other to harden in the mainsheet. [55] Back through Felixstowe Road she sailed, steering for the Beach End buoy. Then this truly royal yacht, so beloved by the public, turned into the last leg past Landguard Fort to the finishing line. In those days there were mark boats in the harbour and the race officials were stationed by the R.H.Y.C. flagstaff on the head of the original Felixstowe Pier. To the immense delight of all the new-rigged *Britannia*, after six hours of racing in mainly light airs, was eleven minutes in the lead. Her many successes usually came in heavy weather. It was indeed a sight to be remembered, for the King of England stood proudly at her helm, doubly happy in the knowledge that by his own example he had revived big-class yachting after a disastrous war.

Now, sixty years onwards and safely through another war in which the Netherlands and British navies fought on the same side, it is the crowded starts of the North Sea races which provide the chief yachting spectacles at Harwich. Each month of May sees many a happy Dutchman and a host of equally cheerful Englishmen sailing out past Landguard Fort in friendly rivalry on their annual jaunt to The Hook.

Landguard trading token
1667 (enlarged)

# CHAPTER ELEVEN

# The Last Days of the 1626 Fort and the Later Constructions

C OPPER half-penny and farthing tokens were issued, probably to com-
memorate the successful defence of the fort but also to alleviate the
chronic shortage of small change. The obverse of these pieces bore the now
proud name LANDGUARD together with a lion rampant. The reverse was
inscribed POYNT. FORTE. 1667 = OB with a cross pattée device, the *obolus*
letters being omitted in the case of the farthing. One can imagine this coinage
changing hands for many a mugful in the Sutler's premises until all traders'
tokens were cried down by royal proclamation in 1672.

Meanwhile, during the years 1668-1671 Anglo-Dutch relations had
become considerably less strained, helped by the Triple Alliance of England,
the United Provinces and Sweden. Nevertheless Charles II was also plotting
with the French, who coveted the Spanish Netherlands, and this scheming
came to a head in 1670 when the secret Treaty of Dover was signed. This was
the real reason for the Third Dutch War of 1672-74, though every effort was
made to heap the blame for it upon the Dutch. Previous pretexts for hostilities,
however trivial, were resurrected, and most unworthy of all was a deliberate
provocation concerning the Dutch promise to honour the flag of any royal
ships they chanced to meet within the Narrow Seas.

In 1671 the royal yacht *Merlin*, the same vessel later based on Harwich for
the Greenvil Collins sea surveys, brought Lady Temple, an ambassador's wife,
to England. It is said that her captain was ordered to sail through the Dutch
fleet and "to make them strike their topsails or to fire upon them until they
should return his fire".[56] Rather surprisingly the Dutch admiral took this show
of bravado in very good part, even going aboard the yacht to pay his respects.
He said that he would not lower topsails, as demanded, but he did compliment
the yacht with a gun salute. The *Merlin's* captain, feeling that honour had
thus been largely satisfied, resumed his journey home but on arrival he found
that his superiors thought otherwise. So he was promptly committed to the
Tower for neglect of orders.

The fresh outbreak of hostilities found Landguard Fort unprepared, to
say the least. Sir Charles Lyttelton, successor to Major Darell, reckoned the
place "in the most miserable condition of any fort in Europe". He was

unhappy, too, in having a much smaller number of defenders than the Dutch had faced in 1667, the few available to him being two companies of the Lord High Admiral's Regiment, a company of Colonel FitzGerald's Regiment stationed "on the hill" and two troops of horse. Lyttelton happened to be n Aldeburgh on 28th May, 1672, the day of the Sole Bay battle, and there he found the entire view from the coast obscured by drifting gunsmoke. He was back in Landguard Fort by eight o'clock that evening and from there "could scarce discern the Beacon Hill". The cannonade had continued meanwhile, with hardly any intermission, and the windows and structure of the Governor's

Colonel Sir Charles Lyttelton, Bart.
*From J. H. Leslie's History of*
*Landguard Fort*

house shook terribly. There was some improvement in the fort's intelligence as every day a small vessel was specially sent to sea to collect information, but it was soon apparent at Landguard that there was no need for worry. After the great, but indecisive, sea battle which had begun off Southwold and the speedy overrunning of four of the seven Dutch provinces by the French, there remained no threat of another Dutch landing.

In fact the Treaty of Westminster, signed in February, 1674, brought about a peace with the Dutch which lasted for more than a hundred years. Thereafter the old fort was lightly garrisoned and, over the next thirty years or so, its structure gradually deteriorated until it was past repair. The Third Dutch War still had six months to run when Captain Edward Talbot felt obliged to tell the Master General of Ordnance that the garrison was out of repair in all respects. "I neavor did see anything like it", he said, and he wrote also of "the Draw Bridge haveing been faulne down long since and nothing yett done towards repairing it." Some patching was carried out from time to time, however, and companies of the Lord High Admiral's Regiment, Colonel John FitzGerald's Regiment, the Barbadoes Regiment, the Royal Regiment of Foot Guards, the Holland Regiment (later the Buffs), the 12th Foot (later the Suffolk Regiment), Lord Lucas' Regiment and finally the Invalid Companies successively suffered an uncomfortable existence in the fort. In May, 1702, the famous essayist Richard Steele, then a Captain in Lord Lucas' Regiment, described his hours of duty there:

> "Yet have I been forced to creep up cursed Bleak Batteries at midnight, the wind being fair for French Privateers and not for any of our ships to come and Guard the road afore the Fort, so that I am obliged to visit my sentries at all hours they are so raw and ignorant."

In his somewhat love-lorn state he further declared to the Duchess of Marlborough, ". . . my passion gives me double torture and had I but the least grounds for hope of mercy in another World I would end my cares by throwing myself on my sword". By September his cares were even greater, for in his company there were two sergeants, two corporals and nine sentinels so ill they could not do duty. Because of the state of the barrack windows and tiling some of these men were lying in their beds "expos'd to all injuries of the Weather".

Major Leslie's history deals at some length with the life histories of all the Governors of Landguard Fort. During the long run-down period of the 1626 structure, Sir Charles Lyttelton, the grave Cavalier officer who had survived the Siege of Colchester and was later the Governor of Jamaica, held the post between 1670 and 1680. His successor, Sir Roger Manley, also a Royalist who afterwards served with the Holland Regiment and the Foot Guards, was an author and historian of some note. Lieutenant-Colonel William Eyton, who had commanded the second battalion of the Foot Guards at Sedgemoor, then took office but only for a few months as he died in January, 1688. Next appointed was Admiral Henry Killigrew, the sole naval occupant of the post. He was so listed until 1697, but he does not appear to have resided at the fort or to have dealt with its affairs to any extent. His successor for fourteen years was Edward Jones, a retired Lieutenant-Colonel of the Coldstream Guards and a particular friend of Richard Steele. Then came Captain Francis Hammond, late of the Foot Guards and first Lieutenant-Governor of the fort since 1687. His thirty-two-year association with it ended with his death in 1719; as will be seen in the next chapter, he was a man of somewhat tyrannical nature. Nevertheless, a harsh man seems to have been needed when the residential office of Lieutenant-Governor was created as this followed complaints of "damage daily done to the country" by the garrison and "the Embezlement of Stores of the said Fort". Hammond would have been in his late seventies in 1716 when the Surveyor General of Ordnance reported Landguard Fort "in so

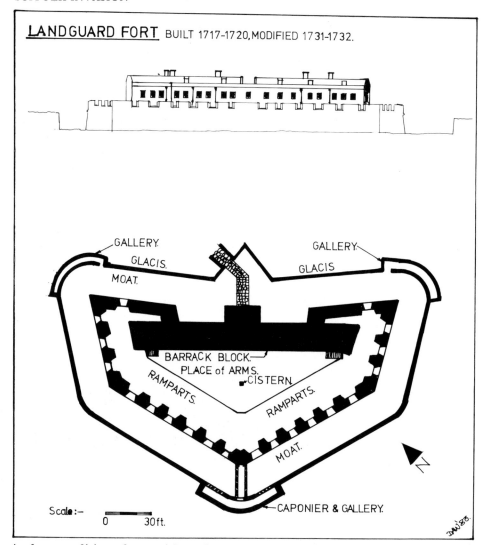

LANDGUARD FORT BUILT 1717-1720, MODIFIED 1731-1732.

GALLERY.
GLACIS.
MOAT.
GALLERY.
GLACIS
BARRACK BLOCK.
PLACE of ARMS.
CISTERN.
RAMPARTS.
RAMPARTS.
MOAT.
N
Scale:−
0    30ft.
CAPONIER & GALLERY.

bad a condition that neither the Fort, Barraques or Storehouses can be repaired".

An estimate to rebuild the fort on the same plan came to a minimum of £21,556, so a very much less ambitious scheme was substituted. This was to construct a battery of twenty guns overlooking the harbour entrance but without any defence on the land side. It was to have barracks for twenty or thirty men and the estimate of cost was only £2,975. [57] This proposal was first put before the Duke of Marlborough and the King in April and May of 1716, and directions by the Prince of Wales for its immediate building were

130

conveyed in a letter of Christmas Eve of the same year. The work, in the form of a closed lunette,[58] was completed in 1720 and meanwhile, except for a guard over the building materials, the company of Invalids was temporarily accommodated at Harwich.

Daniel Defoe described the fort as "one of the best and securest in England" but its approved armament in 1727 was only ten eighteen-pounders and ten nine-pounders, as compared with sixty-three guns in the old fort. This, however, was increased in 1731 when a ten-gun battery was constructed at the foot of the glacis. In 1731-32 the barracks were also extended and raised to three stories. Mr David Wood and Mr Charles Trollope have recently come across plans of this long-forgotten fort which was sited somewhat nearer to the estuary than its predecessor. The "Queen Anne style" fort which Major Leslie dates as 1716 was not in fact built until twenty-eight years later and its interior buildings were not completed until 1751. It was said that, owing to the nature of the soil, "the foundations were not laid without great labour and expense".

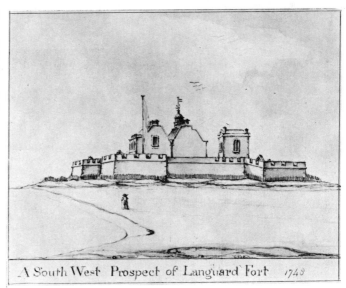

"South-west Prospect of Landguard Fort, 1748", a pen and ink sketch giving the earliest view of the new fort built in 1745-51.

*Ipswich Museums*
*(R.1967.102)*

A South West Prospect of Languard Fort 1749

A most interesting report and estimate by visiting surveyors in 1749[59] reveals that it was in 1744 that the Board of Ordnance proposed "to reform the old battery and build a new fort in the form of a Pentagon with 5 Bastions and Curtains". Only the Governor's and officers' houses were then uncompleted and the report further says:

"This fort is surrounded with a very good covid way and Glacis, has a dry ditch with a bridge and drawbridge over it at the main entrance. The Scarp, Counterscarp parapet all of sufficient thickness well fac'd good

131

A view of the fort of 1745 looking towards Landguard Point.

*From J. H. Leslie's History of Landguard Fort*

brick work and altho the Bastions and Curtains are too small yet the Rampart being 30ft. wide is of sufficient breadth for the recoyl of great guns and will afford good defence to the Harbour and land sides.

"Besides there is at the foot of the Glacis next the sea shoar a very good Battery which flanks the entrance into the Harbour, but as only one gun of this lower battery can conveniently be travers'd to fire at an enemy's ship on their first coming into the channel the Sury. Gen. [Surveyor General] Capt. Watson to make a project for erecting a new battery on the Glacis fronting the point of the South Bastion for the better defence of the mouth or entrance of the Harbour."

High tides had encroached upon the foot of the glacis opposite the point of the north-west bastion, so the alteration of one breakwater and the provision of two new ones was directed. Also included in the estimate was £30 for the building of a clock turret over the centre of the new barracks and £67 "for a good eight day clock as proposed by Mr Thos. Moore of Ipswich". The movement is still in existence, and so is a clock bell with an inscription said to read ANDREAS SCHACHT 1733 but which probably refers to Andrew Schalch, Master Founder at the Royal Brass Foundry at Woolwich from 1716 to 1770.

132

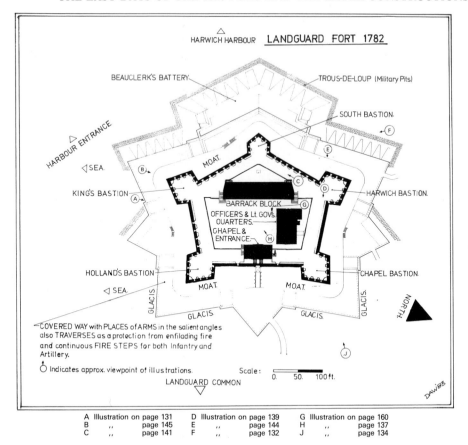

HARWICH HARBOUR  LANDGUARD FORT 1782

BEAUCLERK'S BATTERY

TROUS-DE-LOUP (Military Pits)

SOUTH BASTION.

HARBOUR ENTRANCE

SEA.

MOAT.

F

E

KING'S BASTION

B

A

C

D

HARWICH BASTION.

BARRACK BLOCK

G

OFFICERS & Lt. GOVS.
QUARTERS.

CHAPEL &
ENTRANCE.

H

HOLLAND'S BASTION

CHAPEL BASTION.

SEA.

MOAT.

MOAT.

GLACIS

GLACIS.

GLACIS.

GLACIS.

NORTH

COVERED WAY with PLACES of ARMS in the salient angles
also TRAVERSES as a protection from enfilading fire
and continuous FIRE STEPS for both Infantry and
Artillery.

Indicates approx. viewpoint of illustrations.

Scale:
0.   50.   100 ft.

LANDGUARD COMMON

DAWES

| | | | | | | | |
|---|---|---|---|---|---|---|---|
| A | Illustration on page 131 | D | Illustration on page 139 | G | Illustration on page 160 |
| B | ,, page 145 | E | ,, page 144 | H | ,, page 137 |
| C | ,, page 141 | F | ,, page 132 | J | ,, page 134 |

This then was the fort ruled over by the notorious Philip Thicknesse and pictured by Gainsborough in 1753. Its early appearance is also shown in a small, unsigned pen and ink drawing in Christchurch Mansion, Ipswich, entitled "A South-West Prospect of Landguard Fort" and doubtfully dated 1748, and by a water-colour drawing used as an illustration by Leslie which looks down the estuary towards the point. Neither picture, because of its aspect, reveals the pentagon plan. The lower battery at the foot of the glacis, mentioned in the report of 1749, also does not appear. A distant view of the fort from the Harwich side of the harbour entrance can be seen in a sketch and also in a painting of Princess Charlotte's arrival in 1761, both by Dominic Serres. A portion of the sketch, which includes the fort and the *Royal Charlotte*, is copied in a print issued by Edmund Orme in 1806.

Interior views of the fort are shown in various eighteenth-century pen and wash drawings attributed to Francis Grose. These are among the Fitch illustrations in the Ipswich branch of the Suffolk Record Office. A watercolour

drawing, made on the top of the fort's Harwich Bastion on August 7th, 1769, probably by the artist who drew Leslie's interior view of that year, looks towards the high ground at Felixstowe. It shows a paved garden on the battlements opposite the Lieutenant-Governor's house and in the middle distance of this view, which is now in the Colchester and Essex Museum, is a large house on the common outside the walls. This also appears in the Gainsborough and other views and was originally the Governor's house. Around 1775, however, it was converted into a "Suttling House" and, according to Leslie, still existed in 1898 as the fort canteen. An advertisement of 1771, concerning a boat which had drifted away from the beach, requested that the finder should bring her to "John Coveney at the Marquis of Granby at Landguard Fort", so perhaps this was the title and sign of the sutler's premises?

Major Leslie, Lindsey and many other writers have been intrigued by the extraordinary Captain Philip Thicknesse, "an unprincipled, eccentric, impetuous and curiously constituted being, possessing probably the worst temper that man was ever cursed with". Many people, including John Wesley, felt the whiplash of his pen and tongue. As a young man he lived in Georgia, Jamaica and Gibraltar and had several escapes from death, two on the same ship, when a barrel of rum ignited and later when she was badly pooped. He was appointed Lieutenant-Governor of Landguard Fort in 1753 and, in the very next year, again escaped an untimely end when he was held up by two footpads on the Colchester-Ipswich road. One man fired at him but missed and the captain's return shot not only missed but also broke the stock of his pistol and bruised his hand.

Two years later Philip Thicknesse actually sent his troops into action. [60] In 1756 about sixty impressed men, held on the *Delight* tender in Harwich

**Opposite:** Pen and wash drawing of 1767 showing the approach road winding through the glacis past the palisades to the covered way and drawbridge of the fort entrance.
*Felixstowe Town Council*

**Right:** A print of 1816 showing Felixstow Cottage, supposedly copied "from one of the earliest productions of Gainsborough".
*Author's collection*

Harbour, decided to make a run for it. They overpowered the officers and crew, took charge of the vessel and set her aground near Landguard Fort. Then Thicknesse, "having Notice thereof", put some of his soldiers aboard a sloop and retook the *Delight* while she still had about forty of the mutineers aboard. When the troops shot back, after first being fired upon, they killed one man and wounded several more, of whom four or five subsequently died. In October of the same year an advertisement appeared in the *Ipswich Journal* repudiating "a most malicious Report" that the Lieutenant-Governor had introduced Romish priests into the garrison.

Thicknesse bought for his second wife, Lady Elizabeth Touchet, a small fisherman's cottage nestling under Felixstowe Cliff where ninety years before the Dutch had landed. This the pair extended, making it into a very attractive seaside dwelling which became known as Felixstowe or Landguard Cottage. One room was called the Roman parlour "from its being entirely paved with Roman brick" taken from the ruins of Walton Castle. Among the beach-stones, shells, talc, spar and small pieces of looking-glass which decorated the fabric was a large number of small copper coins from the same source. In the late eighteenth and early nineteenth centuries the house, further embellished, was the summer residence of Sir Samuel Brudenell Fludyer and earlier of Lady Bateman, his widowed mother. It was eventually owned by members of the Cobbold family but it was replaced in the eighteen-eighties by the present building, known as the Lodge, which is now part of Felixstowe College. What was known as Cottage Point became Cobbold's Point, but many yards of garden which formerly stretched seaward were lost by coastal erosion.

Lady Thicknesse herself wrote of the cottage terrace being within a bowsprit's length of the sea but, presumably, she was thinking of former occupants when she said "The inhabitants of the cottage were very much alarmed early one morning, on seeing a large Dutch ship of war . . . with the end of her bowsprit within the boundaries of the garden; nor was she able to be got clear off till it was high water". She confirmed the existence of the old common when she wrote "Between the rock and the margin of the sea was a most beautiful sod, that both in summer and in winter had the appearance of rich velvet. Upon this grew many a purple thistle and also the eringo or sea holly".[61]

In 1762 Lady Elizabeth Thicknesse died at Landguard and was buried in the fort's graveyard. Then, only six months later, Thicknesse married Miss Anne Ford in the fort chapel, receiving his third wife "from the Hands of his Colonel" while dressed in the uniform of a private of the Norfolk Militia which he had joined as a volunteer. The liveries and dresses of the three hundred wedding guests were of the most gorgeous description and the bridegroom's beautiful carriage "was drawn by two fine white horses, with their tails tied up and their manes plaited with ribbands". Thicknesse is supposed to have introduced the tamarisk tree from Spain into this country and one, seen in several pictures, in fact grew to a fair height on the fort battlements. It is also said that he maintained a printing press in the fort for his own amusement. Even his demise in 1792, twenty-six years after he was relieved of his Landguard appointment, was somewhat odd. He died of a seizure when on his way to Italy, "mort dans sa chaise de poste en quittant Boulogne".

The 12th. Foot, later the Suffolk Regiment, passed through Landguard in 1757 on their way to the Seven Years War and their valiant part in the Battle of Minden. In August, 1776, German recruits were quartered both at Landguard and Harwich before their embarkation "by Blenheim transport". Two years later France declared war against England and instructions were sent to the Governor "to keep the guns loaded". Spain followed suit in 1779 and, when the Dutch joined our enemies in 1780 and England temporarily lost command of the sea, the need for an all-round defence against invasion again became evident. Thenceforth there were many developments of the Landguard and Harwich defences. So many in fact took place over the next hundred and sixty years that they are well worthy of a book in themselves, and the hope must be that one or more of the gentlemen engaged on this research will in time bring out this much-needed addition to the history of fortifications. Meanwhile, thanks to their efforts, there is already a sufficient assembly of details to sketch in a broad outline.

In 1745 ten eighteen-pounders were added to the new fort's armament and it is reasonable to assume that the battery "on the glacis fronting the point of the South Bastion" recommended by surveyors in 1749 was built some four years later when Lord George Beauclerk became Governor of the fort. The first mention of it as "Beauclerk's Battery", however, arises in a report of 1779.

136

A pencil, pen and wash drawing of the interior of the fort of 1745, looking across from the chapel towards the barracks and King's Bastion.     *Suffolk Record Office, Ipswich (HD480/2)*

At that time it was armed with 42-pounders and this, the real strength of the fort, can be identified at the top of the glacis as an improvement of the covered way in plans of 1781 onwards.[62]

The purpose of Beauclerk's Battery was to prevent entry to Harwich Harbour by ships of a hostile navy, but that construction could avail nothing against a land attack after the Dutch pattern of 1667. It was thus inevitable that the invasion threat of 1780 should bring about a hurried construction of extra defences. The "New Works", completed in 1782, are well shown in the *Plan of the Fort and Defence Works — 1785*, a plate of Leslie's book. This drawing shows a North Battery and a South Battery, both of considerable size, on the common beyond the glacis of the fort. There is also a large detached fortification named Rainham Redoubt sited by the shore to the east of the fort. Also spread across the common are two rows of storehouses, magazines and guardrooms known as King's Lines and Prince's Lines respectively. Northwards of all these, across the narrow neck of land and behind a small

137

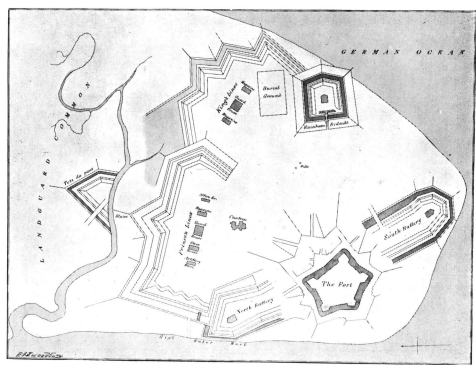

A plan of 1785 showing the New Works.        *From J. H. Leslie's History of Landguard Fort*

creek, are most elaborate outworks, and the landward approach to these, beyond the creek, is defended by yet another work entitled *Tête du pont*. Completed in 1782 and armed with over a hundred guns, these "New Works" were no doubt thought to be the ultimate answer to any threat by land. The entrenched camp and Rainham Redoubt were, however, razed in 1803, after a recommendation by Major Bryce, and Leslie in his history of 1898 said that only a few traces of earth embankments and walls then remained near the external married quarters.

The invasion scare of 1780 completely subsided when the Versailles Treaty of 1783 was signed and, despite a further outbreak of war with France ten years later, Landguard saw out the rest of the eighteenth century in an atmosphere of peace. A water-colour of 1791, by a Captain Hanchett, shows a garden flourishing in the fort ditch, with lawns, gravel paths and trees at least thirty feet high.[63] When the Cambridgeshire Militia were camped outside the fort in 1795 they were fortunate enough to have the use of the old canteen in the fort for their mess. The sutler supplied them with a dinner and small beer

A water colour painted from Harwich Bastion on 7th August, 1769, showing the Lieutenant Governor's house with battlement garden, the Governor's house outside the fort and the view of the low ground at Felixstowe.                                   *Colchester and Essex Museum*

for 1s. 6d. and if they wanted port it cost them three shillings a bottle. A supper of cold meat, bread and cheese, with beer for those who wanted it, could be had for sixpence. A simple breakfast cost eightpence, but with eggs and cold meat it was a shilling. A civilian waiter and a mess man from the regiment were on hand and a drawing room was also provided.[64]

Nevertheless, a young man's ambitions were about to spoil the scene. Napoleon reached his initial height of autocratic power in November, 1799, when he became First Consul of France, and by July, 1801, fears of invasion were again at a height in Harwich. Armed barges were stationed at the mouth of the Deben, at Orford and off Ramsey. A man-of-war arrived in the harbour as a guardship "to be manned by the pike-men of the different sea ports of the Essex and Suffolk coast". Fishing smacks were hired by the Government to be sent to the buoys of the Swin "to cut them away at the first alarm". Admiral Nelson, who was responsible for the Sea Fencibles on the East Coast, came in the *Medusa* frigate with several cutters under his command but he sailed for the Nore after only two days at Harwich. With him went Graeme Spence, a

139

marine surveyor from Ipswich, to pilot the frigate over the Naze flats which local pilots had always considered to be unnavigable by ships of war. The feat caused quite a stir and the *Suffolk Chronicle* forecast that this way out of Harwich would in future be known as "Nelson's Passage", but the name of the ship took pride of place and the Medusa Channel it will always be.

The Peace of Amiens hardly brought a breathing space after ten years of hostilities. It failed when only fourteen months old and 1803 saw the resumption of widespread and most exhausting warfare. Although the threat was practically eliminated by Nelson's victory off Cape Trafalgar, there came yet another and very disturbing fear of invasion. Such was the panic engendered by thoughts of a million raft-borne Frenchmen, said Richard Hall Gower of Ipswich, that it induced many families on the coast to provide themselves "with their cave, or cottage of retreat, away from the haunts of man, in which to take refuge, when the dreaded night should come, with their plate, jewels and conveniences". Some people in Suffolk, it seems, were back to dane-hole days.

The Militia which had been called up during eighteen years of the eighteenth century and the first two years of the next was again embodied in 1803. Then regiment after regiment was stationed at Landguard Fort in addition to the normal garrison. The Cambridgeshires, the 3rd Lancashires and the South Essex Militia followed each other and, late in 1804, the 15th Battalion of the Army of the Reserve arrived by sea from Scotland. There was a dreadful tragedy in April, 1807, when a detachment of "the gallant highland regiment that signalised themselves in Egypt" was being transported across the estuary to Harwich. Their craft, "a crazy vessel called a Bugg", upset and of the hundred and fifteen people aboard, Captain Dawson, 73 soldiers, thirteen women, eight children and three sailors were drowned.[65] In July of the next year the 2nd and the 20th Regiments were marched in excessive heat for embarkation at Landguard Fort. Three soldiers perished immediately on arrival and one of a number of stragglers, who were ordered to remain on the beach all night, died later. More casualties occurred in October, 1811, when "a smuggling vessel laden with 600 tubs of spirits, and a large quantity of lace, ran ashore at the end of the beach at Landguard Fort". The crew threw the liquor overboard but, failing in their attempt to free the vessel, then made their escape. As for the liquor, "the soldiers of the garrison fell in with it, and 4 of them drunk to such excess they are since dead".[66]

From 1809 onwards many martello towers were built along the coast, also two at Shotley and another on the estuary shore near the Walton Ferry inn. The circular Harwich Redoubt arose where the Pain Tree once stood. Batteries, long vanished, were built below all but six of the towers and those near the present site of Felixstowe's Pier Pavilion and the Bartlett Convalescent Home can be seen in one of Emeny's old photographs and an early 19th century drawing. Greenwood's map of 1831, which is based on a survey of 1823-24, marks these batteries as "forts" in front of martello towers at Bawdsey and Alderton. Post-war economies soon ruled, however, and by 1833 Gower was saying of what he called "the one-gun towers", "many have been sold, many have gone to sea and the rest left to rot of time". Nevertheless in their heyday all the East Coast towers had three guns mounted, except at Aldeburgh which had four, and, from 1818 onwards, it seems that most had keepers or were being used by the Revenue men.

Landguard Fort led a very quiet existence during the thirty-five years which followed Waterloo, this despite growing concern in the 1840s regarding the rapid rise in French military capacity. Even the assaults of the waves had receded, except in the vicinity of the old burial ground, where erosion followed the dredging away of Felixstowe Ledge by the stone boats. An Admiralty survey of 1843 shows the uncovered end of Landguard Point no less than 600 yards from the King's Bastion, which at one time was threatened by the sea. In consequence John Rennie's new Harwich lighthouses, built in 1817-18, became of less and less use to incoming mariners and were supplemented in

A pen, pencil and wash drawing of barracks, cannon, etc., with the view from Harwich Bastion of the ramparts on the estuary side of the 1745 fort.

*Suffolk Record Office, Ipswich (HD 480/2)*

1848 by a light exhibited by permission of the Board of Ordnance from Landguard Fort. Beacons were also set up at Landguard in 1857 and the picturesque Landguard lighthouse and its adjoining cottage were erected near the point in 1861. Following some tragic wrecks in the harbour approaches a lifeboat, designed by Captain R. H. Gower of Ipswich, was stationed during 1821 on Landguard beach. She had been paid for by a public subscription launched in Ipswich by Admiral Page. In March, 1827, however, she was up for sale as a "Life Boat Yacht" at Bayley's shipyard.[67]

The much-longed-for peace brought a minor boom for Harwich as a seaside resort and its "fair visitors" were induced by the convenience and safety of its pleasure boats "to inhale the invigorating and refreshing breezes in gypsey parties, upon the luxuriant and picturesque shores of the Orwell and the Stour, and the delightful and amusing beach of Landguard Fort". Richard Cobbold's *Valentine Verses* tell of a water party in the *Fly* pleasure boat of Ipswich on 1st August, 1826:

"Beneath the battlements of Landguard Fort,
We wandered playfully the time away,
And found that pleasure of a cheering sort,
Which says be thankful and enjoy the day."

And Lindsey, too, wrote in 1851 of holidaymakers landing under the walls of the fort. They proceeded over the drawbridge and through the entrance under the chapel to inspect the interior "commodiously arranged for the soldiery".

Lindsey remarked that the Government had recently determined to

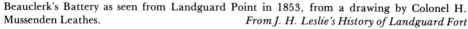

Beauclerk's Battery as seen from Landguard Point in 1853, from a drawing by Colonel H. Mussenden Leathes. *From J. H. Leslie's History of Landguard Fort*

augment the artillery arm and to improve the country's defences generally. This they had already done at Landguard "by mounting a battery of eleven heavy guns, on revolving frames: which, with twenty-five others of various calibres, now give the fortification a very formidable appearance". He was speaking of Beauclerk's Battery which was reconstructed in 1850 along two faces of the glacis. Its armament consisted of four 8-inch smooth-bores of 65 cwt., seven 32-pounder smooth-bores and a mortar with its own portable iron furnace for heating shot which was added later. What Lindsey saw from the beach appears as a vignette in his *Season at Harwich* but the battery is better shown in a sketch made by Colonel H. Mussenden Leathes when he was there in 1853, training with the Suffolk Artillery Militia.

Suspicions regarding the ambitions of Napoleon III had motivated the improvements of 1850 but, as things turned out, England and France fought on the same side during the Crimean War. In March, 1854, those at the fort would have seen the Mayor of Ipswich and a large party sailing past in the *Orwell* steam packet on their way to view the fleet which was about to depart for the Baltic. At that time Landguard Fort was "by no means an unpleasant place to be quartered in". Colonel Leathes wrote of the beautiful garden, abounding in fruit, and of a pond full of goldfish, also of the tamarisk tree still growing on the battlements. Spare time, he said, could be pleasantly occupied in wildfowling and also in the fives-court and billiard-room. From an old water-colour of a peter-boat yacht, with Landguard Fort in the background,[68] it is likely that some of its officers indulged in fishing and pleasure sailing. Locally there was a large and lucrative trade in coprolite and, for the beachcomber, shark's teeth, amber and jet were always to be found after an easterly gale.

Apart from an added porch, early photographs taken in the eighteen-sixties show the old Lieutenant-Governor's house and the chapel block, enclosing the entrance, just as they were painted a hundred years earlier. Beauclerk's Battery, fully armed, was still the main armament and inside the fort, according to Leslie, there were only two 32-pounder smooth-bore guns and three 12-pounder carronades. It was not the practice, however, to keep all guns mounted in peace time. In 1853, for instance, although all nineteen 12-pounder carronades were mounted in the fort proper, only two 32-pounders of its thirteen other guns were in position. Elsewhere, however, there were great advances in rifled-bore artillery and the ironclad, the new and very formidable adversary of all coastal forts, was already over the horizon. At long last the old days were over at Landguard and in 1871 the War Office decided that the fort should be brought entirely up to date and rearmed. Rebuilding proceeded over the next five years and meanwhile the garrison consisted of only seven men of the Coast Brigade, Royal Artillery, who were there in a caretaking capacity.

A paper negative photograph showing an old gun, presumably of Beauclerk's Battery, with Harwich Bastion and the barrack block in the background.     *Suffolk Record Office, Ipswich*

By 1875 the builders had completely transformed the fort, giving it a much lower and rather sinister profile. Gone was the imposing pile of interior buildings, the most prominent of which had been the many-windowed, three-storied barrack block, with its double-pitched roof and crowning cupola. Beauclerk's Battery had been razed and, rising in an arc above the dry moat on the harbour side, a range of seven massive, granite-faced casemates, closed by steel shutters, now overlooked the harbour channel. Further covered embrasures and open gun emplacements had been constructed on the old bastions and also on the curtain walls which faced the sea and the approach from Felixstowe.

At that time there were probably a few large smooth-bore guns left over from the previous era, but the principal and devastating new armament consisted of huge muzzle-loading rifled cannon, each of which ranged over the arc of fire from its embrasure on an iron-tracked carriage. Thirty-eight-tonners of 12.5-inch calibre and eighteen-tonners firing 10-inch projectiles faced the sea and the harbour entrance. Armour piercing and high-explosive shells were already available for distant targets but around 1900 a type of cannister shot was provided for use against any light craft which penetrated the outer defences. For the 12.5s this shot contained no fewer than ninety 3½lb. chilled steel balls and that for the 10-inch guns contained sixty. An ingenious sighting and fire control system was installed for such close-quarters action, the whole operation being known as "Running Past". Details of the

144

A paper negative photograph showing King's Bastion and the barrack and chapel blocks, taken by a pioneer amateur photographer, Richard Dykes Alexander, of Ipswich.

*Suffolk Record Office, Ipswich*

casemates and their interesting ammunition storage and supply facilities are steadily accumulating as a result of Mr David Wood's patient on-the-spot research. Meanwhile the thought of sundry bits and pieces arriving in a shower over Harwich and Dovercourt adds weight to learned counsel's remarks of 1876.

A most intriguing feature of the rebuilding is the caponier with a massive quarter-sphere bomb-proof construction at its outer end. Its purpose was to cover the harbour ditch against infantry assault and it stands approximately on the site of the demolished fifth bastion of the 1745 fort. Also of note is the manner in which the new barrack block stretches round almost a semi-circle as a separate construction some distance inside the old curtain walls. The enclosure of the inner parade ground is completed by the curving casemate section and, since the outside wall of the barracks is itself of great thickness, the result is a strong and separately defendable citadel. A plan at embrasure level and a photograph or two can tell more than many lines of print. A flat asphalte expanse roofs over the entire structure and parts of the 18th century curtain walls are about all of the subject of Gainsborough's picture which now remain.

The year 1882 is notable for the mention of two Gatling machine-guns at Landguard, the twenty-year-old brain children of an American steam plough inventor, but such were the other advances in the art of war that the new fort, the pride of its builders and garrison, was already outmoded. A witness before

145

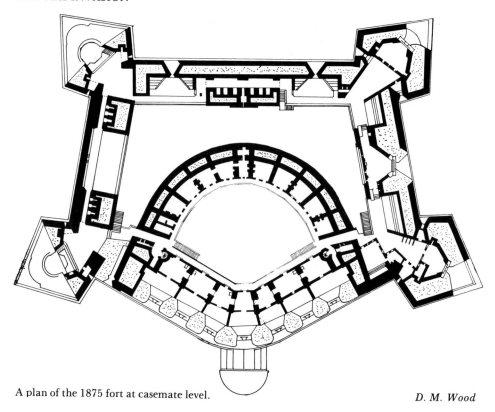

A plan of the 1875 fort at casemate level.                    *D. M. Wood*

the Stanhope Commission of 1887 declared that at only 700 yards range "the guns which are in the fort at present are not capable of piercing any very heavy armour". Although suitable for use against an armoured cruiser they were not expected to be very effective against the latest ironclads but, presumably, some useful results could be hoped for from the submarine minefield which had been installed about 1878. The latter was mentioned in the following recital of the fort's armament in 1887:

> "The guns in the casemated battery are four 12.5 R.M.L. guns, three 10-inch R.M.L. guns; in King's Bastion, one 10-inch and ten 12.5 inch; in Holland Bastion, one 10-inch; in East Curtain, two 64-pr. R.M.L.; in Chapel Bastion salient, one quick R.M.L. and two 8-inch R.M.L. howitzers; in Harwich Bastion, one 9-inch and some S.B. guns. Then, besides that, there is a minefield, with all the buildings, just on the outside of the fort, and sheltered by the fort."

In reply to a question as to what were the main weaknesses in the defence of Harwich and the river, the same witness said: "A want of long-ranging guns,

146

a general deficiency of fire power over the entrance and over the higher water" — this in spite of all the guns at Landguard, Harwich, Shotley and Walton Tower Battery! It is clear that Harwich Harbour and the Felixstowe shore were still regarded as tempting targets for a would-be invader, and much can be gleaned on the entire subject from this interesting record which also covers the Thames and other places. As always the Royal Navy was the first line of defence but, then as now, it could not be expected to be at every danger point at once.

The greatly outranged muzzle-loaders at Landguard were kept in some sort of service until 1904-5 but the chief result of the Stanhope enquiry was the construction of an entirely new and almost invisible battery outside the curtain walls of the fort. In 1890, Wing Battery, later known as Left Battery, was built facing the sea from alongside the approach road across the common. Over at Harwich a new fort, the first of its kind, had already been built on Beacon Hill during 1888-89 [69] and there the circular redoubt was now regarded as more or less obsolete. It had been decreed that the new batteries were to have 10-inch

Two of the granite gun embrasures, with caponier and ditch.          *Mrs Winifred Cooper*

and 6-inch breach-loaders on disappearing mountings and that quick-firers were to be installed for close-quarters action.

In 1891 a most impressive photograph was taken of the immense 10-inch breach-loader at Landguard on its disappearing Easton & Anderson hydro-pneumatic mounting in a circular emplacement. It fired a 500 lb. projectile no less than 10,000 yards. Also in Wing Battery was a 6-inch breach loader, rather similarly mounted, and this was joined by another in 1899.

Between 1898 and 1901 Right Battery was constructed on the common southwards of the fort. In 1910 it was armed with two 6-inch guns and one 10-inch gun, but it was substantially altered later. A plan of Minefield Battery, dated 1902, shows proposed armament of two 4.7s in barbette emplacements. This new work, overlooking the harbour entrance beyond the RML casemates and the ditch, was in effect a successor to Beauclerk's Battery. [70] In 1940 it was rebuilt and armed with two twin six-pounders. Its name had been changed by 1906 to Darelli Battery, altered to Darell's in 1907 when a tablet was erected in honour of the brave defender of 1667.

The minefield itself was operated by men of the Royal Engineers and the Royal Engineers Militia, for whom quarters were built outside the fort. Detonation was originally achieved by electrical means from two look-out stations ashore but it was said that all mines laid during the 1914-18 War were of contact type. After 1905 the minefield became the responsibility of the Royal Navy, and it eventually fell into disuse.

Over the years a great variety of constantly up-dated artillery was placed in the three batteries of the fort. Six-inch guns became the main standby, with 4.7s, 12-pounders and 6-pounders for the shorter ranges. All were assisted by searchlight positions which occupied a number of buildings on the common and along the estuary shore. Also concerned with the defence of the harbour approaches were the famous Harwich Force of 1914-18 and the seaplane and flying-boat units of the Royal Air Force, originally the Royal Naval Air Service. Two of the great hangars still remain amid the port installations on the neighbouring estuary shore, but it is not so well known that there was once an airstrip for land planes on Landguard Common. Many complex details are

**Opposite:** The 10-inch breach-loader on its disappearing Easton and Anderson hydro-pneumatic mounting in 1891. *The Royal Artillery Institution, Woolwich*

**Right:** Darell's Battery six-pounders. *Soldier Magazine*

149

An aerial view of Landguard Fort as it was when the Army departed in 1957. Many of the external buildings have since been demolished and Darell's Battery at upper left is now in a ruinous condition. *East Anglian Daily Times*

**Opposite:** The casemates of Landguard Fort in an engraving of 1888.

steadily being investigated and in time the full story of military activity on the Landguard peninsula will emerge. Meanwhile a fine collection of plans has already been accumulated.

Barrage balloons were the heralds of the 1939-45 War and before very long the "Little Ships" of Light Coastal Forces crowded the nearby dock. Entrance to the harbour was controlled by a boom defence operated by two vessels stationed near the tidal gauge. The beaches and the common were mined and a fresh assortment of artillery for all purposes was set up around the fort. Apart from the six-inch guns and the twelve and six pounders, there is mention of 3.7in and 20mm anti-aircraft guns, 40mm Bofors also, as well as 2-pounder anti-tank guns and machine guns of .303 and .5in calibre.

Those who served this artillery must have many a tale worth the telling but, as yet, hardly a handful have written about their experiences. It is to be hoped that many will search their memories and record a few hectic and amusing moments which relieved long periods of boredom. The shooting

down of over twenty flying bombs has at any rate been mentioned elsewhere. [71]
There followed a very quiet period after the coming of peace and it seems that
the only interesting activity concerned some experiments with anti-aircraft
artillery.

Units of the Coastal Artillery were disbanded in 1956 and, with the
departure of the military on June 24th 1957 [72] and the closing down of the fort,
this historic building was scheduled as an Ancient Monument in 1961 and
placed in the guardianship of the Department of the Environment in 1975.
Although constructed to keep out invaders, and most firmly locked and
barred, it sadly proved no match for local vandals who soon smashed many
windows in the interior and did a great deal of other damage. Even the
restoration efforts of the four-year-old Felixstowe History and Museum Society
have suffered in this respect, but a fine beginning has now been made in the
Ravelin Block which was once the headquarters of the submarine mining
operation. Here outside repairs and rewiring have been carried out by the
Department of the Environment and interior repairs and redecorations by the
very active sub-committee headed by Mr and Mrs B. E. Rayner. The upshot is
a permanent headquarters for the society and an already well-stocked museum
which was opened by the Mayor of Felixstowe on 18th September, 1982. It is
hoped that work can be started next year on clearing the interior of the fort
itself, with a view to its being eventually opened to the public.

Such a combination of local fund-raising and extremely hard work
deserves the greatest encouragement, for here is an opportunity to develop a
unique museum covering the whole coastal region with perhaps some sections
for the history of artillery and yachting too. This brings visions of centuries-old
breach-loaders trawled up off the Suffolk coast and of dioramas in some of the
casemates which could rival those of St Malo's famous "Quic-en-Groigne".
The most has yet to be made of this historic viewpoint and the natural history
attractions could also become a popular feature. With ferry and landing
facilities for yachtsmen and Essex visitors, and with value-for-money seasonal
catering facilities, the whole could become a major tourist attraction and a
fitting complement to the endeavours of the great and successful port area.

# CHAPTER TWELVE

# The Last Salute

WHEN ordered to jubilate, honour or mourn it has long been the custom of gunners everywhere, ashore or afloat, "to shoote off their pieces after the manner of warre". On May Day, 1535, the opportunity was taken to fire thirty-two newly cast guns at Calais both in salute of Henry VIII and as a proving operation. Each gun was shot three times, "once for your Highness, secondly for the founders, thirdly for the better proof thereof". Sheer noise, it seems, was an important factor since Lord Lisle, the King's Deputy, said "in my life I never heard vehementer pieces". During the previous October John Husee informed Lord Lisle that Henry VIII "willed his lordship to cause a CL shoot" for Philip Chabot, the Great Admiral of France. In 1537 there were gun salutes in various places to celebrate the Queen's pregnancy and two years later, as her successor Ann of Cleves entered Calais, the 150 guns of the King's ships *Lion* and *Sweepstake* "made such a smoke that one of her train could not see another".[73]

The artillerymen at Landguard Fort were no exception, and the clinging gunsmoke of their usually harmless discharges rolled away across land and water for more than three hundred years. At sea, whether accompanied by a gun salute or not, it had become the established custom to dip ensigns and even to lower topsails in friendly greeting. King's ships always had precedence over merchantmen but there was also the claim of the English monarchs that foreign warships, too, should strike their flag if they met with a British man-of-war in the Narrow Seas. Thus the question who dipped first to whom was at times most delicate and failure to pay the compliment was cited more than once among the causes of the Dutch Wars. There was trouble on the home front, too, because the seventeenth-century rule-makers seem originally to have neglected to decree what should happen if King's ship met King's fort.

Maybe the first gun salutes from Landguard Point were fired by men of the bulwarks in 1588 after the harbour had filled with ships bringing news of the Armada's defeat. The first record concerning compliments, however, came three years after completion of the fort proper. In 1629 an English man-of-war came into the harbour "to presse 40 men" and to take in fresh

Landguard Fort saluting the arrival of Queen
Maria de Medici in 1638.   *Essex Record Office*

153

water. Her captain, Richard Plumleighe, refused to strike his ensign when commanded to do so by "the Officers of the Fort" and he later reported to the Admiralty Secretary as follows:

> "I told them that without an Order from the Counsell or Commissioners of the Admiralty I durst doe noe such obeisance, they answered that if I refused it they would sinke me and that they had warrant from my Ld. of Warwick soe to doe. I slighted that Authority and replyed that I thought my selfe as able to beate their paper fort to pecies with my Ordinance as they to sink me, and bidde them take heed how they made the first shott, upon this wee fell to worse wordes and at length to some blowes in which they had nothing the better." [74]

It should not be inferred, as elsewhere, that this led to gunfire since it was probably just a couple of boarding officers, threatening to pull down the warship's ensign, who received some rough handling. Further on in the same letter Plumleighe said "in fine I maintained my Flagg in peace without having any shott made against it and so past out". Even so, there must have been a very uncomfortable feeling aboard that man-of-war as she slowly made her way to sea within a biscuit's toss of the fort. After five or six windbound days

Queen Maria de Medici's voyage to England in 1638.

*Essex Record Office*

the enterprising Plumleighe warped his vessel out of harbour, a process which local pilots declared they had never seen used before to get out of Harwich.

In 1638 King Charles the First's mother-in-law was welcomed in more peaceable manner. After voyaging for seven days in rough seas, and being unable to disembark as planned at Dover, Queen Maria de Medici, widow of Henry IV of France, landed unexpectedly at Harwich. An illustration in a contemporary account of her travels by Puget de la Serre shows her stormy "navigation" over a sugar-icing sea in a three-masted ship of war, and it is said that although the Queen was "insensible to the fatigues of the sea" her ladies were a little in disorder, having been more attentive to alleviating their uneasiness than to preserving their beauty. [75] A second woodcut pictures Landguard Fort firing a salute in the distance while the Queen is being welcomed at Harwich Town Quay by a local dignatory on bended knee. That evening the soldiers and the burgesses celebrated with "feux de joye" and "a thousand different pastimes whereof the violins, pipes and drums enhanced both the sweetness and the grace". During Queen Maria's stay at the Mayor's house, one hundred and fifty people of the baser sort were attracted by the force of curiosity to crowd daily into her appartment to watch her dine. No doubt this was a great week for old Harwich, and perhaps for those at Landguard too, but in truth the King's crusty old mother-in-law became such a nuisance elsewhere that Parliament voted £10,000 three years later to defray the cost of shipping her back to Holland.

Although there were fears of attack by royalist ships and a royalist detachment once briefly occupied Harwich, the only record of guns being fired at Landguard during the Civil War came when hostilities were virtually at an end. Besieged Colchester surrendered on 28th August, 1648, and on 7th September the victorious Lord Fairfax crossed over from Harwich to Landguard with some troops and was there saluted "with abundance of Ordnance". With this compliment over, the general marched to Ipswich.

There is no mention of salutes in Commonwealth days and on 14th June, 1652, the stores at the fort were down to "Barrells of Pouder 92" and only 1,570 shot of various kinds. A letter of the same date, detailing the stores and ammunition needed to make the fort efficient, also said "there are likewise flaggs wanting very much, but being things of ornament not strength, I leave it to your Honors, only adding that those thinges give testimony of the side wee hold too, though none of our abillityes to defend that side". Doubtless there was enough powder in stock to salute the Restoration when it came along eight years later. Ipswich at any rate was prepared to welcome Charles II with "fyve or six great guns provided readie att the Common Key to discharge att the same time". [76] Presumably a salute was also fired when Charles II visited the fort in 1668.

On 3rd June, 1669, the serene Prince Cosmo III, Grand Duke of Tuscany, arrived at Landguard Fort and, according to the *London Gazette*, was received by the Governor "with all the honour and military ceremony which could be given him in that place". He had been provided at Ipswich with boats to transport him and his suite down the Orwell and before evening he crossed over to Harwich. There is a sketch of the harbour, with a distant view of Landguard Fort, in a book of Cosmo's travels in the Laurentian Library at Florence. It is there stated that when the Grand Duke departed for Holland in a royal yacht she was "saluted by the fortress, as she went out of harbour, with discharges of cannon, which were duly answered". There is some doubt as to whether the yacht was the original gift vessel from Holland, as claimed in the book, but it is beyond question that the Grand Duke had a rough passage. "There was no person on board but what, in the course of the night, suffered sea-sickness and lightened his stomach without the aid of medicine." [77]

Three years later the guns at Landguard Fort were fired in mourning for Pepys's great patron, the Earl of Sandwich, who was drowned after leaping from the burning *Royal James* during the Battle of Sole Bay. His body was found floating in the sea a few days later and brought to the fort. There, after embalming, it lay in state in the chapel for over a fortnight. "Serjeant Chirugeon Knight" of Ipswich went down to assist and, as the late Major E. R. Cooper remarked, "how the doctors fell out over the job can be read in the State Papers". [78] Then, on 19th June, 1672, the admiral's body was embarked on board the *Fan-Fan* for transport by sea to London for the funeral in Westminster Abbey. Some of the local gentry, the Mayor of Harwich, Captain Taylor "and ye principall of ye Towne" had been invited to Landguard by the Governor. Sir Charles Lyttelton's and Colonel Buller's companies of the Lord High Admiral's Regiment provided a guard of honour to the waterside. Some volleys of small shot were fired when the body was embarked in a boat and these were followed by a twenty-one gun salute from the fort. "I thought it undecent to part without some such", Lyttelton said, "because it being heere so publikely known, though they have order to pass through the Fleet with all privacy".

Five years later, there being peace at last with Holland, William, Prince of Orange, a nephew of Charles I, came over to marry Mary, eldest daughter of the Duke of York. The royal yacht *Mary*, the second of that name, brought him from Hellevoetsluis to Harwich where he landed on 9th October, 1677. Perhaps there was a welcome from the guns of Landguard Fort, but it was the Honeymoon Voyage of a whole fleet of yachts from the Thames in November which produced the well-known series of sketches by the elder Van de Velde.

Charles II died in 1685, James II reigned shortly until 1688 and then William the Dutchman reigned jointly with his Mary until 1694 and continued alone until 1702. Queen Anne, who followed, was nine years on the throne before the next surviving record of a salute at the fort. Nevertheless in the meantime it is certain that these royal changes, the presence of William III several times in the harbour, the occasional victory or the signing of a fragile peace and the need to celebrate certain other "Rejoicing Days" with Harwich would have necessitated a continual and considerable expenditure of gunpowder at the fort. The salute of 1711, however, is unique because it arose from an extraordinary private hilarity.

On their way to tour Holland, Flanders and France the famous artist James, later Sir James, Thornhill and three companions spent some time in Ipswich and Harwich. They made excursions in Suffolk and Essex and the first of four visits to Landguard Fort took place during the evening of 25th May, 1711. There the visitors drank "a bottle of excellent Barcelona at ye Suttlers in ye Fort" for which they paid two shillings and at the same time met some boon companions. On 28th May they were invited to dine at the fort with Mr Marshall, the Master Gunner, Dr Rust of the nearby township of Walton, who was the fort's chaplain, and a Mr Scot. Since Rust was "a Man of Wit" and well known for "sitting up and playing with Coblers, Tinkers &c. all night at an alehouse and going from thence to Church" the dinner conversation was of a distinctly Rabelaisian character. Thornhill noted "Some of the Parson's worthy sayings and Storys"[79] but it is the later course of events which made this guest night so truly memorable. The diners repaired to the battlements and there, as this lively diary records, "Every one fird a Gun and I fired 2—Mr Marshall gave us 15 Guns which with our own made 20". Things were not at all quiet on the next day either as Thornhill explains:

> "[May the 29th.] We went again to Landguard fort, being the Anniversary of Charles 2nd. Restoration—the Fort fird 21 Guns, Dr Rust preacht a sermon in the old Chappel there, after which we were entertained by Mr Scot, Mr Marshall &c. very well."

On Wednesday, 6th June, the friends were over at Landguard once more, dining with Mr Marshall. It was then that Thornhill took the opportunity to make a sketch of three guns on one of the pages of his diary.

Four years later Captain Francis Hammond[80], who had held the Lieutenant-Governorship since 1687 and the Governorship since 1711, had an information sworn against him by the master of a Yarmouth ship. The latter alleged that "when sailing out of the harbour of Harwich his ship was fired at by the Governour of Landguard Fort". No doubt this arose from a failure to pay proper compliment to the fort and it was not by any means the only such occurrence, for the captain of a Wisbech ship said the fort had fired a gun at him, and in 1715 no fewer than sixty-one masters made similar allegations. However, the accession of George I in 1714 had already heralded a busy century for the saluting batteries because the port had then become used by royalty and other personages going back and forth to Hanover.

157

A water colour drawing by Dominic Serres of Princess Charlotte's arrival at Harwich in 1761. The gunsmoke from Landguard Fort's salute can be seen on the extreme left.

*National Maritime Museum, London*

The great spectacle and drama of a royal embarkation was well captured by John Cleveley the Elder round about 1750 when the new *Royal Caroline*, a three-masted royal yacht, was at Harwich with other yachts and warships to convey King George II and his suite to Holland. It was such an occasion as this which induced Governor Philip Thicknesse to request Thomas Gainsborough to paint a picture of the fort.

"Soon after this the late King passed by the garrisons under my command, and as I wanted a subject to employ Mr Gainsborough's pencil in the landscape way, I desired him to come and eat dinner with me, and to take down in his pocket-book the particulars of the Fort, the adjacent hills, and the distant view of Harwich, in order to form a landscape of the yatchs passing the garrison under the salute of the guns." [81]

The picture itself did not survive the effects of salt in the mortar of the wall of the Governor's house at Landguard, but fortunately some prints were made from it by T. R. Major, a London engraver, and published in 1753. Their historical interest lies chiefly in Gainsborough's view of the low ground leading to the fort since, apart from the appearance of the new fort structure of 1745, the scene could hardly have changed since the Dutch marched that way in 1667.

A fair proportion of the salute-worthy traffic to and from the Continent concerned the exports and imports of English and foreign princesses. Among such occasions was the much-pictured arrival at Harwich in 1761 of Princess Charlotte of Mecklenberg Strelitz, who came over to marry King George III. Dominic Serres shows a fleet of royal yachts sailing past Landguard Fort, with smoke billowing from the saluting battery. John Cleveley the Elder painted the scene within the harbour, and this was also graphically described in the *Ipswich Journal*:

> "We hear from Harwich that during Her Majesty's Stay at that Harbour, she behaved with the greatest Affability to all the Spectators; and after condescending to draw down a Sash in her Apartment on board the Yacht, she paid her respects to all Ranks of People that were continually rowing around in Boats, who testified their Joy by loud Acclamations. On her Departure from the Yacht, she was saluted by the firing of Guns from all the Ships in the Harbour, and was attended by his Majesty's Band of Musick to the Shore, when the Mayor and the rest of the Corporation, in their Formalities waited for her Landing."[82]

Captain Philip Thicknesse.
*From J. H. Leslie's History of Landguard Fort*

The *Royal Caroline* had been renamed the *Royal Charlotte* in honour of the Princess and her crew had been "cloathed at his Majesty's private expense in a red uniform with gold laced hats, light grey stockings, buckles and pumps".[83]

It was in the early seventeen-sixties, too, that Lieutenant-Governor Thicknesse sent a wooden gun by way of a present to Lord Orwell. Although hardly in the nature of a salute, the dispatch of this dummy gun is worth recording since it had an astonishing sequel. The recipient of this studied insult, which implied a lack of personal courage, had recently presided over a court-martial at the fort. The prisoner was acquitted and Thicknesse, who had brought the charge, was himself reprimanded "for want of temper". The upshot was a civil action in which it was held that the dummy gun constituted a libel and for this Thicknesse was fined £100 and sent to prison for three months. This he duly served in the King's Bench prison, but his gaiety did not forsake him. "Over the door of his apartment, which was afterwards occupied by Mr Wilkes"[84], he placed a painting of a gun and the "Gun Room" it was called for a long time afterwards.[85]

While Thicknesse was so incarcerated his temporary successor, a Captain James Marsh, made an attempt to lift the dull life on desolate Landguard Point. To this end he indulged in antics which are best explained by quoting one of the four charges made at his subsequent court-martial. In this Captain Marsh was arraigned:

"For having in the most public and shameful manner, in direct violation of the Articles of War, and his Majesty's Royal Proclamation to discourage Vice and Profaneness, assembled a large number of People of both Sexes in the Chapel of the Garison under his Command, and though his Majesty's said Proclamation was pasted on a pillar before his Eyes in the said Chapel: yet he, in defiance of the laws of God and the Commands of his Sovereign, allowed and encouraged, by his Example, revelling and rioting with musical Instruments, and dancing Country Dances therein, the greatest Part of a whole Night, thereby profaning a Place fitted with all the Externals, and dedicated only to Divine Worship, to the disgrace of Religion, the Corruption of the Troops, and the great Offence of the whole Neighbourhood."

"Chappel at Landguard Fort", a water colour dated 20th July, 1769.   *Felixstowe Town Council*

The chapel was a fine room over the entrance arch of the fort and capable of holding three hundred people. It apparently once had an organ "eight feet high of elegant structure and six stops", since one was advertised for sale at the fort in 1757. The Communion table, Thicknesse said, was used for the punch and negus and the ball itself must have been a great success, since it did not break up until about four o'clock on a Sunday morning. Sir John Barker and many of the gentlemen were "compleatly drunk". With such overwhelming evidence Captain Marsh was found guilty of "Indiscretion", but this verdict does not appear to have affected his military prospects because he commanded the 43rd Regiment of Foot in 1775.

In February, 1763, the fort saluted the departing royal yacht *Katherine* with the two Princes of Mecklenberg aboard and on 13th January, 1764, the guns were at it again to greet Charles William, the Hereditary Prince of Brunswick. The latter, "an extremely personable and active man", had come over to marry Princess Augusta, the eldest sister of George III. The royal wedding took place in London on 16th January but bad weather delayed the embarkation at Harwich for thirteen days. The Princess, dressed in scarlet damask made up in the German fashion, went on board the *Fubbs* and her husband, in blue cloth trimmed with gold lace, followed on board the *Augusta*. [86] The royal yachts *Fubbs, Augusta* and *Katherine* each saluted the standard of the Princess with seven guns and the same salute was given half an hour later when the Prince's standard was raised above the port quarter of the *Augusta*. [87] For good measure the *Happy,* escorting sloop, then honoured the Prince and Princess with a combined salute of fifteen guns, but bad weather postponed the departure until the next day. Then salutes were again in vogue. The *Happy* gave the Princess eleven guns as the *Fubbs* got under way and another eleven guns followed for the Prince. Then, as the *Fubbs* sailed down to Landguard Point the fort fired a salute and the yacht replied.

This Honeymoon Voyage of 1764 was among the stormiest of North Sea passages but, following the good example of her sister-in-law Charlotte, who in 1761 was "gay the whole voyage, sang to her harpsichord and left the door of her cabin open", Princess Augusta remained "surprizingly cheerful notwithstanding the badness of the Weather and never once shew'd the least apprehension of danger". She certainly deserved the cheers and twenty-one gun salute given her at Hellevoetsluis when she transferred from the *Fubbs* to a yacht provided by the States General.

A National Trust painting in Waddesdon Manor shows a scene from the Rolling Ground in which Landguard Fort is firing a salute as several royal yachts leave the harbour. The leading vessel wears a Danish flag at the mizzen masthead, so the picture almost certainly concerns the last big royal yacht occasion of Georgian times at Harwich. This was the sailing in October, 1766, of Princess Caroline Matilda who had just been married by proxy in London to

King Christian VII of Denmark. The young queen was only sixteen years of age and, like many a North Sea traveller before her, she was forced to stay a night ashore at Harwich because of an adverse wind. She also had another night on board the *Mary* in the harbour before the yacht could get away. Nevertheless she was in good spirits and "was graciously pleased to come often upon Deck that the People who were continually going near the Yacht in Boats might have an opportunity of seeing her". [88] Next day the *Mary* left, escorted by the royal yachts *Katherine*, *Augusta* and *William & Mary*, but fate thereafter was most unkind to the poor girl, who finished her life imprisoned.

The next record of a salute from Landguard Fort concerns twenty-one guns fired on 25th November, 1769, to compliment the Russian Ambassador as he left the harbour in the *Dolphin* packet. Then, in 1775, came an incident reminiscent of Governor Hammond's regime. One evening in October a fleet of seventeen transports entered the harbour towards dusk and was immediately ordered by the gunner to strike to the fort. They did not do so and, after due warning, the gunner fired a blank. As this had no effect he loaded with shot and carried away the fore-topsail yard of one of the ships. An officer of the garrison then went out and demanded a fee of 13s. 8d. which the fleet commodore refused to pay. The charge was remitted, however, when it was found that the ships were in government service. [89]

In fact the seventeen-seventies at Landguard must have been noted for the sound of gunfire, as lengthy experiments or proofs of artillery took place there and were reported on in detail in 1774, 1776 and 1780, when men of the Royal Regiment of Artillery and various kinds of guns and ammunition were sent down from Woolwich by water. It was said that bomb-shells were thrown three miles with great exactness. Most of the firing seems to have been carried out over the land towards Felixstowe cliffs, however, since first, second and third grazes were recorded and there was yet another column for length of roll. Shots lodged in marshes, ditches and a hill and one rolled into the sea. As a result of these experiments the use of langridge shot was discontinued by the Navy, the superiority of grape having been proved. All this makes it very clear that traverse of the low ground at Felixstowe must at times have been a risky business.

The early seventeen-eighties, however, saw even greater activity at the fort since it was considerably strengthened in view of hostilities with France. The construction of three redoubts and very extensive outworks to make the fortress less vulnerable from the rear has already been mentioned. Major Leslie, the fort's historian, thought it unlikely that these defences were ever armed with guns, but he was wrong, since the *Ipswich Journal* of 8th June, 1782, proudly announced that "Tuesday being his Majesty's birthday 110 pieces of new heavy cannon planted on the new works at Landguard fort were discharged".

Notwithstanding the hostilities, the export of princesses continued and during April, 1797, the Prince of Wurttemberg arrived at Harwich on his way to London to marry Charlotte, the eldest daughter of George III. He came from Cuxhaven in the *Prince of Wales* packet and all the cutters and packets in Harwich Harbour gave him a gun salute. On shore the Hertford Militia provided a guard of honour. Next morning, after spending the night in the Three Cups, he was saluted twice by the *Black Joke* lugger with nineteen guns. [90] The royal couple were married in London on 18th May, the ceremony causing some amusement as there was great trouble in finding the ring, and three weeks later they travelled to Harwich. Three frigates had been sent round from Portsmouth to take the bride and bridegroom and their suite to Cuxhaven but for some reason the 40-gun *Revolutionaire,* the 40-gun *Virginia* and the 36-gun *Melampus* had to lie out in Felixstowe Road. Presumably all three vessels and the fort saluted when the Prince and Princess embarked on 10th June. They had to use a fishing boat to take them out of harbour, there being no other vessel available for this purpose. [91] The bride was attired in a blue riding habit and a straw bonnet and she had the Star of St Catherine on her breast. She "shed tears of gratitude" in return for the applause of the "numerous and loyal multitude", but maybe her thoughts were really akin to those of the fifteen-year-old Mary who one hundred and twenty years before had wept for a day and a half when she learned that her fate was to marry Prince William of Orange.

Landguard no doubt celebrated the Camperdown victory over the Dutch. At Harwich "the bells rang the whole day, a number of transparencies were displayed at different parts of the town and the West Norfolk Militia fired three vollies on the occasion". [92] Trafalgar, the jubilee of King George III in 1809 and the triumph at Waterloo would hardly have gone by unsaluted. Certainly in 1808 there was ceremony to mark the safe arrival of the Countess de Lille, consort of the self-proclaimed Louis XVIII of France. On her departure for the shore the frigate *Euryalus* manned her yards and fired a royal salute and the bells of St Nicholas at Harwich rang for the rest of that day to celebrate this deliverance from "the vengeance of that scourge of Europe, Bonaparte". [93]

With the eclipse of Napoleon there came a much-needed peace to the North Sea, but it brought about a rapid and great decline in the fortunes of Harwich Harbour. The profitable naval and military activity almost ceased and the adoption by mail services elsewhere of the newly invented steam vessels eventually forced the shutdown of the Harwich sailing packet service in 1832. Furthermore there was a great reduction in the fishery and, unfortunately, the dredging of septaria for the Roman cement manufactory, which had proved a useful substitute, soon brought about the temporary ruin of the entrance to the haven. Therefore it is likely that there was already a suitable air of gloom when, in 1821, the body of the much maligned Queen Caroline was brought to Harwich. The frigate *Glasgow*, with escorts *Garnet* and *Wye*, had been sent round for the passage to Cuxhaven. As soon as the coffin had been placed on a rowing boat for conveyance to the schooner *Pioneer* and thence to the frigates, the firing of minute guns commenced at Landguard Fort and continued until sunset. [94]

An order of 27th June, 1827, from the Master General of Ordnance terminated the firing of the Evening Gun at Landguard. This practice, which had been in force "since earliest times", and for which a reference of 1738 had been quoted, had consumed 261 lb. of powder during 1826. Whether sunrise was ever similarly greeted at Landguard is very doubtful, but it was certainly punctiliously saluted with a gun by some early yachtsmen. The firing of a noonday gun was also a custom in some military establishments.

For the older people of Harwich it must have been a welcome flashback to the colourful past when, most unexpectedly, in October, 1827, the elaborately decorated, three-masted, square-rigged *Royal Sovereign* came into the harbour attended by two steamers. On board the royal yacht was the Dowager Queen of Wurttemberg, the same princess who had left Harwich thirty years earlier in a fishing boat, but, although pressed to do so, she declined to come ashore. Colours were soon hoisted on all vessels in the harbour and on public buildings in the town, and the bells of St Nicholas rang a merry peal. It is not recorded whether there was a gun salute from Landguard Fort when the Princess Royal left the following morning but the arrival of the yacht, wearing the Royal Standard of England, certainly put Hellevoetsluis in a ferment three days later. [95]

Next year the first Harwich Regatta took place "in honour of the Lord High Admiral's birthday". He was "Sailor Bill' Duke of Clarence, and doubtless the fort guns were firing in 1831 to celebrate his coronation as King William IV. Queen Victoria's coronation in 1838 was properly marked at Harwich and in the Harbour, as will be observed:

> "The morning of the Coronation was ushered in by a choir of singers parading the streets. At 8 o'clock the bells began to ring and colours were seen waving in different parts of the town, and a band of music enlivened the scene. At 12 o'clock a royal salute was fired from the circular redoubt, whilst the soldiers in the barracks were drawn up on the Glacis and fired a *feu de joie*. At one, Landguard Fort, H.M.S. *Fairy* and three Revenue Cruizers fired a royal salute. Soon after the Regatta commenced but there was not sufficient breeze to give the desired effect to it." [96]

Since Landguard Fort was one of twenty-three saluting stations in Great Britain and of sufficient importance to fly the Union Flag every day, and also had the rare privilege of substituting the Royal Standard on royal anniversaries

The *Kronprins Frederik* leaving Harwich Harbour in 1951 with the King and Queen of Denmark on board. Five minutes after the picture was taken Landguard Fort fired its last salute. The frigate with crew manning the rails is H.M.S. *Bleasdale*. *Photograph by the author*

and state occasions, the rest of the nineteenth century would certainly have been punctuated with regular and noisy celebrations. Round about 1860 three 12-pound carronades were used for saluting purposes, but presumably these were replaced by breach loaders later. Queen's Birthday, Coronation Anniversary, Silver, Golden and Diamond Jubilees and other national rejoicings would all have been saluted at the appropriate time, and doubtless there were mourning guns for Prince Albert in 1861 and a long forty years afterwards for the old Queen. Sixty minute guns were certainly fired by the fort to mark the death of the Duke of Clarence in 1892. The resumption of the packet service after the very late railway link with London would have brought a number of important arrivals in the harbour, but the last hundred years and more have yet to be exhaustively researched. A paragraph, spotted by chance, reveals that in 1894 Landguard Fort showered Harwich with bullets during machine gun practice, but presumably there were other salutes of a less haphazard kind.

In August, 1891, the royal Yacht *Victoria & Albert* (the second of that name) took the German Empress and her children from Felixstowe to Flushing. The Empress had come down from London on July 13th after a state visit and the five princes had landed at Felixstowe five days earlier. The German royal yacht which brought them over was said to have damaged eight

paddle-floats on the way. Nine-year-old "Little Willie", the Crown Prince, had good reason to remember that holiday for the "hearty clip on the ear" which he received from Tom Winks. The latter was never tolerant of youngsters who jumped up and down in his beached boats and the Empress, sensible lady, most kindly told Winks to re-apply the same treatment if it proved necessary. It was not until 1921 that the third *Victoria & Albert* attended Harwich Regatta, and she was there again in 1923. King George V was aboard her when not sailing in *Britannia* or visiting upriver at Orwell Park.

So the story continues, through the two world wars when, except for the firing of a round or two when a friendly ship failed to give the recognition signal, only the anti-aircraft guns, searchlights and barrage balloons saw action. Then came Friday, 11th May, 1951, an unforgettable day on which the King and Queen of Denmark left Parkeston Quay at the conclusion of a state visit. On this sparkling morning of bright sun and lively water in the harbour the scene was brought fully to life by two score of yachts as they jockeyed for the start of their annual race to The Hook. All moored vessels were dressed overall and a thousand flags fluttered in the breeze. There was a continual flashing of bright colours from wet paintwork as the racers turned and heeled in the sun, a fitting contrast to the creamy whiteness of hard-driven sails above.

After the yachts had departed a gallant convoy sailed from Parkeston Quay. The handsome packet *Kronprins Frederik* came proudly down harbour wearing the royal standard of Denmark. Her sleek grey escorts, HMS *Zephyr*, HMS *Opportune* and HMS *Savage*, took station with Danish swallowtail at the main. Ensigns dipped everywhere and HMS *Bleasdale*, anchored near Shotley, manned ship and cheered. Then, as the departing royalty passed the point of the low-lying Suffolk shore, the saluting gunsmoke rolled away as it had done a thousand times before. Should any Viking spirits of 885 AD still have haunted Stourmouth they were certainly laid that day, and there was the happiest sense of fitting compliment. This salute, however, was fired from an old saluting base outside the walls towards the point. That Friday morning four 25-pounders of a field battery had travelled over from Colchester behind their Quads to perform this pleasant service. "For security reasons" no photographs were taken on the Felixstowe shore. Six years later, in June, 1957, the fort finally closed down because the development of land, sea and air weapons had made its defences obsolete.

In March, 1958, Her Majesty the Queen and Prince Philip left Harwich Harbour at the commencement of a state visit to the Netherlands. Before

The arrival of Queen Elizabeth II at H.M.S. *Ganges* landing stage at Shotley in 1961. The Royal Yacht *Britannia* is moored in the River Stour.     *East Anglian Daily Times* being piped aboard the royal yacht at Parkeston Quay they made a happy tour through part of Essex and met notabilities at Harwich Town Hall. Then, in time-honoured fashion, the *Britannia* was led out of harbour by the Trinity House Vessel *Patricia* while two RNVR sea-going tenders, HMS *Thames* and HMS *Isis*, provided the initial escort. Waiting at sea were the frigates HMS *Grenville,* HMS *Pellew* and HMS *Paladin.* Some listened hopefully as *Britannia* passed the deserted point but a deathly hush prevailed. At Landguard, with the rejoicing days of twenty reigns behind it, at Landguard which once held fast for England, at Landguard Fort, most sadly, there was no more powder to salute our Queen.

*AFTERTHOUGHT.* The veneer of Civilisation is woefully thin, its protections manifold though often lacking in Time. Ever to be cherished are all loving and long-enduring beliefs, but sadly still essential is an effective and valiant defence against internal and external aggressions of increasing frightfulness. High among the rest is the maintenance of a kindly trade, for in the fair sharing of Man's blessing lies a surer protection than all the forts of old. This happy Jubilee departure from the thriving port of Felixstowe is thus an augury for Peace.

Photograph, *East Anglian Daily Times*

# References and Notes

1. G. Kinsey, *Seaplanes—Felixstowe,* Terence Dalton, 1978.

2. *Suffolk Chronicle,* 8 January, 1876.

3. In the Ipswich branch of the Suffolk Record Office A53/1.

4. *Ipswich Journal,* 19 April, 1794.

5. G. Brandt, *Het Leven van De Ruyter,* 1686, pp. 589-590.

6. The name Heaps, now rarely heard, was used by Thames bargemen for the anchorage on the seaward side of the Spitway.

7. In 1514 John Woodlas of Harwich conveyed the King's ship *Mary Rose* "out of Harwich Haven through a place in the sea called the Slade." L. Weaver, *The Harwich Story,* 1975, p. 13.

8. In this case meaning "anchorage."

9. Bacon, *Annalls of Ipswich,* p. 96.

10. A small fort or earthwork on which the guns were usually protected by circular earth-filled baskets called maunds.

11. J. H. Leslie, *The History of Landguard Fort in Suffolk,* 1898, p. 4.

12. L. J. Weaver in *The Harwich Story,* p. 16, refers also to sakers, bombards, demi-culverins and haggabusses, etc. being moved by lighter.

13. L. Weaver, *The Harwich Story,* pp. 40-41.

14. Calendar of State Papers Domestic, James I, 157.29.

15. *Victoria County History, Suffolk,* p. 226.

16. See Appendix I.

17. The sutler sold provisions and liquor to the troops.

18. These and many other details come from Major J. H. Leslie's *The History of Landguard Fort in Suffolk,* 1898.

19. Dutch fishery claims were based on a commercial treaty concluded as far back as 1285 on the occasion of the marriage at Ipswich of Elizabeth, daughter of Edward I, to John, Count of Holland. J. G. Nall, *Great Yarmouth and Lowestoft . . . chapters on the archaeology, natural history etc. of the district . . .* 1866.

20. For a full account the National Maritime Museum booklet *The Anglo-Dutch Wars of the 17th Century* by Professor C. R. Boxer, HMSO 1974, is strongly recommended.

21. It was returned with trees destroyed in April, 1665, but repossessed by the Dutch shortly afterwards.

22. Wicquefort in a letter of 19th June, 1667, seems to be in error in stating that Jan was son of Pieter.

23. The London street is named after him.

24. Calendar of Treasury Books Vol. I, 7 November, 1665.

25. Calendar of Treasury Books Vol. II, 29 July, 1668.

26. The village of Bawdsey near the mouth of the Deben.

27. Joint Engineer in Chief of Royal Castles and Forts.

28. A shallow anchorage amid the sands off Walcheren.

29. A reach of the Thames immediately below Gravesend Reach.

30. H. T. Colenbrander, *Beschieden uit vreemde archieven omtrent de groote Nederlandsche zeeorlogen 1652-1676*, p. 573, from *Rawlinson MSS* A195 fol. 138.

31. Built in 1666 and paid for by the City.

32. A former shoal in Harwich Harbour entrance.

33. An offshore shoal between the Gunfleet anchorage and Harwich.

34. From at least the time of Elizabeth I there was drawing of gibbets on "haste for your life" letters, but this practice so scared the postboys that it was eventually banned.

35. British Library Add. MS 39.246, f. 15.

36. The sea area off the Deben entrance between Felixstowe Cliff and Bawdsey (Balsey) Cliff.

37. The balance-wheel pocket watch had yet to come into general use and considerable reliance was placed on pocket sundials. Shore times stated at Harwich, however, should be fairly accurate as the shipyard boasted "an excellent pendulum clock".

38. *East Anglian Daily Times*, 8 January, 1926. Article "The Suffolk Militia", by E. R. Cooper.

39. Peewit Hill is the present-day name for the steep track to the low ground at the south end of Grange Road, the former Maidstone Street of John Kirby's survey of 1740-41.

40. The arm of Walton Creek which used to run up as far as the Ordnance Hotel was once known as Ireton's Ditch.

41. For details see Appendix II.

42. Nowadays steps known as Jacob's Ladder give access to the shingle beach.

43. Being windbound, Plumleighe was the first captain on record to warp his vessel out of Harwich Harbour (see Chapter 12). Warping is a process by which a vessel lays out kedge anchors in the desired direction and hauls successively on the warps.

44. The Pain Tree grew on top of the hill between Harwich and Dovercourt where the Redoubt was later built.

45. Saxby Ryde, *British Lighthouses*, 1913, p. 135.

46. There were three Cornelis Evertsens in the Dutch Navy at this time, known as "the elder", "the young" and "the youngest".

47. J. H. Leslie, *The History of Landguard Fort in Suffolk*, p. 44.

48. He died by drowning in 1668 and Pepys failed in his bid for the Parliamentary seat thus made vacant.

49. Presumably the sixth-rate built at Harwich in 1665.

50. The City of London had already subscribed funds for this purpose.

51. *Trans. Essex Arch. Soc. N.S. XXII*, 1940. Article "The Vice-Admiralty of Essex during the Dutch Wars of Charles II", by T. M. Hope, p. 307.

52. The owner of Christchurch Mansion at Ipswich, P.R.O. SPD Charles II 247, 127.

53. C. J. W. van Waning & A. van der Moer, *Dese Aengenaeme Tocht*, 1981, p. 57.

54. *East Anglian Daily Times*, 4 June, 1895.

55. Douglas Dixon, *The King's Sailing Master*, London, 1948, p. 26.

56. Arthur H. Clark, *The History of Yachting*, 1904, pp. 107-8.

57. P.R.O. P.C.1 3/45.

58. A fortified work of more than four sides, with parapet and ditch all round (Leslie, p. 48).

59. P.R.O. W.O. 55-2272.

60. *Ipswich Journal*, 26 June, 1756.

61. *The Harwich Guide*, 1808, pp. 70-75.

62. C. J. N. Trollope, *Beauclerk's Battery*, 1982.

63. Mentioned by J. H. Leslie in *The History of Landguard Fort*, p. 78, but not subsequently traced.

64. J. R. Western, *The English Militia in the 18th Century*, p. 393.

65. L. Weaver, *The Harwich Story*, p. 108.

66. *Ipswich Journal*, 26 October, 1811.

67. R. Malster, *Saved from the Sea*, Terence Dalton, 1974, pp. 54-56.

68. In the author's possession.

69. *Highlight*, Journal of the Harwich Society No. 44, 1981, "Beacon Hill Battery", article by C. J. N. Trollope.

70. Inspection Reports, 9 June, 1906, and 9 July, 1907.

71. *East Anglian Daily Times*, 2 December, 1981, Ken Blowers' review of *The Doodlebugs*, by Norman Langmate.

72. Letter from Mr W. H. Harrison, late 515 Suffolk Coast Regiment, R.A.

73. Muriel St Clare Byrne (ed), *The Lisle Letters,* University of Chicago Press, Vol. II, pp. 268, 479; Vol. IV, pp. 315-316; Vol. V, p. 725. The P.R.O. source references given are L & P VII 1224; v 14. VIII 681. XII ii ll; vii 101. SP/ 1/92 f 52. SP 1/157 f5ᵛ.

74. P.R.O. S.P. 16, 147/18.

75. Joan Parkes, *Travel in England in the Seventeenth Century*, p. 116.

76. Paul Fincham, *The Suffolk We Live In*, 1976, p. 49.

77. *Travels of Cosmo the Third, Grand Duke of Tuscany, Through England . . . 1669,* published London, 1821.

78. *East Anglian Daily Times*, 18 April, 1936.

79. Katherine Fremantle (ed), *Sir James Thornhill's Sketch-Book Travel Journal of 1711,* Utrecht, 1975.

80. His mother was formerly Miss Mary Mennes, sister of Sir John Mennes of Pepys' Navy Board.

81. Philip Thicknesse, *A Sketch of the Life and Paintings of Thomas Gainsborough Esq.*, 1788.

82. *Ipswich Journal*, 12 September, 1761.

83. *Gentlemen's Magazine*, Vol. 31, p. 376.

84. John Wilkes, who denounced George III and the Earl of Bute in his newspaper *The North Briton.*

85. W. Lindsey, *A Season at Harwich,* p. 133.

86. *Ipswich Journal,* 4 February, 1764.

87. P.R.O. Adm. 51/217, 51/378, 51/434, 51/2479, 51/3776. See article by Commander W. E. May in the *Mariner's Mirror,* May, 1958.

88. *Ipswich Journal,* 11 October, 1766.

89. Old *Ipswich Journal,* 30 September, 1775.

90. *Ipswich Journal,* 14 April, 1797.

91. *Ipswich Journal,* 3 and 10 June, 1797.

92. *Ipswich Journal,* 28 October, 1797.

93. W. Lindsey, *A Season at Harwich,* pp. 63-64.

94. W. Lindsey, *A Season at Harwich,* Researches A, p. 34.

95. *Ipswich Journal,* 13 and 20 October, 1827.

96. *Ipswich Journal,* 7 July, 1838.

*NOTE:* The main sources of information for Chapters 4, 5, 6, 7, 8, 9, which cover the Second Dutch War, are Major J. H. Leslie's *History of Landguard Fort* (1898), *State Papers Domestic* for the respective years in calendarised or in transcript form, translations from Gerard Brandt's *Het Leven van de Ruyter* (1686), extracts and translations from H. T. Colenbrander's *Beschieden uit vreemde archieven omtrent de groote Nederlandsche zeeorlogen 1652-1676* (1919) which includes transcripts from the *Rawlinson MSS* in the Bodleian Library, and translations of extracts made by the late Dr van der Kooij from Dutch naval archives. Public Record Office permission to use Crown copyright material in their custody is gratefully acknowledged and the following references concern the numerous *State Papers Domestic — Charles II* items which have contributed to the narrative.

*1664/5* Jan. **110,** 57; *1665* Aug. **128,** 50; *1666* Feb. **149,** 78; June **160,** 56, 64, 112; July **161,** 36, 82, 94, 128; **162,** 51, 52, 73, 76, 144; **164,** 131, 136; **165,** 41, 42, 48, 107; Sept. **170,** 158; *1667* Jan. **188,** 126, 131; April **197,** 20; **198,** 69; **199,** 40, 107, 110; June **206,** 46, 47, 50, 108, 109, 110, 126, 127, 169, 170, 171; **207,** 10, 11, 69, 98, 100, 101, 102, 103, 112, 113, 130, 131; July **208,** 24, 25, 26, 27, 28, 54, 55, 72, 73, 81, 82, 113; **209,** 16, 49, 50, 51, 82, 83, 84, 86, 131, 140; **210,** 102; Aug. **211,** 36, 92; **212,** 46, 117; **213,** 21, 24, 26, 27, 29.

# Work in Progress on 11th October 1626

The circuite of the whole Forte beinge 4 square with his bulwarkes is 164 rodd 4 foote.
There are 4 curtaines everie one of them 12 rodde 9 foote in length at 12 foote to the rodde.
The face of every bulwarke is 12 rodd in length.
The flancke 3 rodd 2 foote in length.
The curtaine is now 11 foote high within the worke, and to perfect it the Workemaister intendes to make it 7 foote higher.
One of the Bulwarkes is alreadie raised to 11 foote high, and above withoute, but is not fullie squared within and is to be raised according to the curtaine.
Another Bulwarke is raised 7 foote and a halfe.
A third Bulwarke is neare 7 foote high.
The fourth Bulwarke hath earth alreadie brought up to make it 6 foote high, but it is not turfed.
The curtaine towardes the channell is at the foote 3 rodd 8 foote broade.
The hight of the rampier of the same Curtaine within is 6 foote.
The breadth of the same rampier is 32 foote.
The breadth of the parapett at the grownd is 17 foote.
The hight of the parapett is 6 foote.
The breadth at the topp is 12 foote.
The foote bancke 3 foote broade 1 foote high.
The other three curtaines 30 foote broad at the grownd 6 foote high; the rampier 21 foote broad; the parapett 11 foote broad at the grownd, 6 foote high, 6 foote broad at the topp.
The foot bancke 3 foote broad, 1 foote ½ high.
In everie corner of the 4 square is a Batterie wheron is a platforme, whereof 2 towardes the channell are 36 foote square, 9 foote high, and have 9 peeces of Ordinance upon them both, 2 demi-cannons of brasse, 1 sacre of brasse, 6 demi-culverings of Iron.
The 2 other platformes are 30 foote square, 9 foote high and have 6 demi-culverings of Iron upon them both.
Before the Porte are two brasse peices, the one a Fowler, the other a Port peice, with two brasse Chambers to eich of them.
The floor of the Porte is 30 foote in length, 10 foote high, 10 foote broade with two doors all of Timber.
The ditch is so deepe as the earth that hath made the Forte hath beene brought out of it, but it is unfinished and the Workmaister intendes to make it 60 foote broad and 12 foote deepe.
The first built howse where now the souldyers lye which is intended for the Magazine is built of brick and tymber, and is 51 foote longe, and 21 foote broade, and hath in it 12 rooms.
There is another howse built all of bricke, being a bricke and a halfe thicke which is 115 foote longe, 24 foote broade, in hight 10 foote, and hath in it 40 severall chambers for Lodgeinges for souldyers, everie one 11 foote broade and 12 foote longe, and 20 of the roomes have Chimnies.
There is also alreadie built one powder house all vaulted with bricke very substantiall 12 foote high, 18 foote longe, 14 foote wide.
There is an aqueduct of very good sweet water with a Conduit house of bricke, the water brought in leaden pipes a mile and a halfe of the howse unto the ditch side and cannot be finished until the drawbridge be sett up, but the pipes of lead lye readie to finish it. We finde by the plott an intencion to build within the forte such another row of Huttes as is alreadie builte, a

Chappell, a house for the Captaine, a Court of Guards, a second powder house, a drawe bridge, and a great Cisterne and a posterne.

There are alreadie two Centry houses builte, and three more are intended to be builte.

We find there great store of bricke and tile, by Computacon enough to finish the worke, and also a good store of lime, and some Timber. We also find there good store of powder bullets and other amunition which by your Lordships order the Earle of Warwick is to deliver up by indenture.

Upon the finishing of the forte the porte is intended to be enlarged 24 foote in length with a Percullis.

We did see 33 Musketiers very proper and able bodied men excercise there, and 3 sicke, in their beddes, besides the Officers and Canoniers.

The Channell lyes from the said forte of Lantguard pointe within 100 rodd.

*P.R.O. State Papers Domestic Charles I, 37, 64.*

## APPENDIX II

# Particulars of Dutch Troops Landed at Felixstowe on 2/12 July, 1667

Sources:  a.  Report of Cornelis de Witt to the States General and respective Admiralties, 3/13 July, 1667.
        b.  Journal of Captain in the Army Jan Maurits de Castillego, Adm.arch. XLVII.16.
        c.  ARA Collection De Ruyter, no. 53.
           (minor variations in name spellings are noted below)

TROOPS under the command of Colonel Thomas Dolman and the Count van Hoorn: —

| | Muskets | Pikes | Transporting ship or its captain as in landing orders |
|---|---|---|---|
| Colonel's Company | 42 | 24 | Capt. van de Haen |
| Lt. Col. van Rheede | 30 | 12 | *Jongen Drost* — flute |
| Major Overschie (also called Sgt. Major) | 30 | 12 | *Postilion* — flute |
| Capt. de Castillego | 30 | 12 | Lieut. Adm. Banckert |
| Capt. Ruysch (Ruys) (30 in a.) | 36 | 12 | Capt. Evert van Gelder |
| Capt. P. Panhuysen (Panhuys) | 36 | 12 | Capt. Jan van Amstel |
| Capt. Lanoy the Elder | 36 | 12 | Capt. van de Haen |
| Capt. Paigny (Pagny) | 24 | 12 | *Gouda* — flute |
| Capt. Lanckvelt | 36 | 12 | "the hoeker laden with soldiers" |
| Capt. Schoonhoven | 18 | 12 | *Gouda* — flute |
| Capt. Rhote | 30 | 12 | *Jongen Drost* — flute |
| Capt. Bonneman (Bennama) | 30 | 12 | *Jongen Drost* — flute |

| | | | |
|---|---|---|---|
| Capt. van Beveren, Ysendoorn Lt. | 36 | 12 | Capt. Jan Paulussen van Gelder |
| Capt. Hamel | 36 | 12 | *Glasemaker* — flute |
| Capt. Nothe (Notke, Note) | 36 | 12 | Capt. van Zyl |
| Capt. Lanoy the Younger | 36 | 12 | *Den Harder* — flute |
| Capt. van de Val (der Wall) | 36 | 12 | Capt. Jan Heck |
| Capt. Drost | 36 | 12 | Rear-Adm. Vlugh |

|  |  |  |
|---|---|---|
| *Totals as in a. & b.* | 486 | 192 |
| *Corrected Totals* | 594 | 228 |

MARINES under the command of Lt. Colonel Francois Palm: —

| | *Firelocks* | | *Firelocks* |
|---|---|---|---|
| Lieut. Colonel Palm his men | | Capt. Brouwer | 36 |
| led by Capt. Dolman | 36 | Capt. van Nispen | 36 |
| Capt. Jan de Witt | 36 | Capt. Padburgh | 36 |
| Capt. Cornelis de Witt | 36 | Capt. Arckel | 36 |
| Capt. Pompen | 36 | Capt. Knoppert (Cnoppert) | 36 |
| Capt. La Court (Lancourt) | 36 | | |
| Capt. Velsen | 36 | | 396 |

*Other names mentioned:* — Capt. de Clarges, Capt. Assendelft, Capt. Paul (volunteer), Commisioner Tuschen, du Blois (engineer)

Castillego summarises as under —

| | |
|---|---|
| SOLDIERS (muskets) | 486 |
| FIRELOCKS | 396 |
| SEAMEN | 400 |
| | 1282 |
| PIKES | 192 |
| | 1474 |

*NOTE:* Brandt also quotes these figures on p. 592 of the 1686 edition but they apparently do not include the companies of the two colonels and a further 36 men (see Chapter 6).

# Dutch Ships Involved in the Felixstowe Action of 2/12 July, 1667, including the Rearguard of Five Men-of-War in the Sledway

| Name | Guns/Men | Captain | Admiralty |
|------|----------|---------|-----------|
| Amsterdam | 62/290 | Joost Verschuur | Amsterdam |
| Calantsoog | 68/320 | Jan de Haan | North Quarter |
| Delft | 62/265 | Rear Adm. Jan Janszoon Van Nes | Maas (Rotterdam) |
| Deventer | 62/290 | Lt. Col. François Palm | Amsterdam |
| Eendracht | 80/370 | Lt. Adm. Aert Janszoon Van Nes | Maas |
| Essen | 50/255 | Jakob Binkes | Amsterdam |
| De Faam — advice vessel | — | Dirck de Munnick | — |
| De Glasemaker — flute | — | | — |
| Gorinchem (also Gorkum) | 36/105 | Pieter Jacobszoon Nanning | Maas |
| Gouda — flute | — | | — |
| Groningen | 70/360 | Vice Adm. Enno Doedes Star | Friesland |
| De Groote Christoffel — boeier | — | | — |
| Groot Frisia | 74/465 | Lt. Adm. Van Aylva | Friesland |
| Den Harder — flute | — | | — |
| Harderwijk | 44/205 | Jan Pauluszoon van Gelder | Amsterdam |
| Harderwijk | 36/105 | Nicolaes Naelhout | Maas |
| Hollandia | 80/440 | Rear Adm. Willem van der Zaan | Amsterdam |
| De Hoope — fireship | — | Willem Meerman | — |
| Het Huis te Oosterwijk | 62/290 | Jan Roetering | Amsterdam |
| Jaersvelt | 46/205 | Pieter Sitter | Amsterdam |
| De Jongen Drost — flute | — | | — |
| Justina van Nassau | 60/310 | Jan Hek | North Quarter |
| De Kaleb | 48/180 | Jan Janszoon Maauw | North Quarter |
| Komeetstar | 68/320 | Jacob van Meeuwen | Amsterdam |
| De Leeuwen | 50/255 | Abraham Ferdinand van Zijl (or Zyll) | Amsterdam |
| Middelburg | 50/224 | Cornelis Evertsen the Youngest | Zeeland |
| Het Noorderkwartier | 60/295 | Pieter Klaaszoon Wijnbergen | North Quarter |
| De Olifant (De Witte Olifant) | 80/525 | Vice Adm. Isaac Sweers | Amsterdam |
| Oostergo | 62/300 | Jan Janszoon Vijzelaer | Friesland |
| Oostersouburg — hooker | — | Daniel Verdiest | — |
| De Posteljon — advice vessel | — | Laurens de Bruin | Amsterdam |
| Postilion — flute | — | | — |
| Prinses Albertina | 50/250 | Joost Michielszoon Kuik | Friesland |
| 'T Raadhuis van Haarlem | 46/205 | Pieter Magnuszoon | Amsterdam |

| | | | |
|---|---|---|---|
| *De Spiegel* | 70/375 | Dirck Schey | Amsterdam |
| *Stad en Landen* | 62/300 | Roelof Janszoon Ketelaar | Friesland |
| *De Stad Gouda* | 46/205 | Michiel Suis | Amsterdam |
| *Tijdverdrijf* | 60/290 | Jan van Amstel | Amsterdam |
| *De Tromp* (also *Muiltromp*) | 46/205 | Jan Gijsels van Lier | Amsterdam |
| *Utrecht* | 62/290 | Hendrik Gotskens | Amsterdam |
| *Veere* | 50/206 | Adriaan de Haaze | Zeeland |
| *Vlissingen* | 50/204 | Rear Adm. Jan Matthijszoon | Zeeland |
| *Walcheren* | 70/316 | Lt. Adm. Banckert | Zeeland |
| *Het Wapen van Utrecht* | 72/340 | Rear Adm. David Vlugh | Maas |
| *Wassenaar* | 56/230 | Cornelis de Liefde | Maas |
| *Westergo* | 58/270 | Wytze Beyma | Friesland |
| *De Windhond* | 34/175 | Jan Pieterszoon Vinkelbosch | Friesland |
| *Woerden* | 68/320 | Hendrik Adriaanszoon | Amsterdam |
| *Vereenigde Provincien* (also *Zeven Provincien*) | 46/205 | Jakob Willemszoon Broeder | Amsterdam |
| *De Zeven Provincien* | 80/460 | Lt. Adm. Michiel Adriaenszoon de Ruyter | Maas |
| *Zierikzee* | 60/264 | Vice Adm. Cornelis Evertsen | Zeeland |
| (unnamed fireship) | — | Willem Gerritszoon Amberlandt | — |

*NOTE:* I am most grateful to Vice Admiral A. van der Moer and to Michael Robinson whose additional research has added to my original list. Dutch historians include the definite article as part of some ships' names but most English authors ignore it because it is customary to prefix all ship names with 'the'. Different sources reveal minor variations in spelling of both ships' and personal names. All the above mentioned vessels can be deemed to have been off Felixstowe with complete or near certainty. There may have been up to half a dozen more, including *De Gouden Leeuw* (80/485 Amsterdam) whose Rear Admiral Verburgh had been invalided home by galliot. Some uncertainty arises because the composition of Lieut. Admiral Van Ghent's flotilla of seventeen ships which had sailed to the north is not at present known. Consideration could also be given to inclusion of the following ships, but with much lesser certainty than those listed above: —

| | | | |
|---|---|---|---|
| *Westvrieslandt* | 78/395 | Lieut. Adm. Van Meppel | North Quarter |
| *De Pacificatie* | 78/385 | Vice Adm. Schram | North Quarter |
| *'T Geloof* | 60/315 | Nicolaes Marrevelt | Amsterdam |
| *Gelderlandt* | 66/250 | Evert van Gelder | Maas |
| *Stadt en Landen* | 62/290 | Jacob Andrieszoon Swart | Amsterdam |
| *Schiedam* — advice vessel | 22/85 | Jacob Pieterszoon Swart | Maas |

Silas Taylor's count was "about 47 sayle besides tenders, besides 5 that lay in the Sledway" at the back of the fort off Felixstowe at about 1 p.m. on Tuesday 2/12 July, 1667. The four ships detached to attack Felixstowe Ferry may have been outside his line of sight. Including men-of-war, galliots, transports, supply ships and oar-driven boats and barges used for the landing the total number of enemy craft off Felixstowe must have exceeded a hundred. The English were in fact threatened by more than 2,400 guns and something in excess of 12,000 Dutchmen.

F.H., March, 1983.

APPENDIX IV

# Some Pictures, Charts and Plans Concerning the
# Landguard Forts

1. Plan of proposed fortifications at "Lunger Pointe" and Beacon Cliff by Richard Lee, now thought to date 1543. (*British Library*, Cotton MS Aug. I i 56)
2. Orwell Haven chart with circular sconce on "Lunger Poynt", temp. Henry VIII. (*British Library*, Cotton MS Aug. I i 58)
3. Gun salute from the fort in 1638, background of a copper engraving in the *History of the Entry of Mary de Medicis . . . into England*, Puget de la Serre. (*Essex Record Office*)
4. The Dutch attack on the fort and Harwich Harbour 2/12 July, 1667, a grisaille (pen-painting) by Willem van de Velde the Elder, signed and dated 1669. (*National Maritime Museum*)
5. Distant view of the fort in a manuscript account of the travels of Cosmo, Grand Duke of Tuscany through England, 1669. (*Laurentian Library, Florence, Med. Pal. 123. c. 1003* [*Veduta di Harwich*])
6. "Ships lying in the entrance to Harwich", pencil and wash drawing by Willem van de Velde the Elder showing Landguard Fort and Beacon Cliff 1685? (*Boymans—Van Beuningen Museum, Rotterdam, MB1866/T559*)
7. "Langer Fort by Harwich", 17th century pen and wash drawing by Francis Place giving a view of the low ground and cliffs at Felixstowe. (*Henry Huntington Art Gallery, San Marino, Cal. U.S.A.*)
8. Print entitled "HARWICH" with a view of the fort from the Rolling Ground. (*Ashmolean Museum*)
9. Chart from a survey c.1683 by Capt. Greenvil Collins entitled 'Harwich, Woodbridge and Handfordwater with the Sands from the Nazeland to Hosely Bay", published 1686. The fort is shown and nearby creeks. (*National Maritime Museum*)
10. Rough plan of the fort on p. 6 of James Thornhill's diary, 1711. (*Victoria and Albert Museum, L.1380. 1961*)
11. Small sketch entitled "Landguard Fort from Harwich Cliffe" on p. 12 of James Thornhill's diary, 1711. (*Victoria and Albert Museum. L.1380. 1961*)
12. "Some of ye Canon on Landg. Fort Wed June 6th" on p. 25 of James Thornhill's diary—1711. (*Victoria and Albert Museum, L.1880. 1961*)
13. "A Prospect of the Towne & Harbour of HARWICH", line engraving by J. Kip, published by Thos. Taylor and Robt. Hulton, c.1714. Some details of Landguard Fort appear to be deficient on comparison with the two following items. This view was reproduced in miniature by Bellin and is copied in many publications. (*National Maritime Museum*)
14. A military surveyor's plan of the 1626 fort and its proposed successor which accompanied correspondence of 1716. Details of the surrounding terrain and the main harbour channel are shown, also the last vestiges of a former turfed sconce surrounding the burial ground, see no. 32. (*Public Record Office PC1,3/45*)
15. A larger plan of the 1626 fort showing a new location for its successor and sections of the moat and ramparts, 1716? (*Public Record Office WO 78/1452*)
16. "A coloured plan of the town and harbour of Harwich, with the soundings marked; drawn in 1725 on a scale of 850 feet to an inch; with a separate plan of Landguard Fort, on a scale of 40 feet to an inch: 2f. 3in. × 1f. 7in." (*British Library XXXIX.61*)

17. Engraving by R. Sheppard showing entrance of Harwich Harbour with the fort answering a warship's gun salute. (Tab. VIII, page 99, of Dale's *History and Antiquities of Harwich and Dovercourt,* 1730.)

18. Board of Ordnance plan c.1731 of the fort built 1717-20, showing proposed battery at the foot of the glacis, breakwaters and a mid-section sketch. (*Public Record Office WO 55/ 2269 MPHH 703*)

19. Board of Ordnance plan dated 1732 showing counterscarp galleries at three corners of the moat and two sectional sketches. (*Public Record Office WO 55/2269 MPHH 703*)

20. "Plans and Profile of the several Floors of the Barracks of Landguard Fort 1732." (*Public Record Office WO 55/2269 MPHH 703*)

21. Chart of Harwich Harbour from a survey by I. P. Desmaretz, 1732, showing the fort, its two breakwaters and the Governor's house. (*History of Harwich Harbour*)

22. "South-West Prospect of Landguard Fort 1748", a pen and ink sketch giving the earliest view of the new fort Built 1745/51. (*Ipswich Museums*)

23. South-east view of the fort, an engraving by T. Major after an oil painting by Thomas Gainsborough, published 1754. The original picture was contaminated by the salt-water mortar of a wall and was described by its owner Thicknesse as "perished and gone". (*Suffolk Record Office, Ipswich branch*)

24. Oil painting (believed 18th century) showing the same view as No. 23 with minor variations, measuring 35ins. × 23½ins. within the frame, formerly in the possession of the late Mr Jennings of Felixstowe. This is one of several oil and water-colour copies which exist.

25. "A two-decker and a frigate off Harwich", oil painting with a distant view of Landguard Fort and nearby coast by Charles Brooking, who lived 1723-59. (*National Maritime Museum*)

26. Pen and water-colour drawing dated 1767 giving a south-east view of the fort with entrance road winding past the palisades and covered way. (*Felixstowe Town Council*)

27. Water-colour dated July 7, 1769, showing the chapel and interior of the fort, the original of Plate VIII of Major Leslie's history. (*Felixstowe Town Council*)

28. Water-colour dated Aug 7, 1769, showing the Lieutenant-Governor's house with battlement garden, the Governor's house outside the fort and the view over the Felixstowe low ground from Harwich Bastion. (*Colchester and Essex Museum*)

29. Pencil, pen and wash drawing showing the Lieutenant Governor's house from Harwich Bastion, much as in No. 28 but with a lower viewpoint which cuts out the ground beyond the fort. (*Suffolk Record Office, Ipswich branch*)

30. Pencil, pen and wash drawing of barracks, cannon, etc., with a view from Harwich Bastion of the ramparts of the estuary side of the fort. (*Suffolk Record Office, Ipswich branch*)

31. Pencil, pen and wash drawing of the fort interior looking across from the chapel towards the barracks and Kings Bastion. (*Suffolk Record Office, Ipswich branch*)

32. Unfinished pencil, pen and wash drawing showing the fort entrance and the view along the moat to the drawbridge and Chapel Bastion. (*Suffolk Record Office, Ipswich branch*)

33. Pencil, pen and wash drawing of the fort Burial ground showing vestiges of the former sconce as in No. 14. (*Suffolk Record Office, Ipswich branch*)
    NOTE: *All five drawings described above are attributed to Francis Grose and are preserved among the Fitch Illustrations — HD 480/2.*

34. Oil painting by Thomas Allen of Lord Anson's departure from Harwich to bring Princess Charlotte to England in 1761. There appears to be a structure in front of the ramparts which is probably Beauclerk's Battery. (*In private ownership*)

35. "VIEW of HARWICH and the Yachts going out with Lord Anson returning the salute from LANDGUARD FORT", line engraving by P. C. Canot after Thomas Allen, 1761. (*National Maritime Museum*)

36. Pen and water-colour drawing by Dominic Serres of Princess Charlotte's arrival at Harwich in 1761 under salute from the guns of Landguard Fort. (*National Maritime Museum*)

37. "A Yacht in a Light Breeze with a View of Harwich", aquatint by J. Clark and J. Hamble after Dominic Serres, published by Edward Orme, 1804. This reproduces a portion of No. 36 and the view is in fact of Landguard Fort. (*National Maritime Museum*)

38. Oil painting by Dominic Serres of Princess Charlotte's arrival as in No. 36. (*National Maritime Museum*)

39. The sailing of Princess Caroline Matilda from Harwich in 1766 under salute from the guns of Landguard Fort. This view, said to be by Serres, is from the Rolling Ground. (*National Trust, Waddesdon Manor*)

40. Colliers off Harwich in 1775, a wash drawing by Francis Swaine with a background which appears to take its detail of Landguard Fort from No. 8 of the previous century. (*National Maritime Museum*)

41. A coloured view of Harwich and Landguard Fort, taken from Harwich Cliffs; drawn by H. Gilder, 1777: 5f. 6in. × 1f. 1in. (*British Library* ⚓ *XIII.15.4.f*)

42. A coloured plan of Landguard Fort, with the proposed alterations, by Thos. Hyde Page, Engineer, drawn to a scale of 40 feet to an inch, with a section on a scale of 20 feet to an inch. (*British Library* ⚓ *XXXIX.62*)

43. "View of Landguard Fort" from the estuary entrance. Coloured print by F. Jukes after A. Callender, published June 12, 1785.

44. "A New Chart of Harwich Harbour with the Rolling Ground, Felstow Road, Goldermore's and Flats of the Naze" by George Burn, published 1787. The fort is marked and the former Governor's House is described as "the Brewhouse". (*History of Harwich Harbour*)

45. A view of the harbour face of the fort engraved by Prattent, published March 1, 1788, by G. Robinson. Plate VII of Major Leslie's history is very similar. (*Suffolk Record Office, Ipswich branch HD 480/2*)

46. Water-colour by Captain Hanchett showing the entrance gate and fort ditch garden with trees in 1791. (*Present whereabouts unknown*)

47. Water-colour drawing of a peter-boat yacht showing Landguard Fort and a signal mast on Beacon Cliff. (*History of the Royal Harwich Yacht Club, Hussey*)

48. "Harwich Harbour and Neighbouring Waters" from a survey by Graeme Spence, 1804. The fort, Rainham Redoubt and South Battery are shown in this, possibly the last chart to show a blunt configuration of Landguard Point. (*History of Harwich Harbour*)

49. Engraving by L. Jeakes, London, of the view across the estuary towards the fort from Harwich town gate. (*The Harwich Guide, 1808*)

50. The fort and soon-to-be-eroded martello tower appear in one of a series of sketches showing Harwich defences against Napoleonic invasion. (*Colchester and Essex Museum*)

51. Oil painting (pre 1830) with a view of the fort and the since-eroded O Martello Tower. (*Felixstowe Town Council*)

52. Ladies' Pocket Book view of the estuary side of the fort with cannon and sentry near the beach, sold by J. Raw of Ipswich and others. (*Suffolk Record Office, Ipswich branch HD480/2*)

53. Admiralty Chart No. 1491 of 1843 showing the rapid prolongation of Languard Point and a northern profile of the fort. (*History of Harwich Harbour*)

54. View across the estuary towards the fort from the low-light at Harwich, c.1850. (*p. 105 A Season at Harwich, Lindsey*)

55. Vignette of the fort c.1850 showing Beauclerk's Battery. (*p. 130 A Season at Harwich, Lindsey*)

56. Pencil sketch by Colonel H. Mussenden Leathes of the fort and Beauclerk's Battery, June 20th, 1853. (*Plate IX of Major Leslie's history*)

57. "The Suffolk Artillery Brigade Militia at Landguard Fort 1854", oil painting by John Duval of a sham fight on the common with the fort in the background. (*Trustees of the Suffolk and Norfolk Yeomanry*)

58. "The Suffolk Artillery Brigade Militia at Landguard Fort 1854", oil painting by John Duval of a drumhead service on the common. (*Trustees of the Suffolk and Norfolk Yeomanry*)
   NOTE: *The fort also appears in numerous nineteenth and twentieth century paintings, drawings and photographs. Collections of plans have been accumulated by the Department of the Environment and members of the Fortress Study Group and the Felixstowe Museum and History Society.*

# A Brief Bibliography

*Calendar of State Papers Domestic* for 1665, 1666, 1667 and 1672 and the many references thereto in the *Victoria County History* for Essex and Suffolk.

Brandt, Gerard. *Het Leven . . . van Michiel de Ruyter*, 1686.
Dale, Samuel. *The History and Antiquities of Harwich and Dovercourt*, London, 1730.
Raw, J. (printer). *The Harwich Guide*, Ipswich, 1808.
Lindsey, W. H. *A Season at Harwich*, Harwich & London, 1851.
Edye, Laurenco. *Historical Records of the Royal Marines (Vol I, 1664-1701)*, London, 1893.
Leslie, J. H. *The History of Landguard Fort*, London, 1898.
Clark, A. H. *The History of Yachting 1600-1815*, New York, 1904.
Tedder, A. W. *The Navy of the Restoration*, Cambridge, 1916.
Colenbrander, H. T. *Beschieden uit vreemde archieven omtrent de groote Nederlandsche zeeorlogen 1652-1676 (2 vols)*, The Hague, 1919.
Tripp, H. Alker. *Shoalwater and Fairway*, London, 1924.
Tripp, H. Alker. *Suffolk Sea Borders*, London, 1926.
Cooper, E. R. *A Suffolk Coast Garland*, London, 1928.
Hughes, B. Carlyon. *The History of Harwich Harbour*, Dovercourt, 1939.
Robinson, M. S. *Van de Velde Drawings in the National Maritime Museum*, Cambridge, 1958.
Rogers, P. G. *The Dutch in the Medway*, London, 1970.
Boxer, C. R. *The Anglo-Dutch Wars of the 17th Century*, National Maritime Museum, 1974.
Fremantle, Katharine (ed.). *Thornhill's Sketch-Book Travel Journal of 1711*, Utrecht, 1975.
van Waning, C. J. W. & van der Moer, A. *Dese Aengenaeme Tocht*, Zutphen, 1981.
van der Moer, A. *Een nabrander van de tocht naar Chatham, Marineblad* (article), Dec. 1981.
Wood, D. A. *Landguard Fort*, Felixstowe, 1982.

Gavin, C. M. *Royal Yachts*, London, 1932.
Naish, G. P. B. *Royal Yachts*, National Maritime Museum, 1953.
McGowen, A. P. *Royal Yachts*, National Maritime Museum, 1977.
O'Neil, B. H. St. J. *Castles and Cannon*, Oxford, 1960.
Hogg, Ian V. *A History of Artillery*, London, 1974.
Hogg, Ian V. *Fortress*, London, 1975.
Duffy, Christopher. *Fire & Stone*, Newton Abbot, 1975.

Of the many sources of Pepys's Diary quotations, the eleven-volume series edited by R. C. Latham and W. Matthews is recommended. A view of contemporary continental history is given in John Stoye's *Europe Unfolding 1648-1688*, published by Fontana in 1969.

# Index

*Illustrations in bold type*

# INDEX

# Index of Ships

188